SUN TECHNICAL REFERENCE LIBRARY

James Gosling, David S. H. Rosenthal, and Michelle J. Arden
The NeWS Book: An Introduction to the Network/extensible Window System

Mark Hall and John Barry (eds.)
The Sun Technology Papers

Michael Russo
A New User's Guide to the Sun Workstation

John R. Corbin
The Art of Distributed Applications: Programming Techniques for Remote Procedure Calls

John R. Corbin

The Art of Distributed Applications

Programming Techniques for Remote Procedure Calls

Springer-Verlag
New York Berlin Heidelberg London
Paris Tokyo Hong Kong Barcelona

John R. Corbin
Sun Microsystems, Inc.
Mountain View, CA 94043

Library of Congress Cataloging-in-Publication Data
Corbin, John R.
The art of distributed applications: programming techniques for remote procedure calls / John R. Corbin.
p. cm. — (Sun technical reference library)
Includes bibliographical references (p.) and index.
ISBN-13:978-1-4612-7753-8
1. Electronic data processing—Distributed processing. 2. Remote procedure call library. I. Title. II. Series.
QA76.9.D5C673 1990
004'.36—dc20 90-10335
CIP

Sun Microsystems, Inc., has reviewed the contents of this book prior to final publication. The book does not necessarily represent the views, opinions, or product strategies of Sun or its subsidiaries. Neither Sun nor Springer-Verlag are responsible for its contents or its accuracy, and therefore make no representations or warranties with respect to it. Sun believes, however, that it presents accurate and valuable information to the interested reader, as of the time of publication.

Typeset by Bi-Comp, Inc., York, Pennsylvania.

9 8 7 6 5 4 3 2 1 Printed on acid free paper

ISBN-13:978-1-4612-7753-8 e-ISBN-13:978-1-4612-2998-8
DOI: 10.1007/978-1-4612-2998-8

This book is dedicated to my parents,
whose many sacrifices over the years made it all possible.

Preface

Sun Microsystem released their first version of a Remote Procedure Call (RPC) Library in 1985. Since then the use of this Library has grown as has the number of vendors that offer the Library. After having implemented distributed systems using this Library, I noticed that the current documentation did not provide enough information to the distributed application developer. This book is an attempt to fill this gap by providing practical information to the distributed application developer. This book should be useful to both new and experienced users of Sun's RPC Library.

I have tried to provide you with all the information about the RPC Library that you will need, but in doing so, the book overlaps with Sun's RPC documentation. I believe that this book provides better insight into using the Library than does the standard documentation. I have tried to take an honest approach to presenting this material that not only includes highlighting the strengths of the Library, but the weaknesses as well.

This book will teach you how to write distributed applications based on the SunOS 4.0 version of the RPC Library. You do not need prior networking experience to understand the text. Any networking information needed is provided. You do not need to be familiar with the UNIX operating system. You should be familiar with programming concepts and with the C programming language.

This book can be used as supplemental text in a distributed systems course, providing the basis for lab assignments. Overall, this book may be too narrow in scope for a distributed programming class as it does not provide a taxonomy of RPC implementations, the theory behind these implementations, or a detailed methodology for developing distributed applications. Even so, this book can provide the student with all they need to know to implement distributed systems using Sun's RPC Library.

There are several ways to present the material covered in the book. I chose to first discuss eXternal Data Representation (XDR) because it is used to represent RPC arguments and results in a machine-independent format, although XDR has other uses as shown in the last section of Chapter 2. Chapter 3 discusses the protocol used by the RPC Library. All of the information in this chapter is optional, although I recommend reading the section on the portmapper to understand how clients *bind* to a service. Chapters 4–6 present the RPC Library routines in order of increasing complexity and include examples of the use of library routines. Chapter 7 covers the *rpcgen* program, which is a protocol compiler for RPC-based distributed applications. This program will be useful to you when you are writing distributed applications. Chapter 8 discusses several issues that you must consider when writing distributed applications. This chapter is a must for distributed application developers. The last chapter covers future directions for RPC mechanisms.

I did not cover the Transport Independent version of the RPC Library in great detail, as this version of the Library was being developed while I was writing the book. TI RPC can be covered in a future edition of the book. The same is true for the SunOS 4.1 version of the RPC Library, although I do cover the differences between the SunOS 4.0 version and the SunOS 4.1 version of the Library in Appendix 4.

Many people have contributed to this book. I would like to give special thanks to Bob Lyon for answering questions and for bringing us Sun's RPC Library, to Dave Brownell for his significant contributions and support, and to Vipin Samar for his significant contributions and thorough reviews. I would like to thank Brian Pawlowski and Mark Stein for their contributions. I would also like to thank the following individuals for their feedback during the review process: Sally Ahnger, Richard Bogen, Brent Callaghan, Rosanna Lee, Karen Maleski, Chuck McManis, Brian Pawlowski, Vicki Schulman, Chris Silveri, Carl Smith, Richard Thio, and Keith White. I would like to thank Donna Frazer and Linda Cwiak for their administrative support, and thank Allen Graves and Eric Liefeld for letting me use their facilities during the review process. I am grateful to my editors John Barry and Mark Hall for helping me through this task.

Contents

Introduction and Overview

1

Significant advances in technology have resulted in the move of computing resources from centralized facilities to the computer user's desktop. Very large scale integration and the advent of data-communication networks have made desktop computers an affordable alternative to centralized facilities. Data-communication networks connect the computers together allowing the exchange of information and the sharing of resources between different computers on the network. Resources can now be concentrated in the computer that best provides the resource; that computer can make the resource available to other computers via the network. An application is no longer confined to the resources available on the local computer, but can now use the resources available to the network.

The full potential of computer networks is only beginning to emerge. Resources that are commonly shared on networks include computers, disks and tape drives, files, databases, modems, printers, plotters, typesetting machines, and other devices. As technology advances, applications and organizations are being structured to distribute the work they perform among resources on the network. Companies use computer networks so that their employees can better work together. This technology lets companies structure their resources to match their organization, as opposed to centralizing the resources unnaturally.

A computer user should be able to access resources on the network without explicitly requesting the network transactions required to use the resource. The computer software can automatically handle locating the resource and transferring information to and from the resource. In other words, access to resources on the network can be transparent, the process of using them is the same as though the resource were available on the local computer. Systems that provide transparent access to resources on the network are referred to as *distributed systems*. Keeping network access transparent, while allowing different kinds of equipment to participate on a network, presents difficult distributed system design challenges. Transparency is easier to achieve if the network is designed for a single kind of equipment—for example, one company's proprietary computers—but this type of network cannot exploit the special capabilities of other computers and devices that may also be on the network, and also does not reflect the reality of the heterogeneous computing environments found in most organizations today.

For some time, developers have needed an easy-to-use platform for writing distributed system software. A platform is a set of routines, typically located in a library, that provide specific functions on which to build your application. It is the "platform" for your application. Ideally, the platform for distributed systems should not be tied to a specific operating system or hardware architecture, but should be an industry standard. The platform should be portable to the various operating systems and hardware architectures. The portability of the platform increases the portability of the applications that use the platform.

The Open Network Computing (ONC) platform developed by Sun Microsystems addresses the above requirements. The platform consists of the Remote Procedure Call (RPC) routines and the eXternal Data Representation (XDR) routines. Both sets of routines are contained within the RPC Library. RPC and XDR were introduced in 1985 and are in wide use today. Sun Microsystems was not the first company to implement an RPC mechanism, but Sun made the RPC/XDR source and protocol specifications publicly available, thus indicating Sun's intentions to make the mechanism non-proprietary. The XDR standard is in Appendix 2 and the RPC protocol specification is in Appendix 3.

You can use the ONC platform to write distributed systems. This platform is portable and widely available today. More than 90 vendors include the ONC platform as part of their operating-system software. Although the majority of ONC implementations are based on UNIX, implementations exist for virtually every major computer system (such as System/370 VM, MVS, VMS, MS-DOS). A version of Sun's RPC Library is also available on UNIX System V Release 4 (SVR4) from AT&T. An overview of the SVR4 version of RPC is presented in Chapter 9.

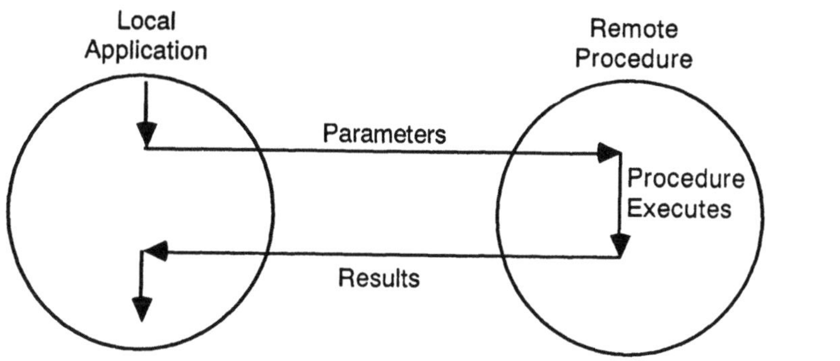

FIGURE 1.1

1.1 Remote Procedure Call Library

The RPC Library enables you to make a call to a procedure that does not reside in the address space of the calling process. The procedure may be on the same computer as the calling process, or it may be on a different computer. A remote procedure call is analogous to a remote *jump to subroutine* call. Figure 1.1 shows how the local application's thread of control for the procedure call is passed over to the remote computer where the procedure is executed and then control is returned to the local application. The RPC mechanism provides function-call semantics for local or remote interprocess communication. This mechanism is a message-passing scheme in which the procedure arguments are in a message sent to the remote procedure, and the procedure return values are in the message passed back to the calling program. You need not worry about how the messages get to and from the remote procedure. The RPC Library handles the message passing.

This book refers to procedures invoked through the RPC Library as remote procedures, even though the procedures may be located on the same computer as the calling application. The book refers to the computer on which the remote procedure is located as the remote computer, even though the remote computer and local computer may be the same. You do not have to worry about whether the procedure or computer is local or remote. Either way, the RPC Library provides the same semantics to the application.

The RPC Library delivers messages using a *transport*. A transport provides communication from one application to another. In the case of RPC, the transport provides communication between RPC mechanisms on different computers. The transport may regulate the flow of information. It may also provide reliability, ensuring that data arrives without error and in the order that it was sent.

One problem with passing RPC arguments and results is that differences may exist between the local and remote computer architectures. This means that the remote procedure may not properly interpret the values passed to it, or the local application may not properly interpret the values returned to it. The XDR routines in the RPC Library allow you to describe the arguments and results of a remote procedure in a machine-independent manner, allowing you to work around any differences in computer architectures.

This book covers Sun Microsystems' implementation of the RPC mechanism and the XDR standard. This implementation includes a programming interface that allows applications to use RPC and XDR. The programming interface is described with C-programming-language-style function declarations. All the examples in this book are written in C and were run under version 4.0 of the Sun Operating System (SunOS). The RPC and XDR Library routines are located in the C Library. Other languages can invoke the RPC and XDR Library routines if they follow the rules for interfacing to C functions. Refer to your programming language manual for more information on interfacing with C functions. Refer to [COUL 88] or [WEIH 89] for more general information about RPC mechanisms.

The source code for the SunOS 4.0 RPC and XDR Library, referred to as RPCSRC 4.0, is a license-free version of Sun's RPC and XDR Library. Anyone developing applications in a distributed-computing environment can use it. RPCSRC also includes on-line documentation, the *rpcgen* protocol compiler (described in Chapter 7), demonstration network services, and sample *rpcgen* input files. RPCSRC is compatible with the 4.2BSD and 4.3BSD versions of the UNIX operating system. Appendix 1 tells you how to obtain RPCSRC.

1.2 Distributed Applications

The RPC Library enables you to write distributed applications consisting of a set of procedures that do not all reside on a single computer. Some of the procedures typically reside on different computers that are interconnected by a communication network. The procedures are invoked using the RPC Library. A distributed application is heterogeneous if the remote procedures are running on computers with different architectures and/or different operating systems from those on the computer where the calling procedure resides.

There are several reasons for building distributed applications. End-users can get a price/performance benefit from building distributed applications. Resources available to an application are no longer limited to a single computer. For example, a computer-aided design (CAD) application may require good graphics capabilities for drawing schematics, a lot of file storage to keep designs and tests, and a fast processor to perform CPU-intensive simulations. Acquiring all these capabilities in a single computer might be very expensive. Alternatively, one could buy a collection of low-priced computers and network them together to reduce costs; a distributed application would use the computers on the network collectively as though they were one large computer. As use of the distributed application grows with an increasing number of users, computing power can be added incrementally to the network to address the demand.

Distributed applications offer the potential for fault tolerance. In the days before networking was widespread, resource sharing and access were limited. If a printer on a computer went down, the application was unable to produce output. Applications today can be designed to access resources on other computers in a network, achieving fault tolerance to minimize the impact on any one computer. Distributed applications can be designed to recover transparently from failure points and redistribute the resource usage. In the case of the printer failure above, the distributed application could simply search the network for another printer. An application, such as a distributed database, offers the potential for high availability of information through replication of critical data on several computers, again improving fault tolerance.

Numerous distributed applications available today are based on Sun's ONC platform. They range from distributed file systems to systems used in the collection of weather-related information, from concurrent-use licensing systems to a distributed clinical information system [BERG 86]. The RPC Library has been used for remote execution, distributed image processing, network man-

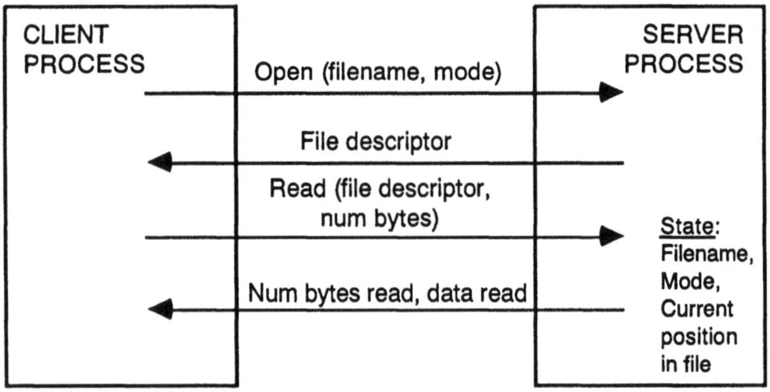

FIGURE 1.2. *Simple stateful file server.*

agement, information backup service, and much more. The number of distributed applications and their diversity is a testament to the usefulness of distributed applications in industry.

1.2.1 Client/Server Model

The RPC Library uses the client/server model, which is popular for distributed applications. In this model, the server offers services to the network which the client can access. An application can be both a client and a server. Another way to understand the model is that servers provide resources, while clients consume them. The terms *client* and *server* do not necessarily denote computers; they could be thought of as a client *process(s)* and a server *process(s)*.

There are two types of servers, *stateless* and "*stateful*". A stateless server does not need to maintain any information, called state, about any of its clients in order to function correctly. A stateful server (that is, one having state) maintains client information from one remote procedure call to the next. Figure 1.2 shows a simple stateful file server that has the *open* and *read* procedures. The client requests that the server open a file, passing in the name of the file and mode associated with the open file. The server returns a file descriptor to the client. The client can then use the file descriptor in a subsequent read operation. Note that the server

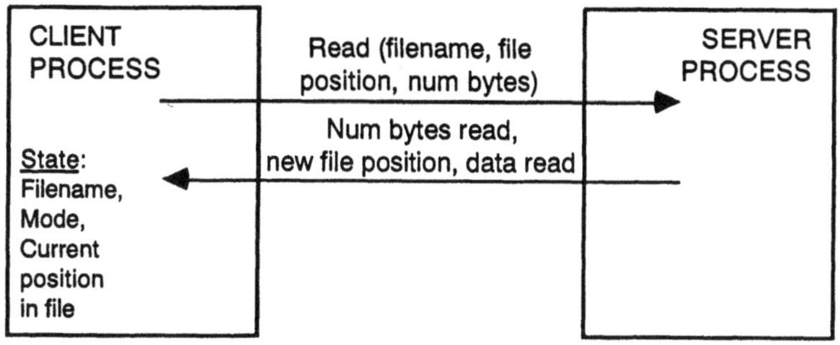

FIGURE 1.3. *Simple stateless file server.*

is maintaining the state of the client's open file. This state includes the file name, the open mode, and the current position within the file. The server must be able to take a file descriptor specified in a read command and map it to the appropriate state associated with the open file. Figure 1.3 shows a simple stateless file server that has only the *read* procedure; it doesn't have an *open* procedure. The client passes all the information into the read request that the server needs to locate the requested data, including the file name, position within the file to begin reading, and number of bytes to read. The server then returns the number of bytes read, the new file position, and the data read. Note that the file state is now located on the client.

In the event of a failure, stateless servers have a distinct advantage over stateful servers. With stateless servers, a client need only retry a request until the server responds; it does not need to know that the server has crashed or that the network temporarily went down. The client of a stateful server, on the other hand, needs to either detect a server crash and rebuild the server's state when it comes back up or cause client operations to fail. If the client crashes, then the server may be holding state that is no longer valid. Stateful servers are typically more efficient than stateless servers, and provide an easier programming paradigm.

Whether to use stateful or stateless servers depends on the application being designed. During the development of a distributed application, it is best to examine the positive and negative aspects of both approaches.

1.2.2 Implementing Distributed Applications

Developing distributed applications is different than developing non-distributed applications. The fact that the application does not reside in a single process's address space introduces new issues that need to be considered and new tasks that need to be performed. Some of these issues and tasks are:

- Which procedures will be local and which will be remote?
- You need to define a protocol that specifies the remote procedures, their arguments and results, and the semantics of these procedures.
- How will the application locate a service on the network?
- What action will the client take when it cannot communicate with a server?
- How will the application handle network communication errors?
- What level of security is needed?
- How will I test and debug the application?

Chapter 8 discusses the issues associated with implementing RPC-based distributed applications.

One tool that can help you develop distributed applications is the *rpcgen* program. Once you have a protocol specification, you can use *rpcgen* to process the specification and generate the RPC layer for your application. The *rpcgen* program is covered in Chapter 7.

1.3 Advantages of using RPC

The RPC Library simplifies the development of distributed applications by providing a familiar programming model. This model effectively hides the details of network programming, allowing you to focus on solving the problems addressed by the application. It is a flexible model that can support a variety of application designs. By structuring a distributed application as a set of procedures that define a service, the RPC Library can be used to construct building blocks of sophisticated applications. These remote procedures may be used in different applications by many clients, and servers may even call other servers to accomplish their work. A network service can be viewed as a library of procedures that are available to the network. The benefits of this library are: added flexibility because the routines are bound dynamically at run-time, and the library routines can be shared and distributed.

The inherent modular nature of distributed applications can be used to your advantage. A collection of specific network services that, together, perform the functions you need to get accomplished tends to be easier to manage than a large network entity such as a distributed operating system. The modular pieces make it easier to implement heterogeneous distributed applications because modules are easier to port than entire operating systems.

The RPC Library hides operating-system dependencies. The only requirement for porting an RPC-based application is that the target computer environment provides a RPC Library that is compatible with the one provided on the computer on which the application was originally developed. Sun's RPC mechanism cannot communicate with other RPC mechanisms that do not employ Sun's RPC message-based protocol. This is also the case for most RPC mechanisms not based on the Sun RPC protocol specification. This problem exists because an RPC protocol standard does not exist. In other words, no prescribed set of rules governs the interaction of RPC mechanisms. There are also no rules specifying the application programming interface (API) for RPC Libraries. This makes it difficult to port your application to another vendor's computer that has different RPC Library routines. Fortunately, Sun's implementation of RPC is available on a wide range of computers and operating systems from different computer and software vendors. Making Sun's RPC implementation "freely available" has freed programmers from the worry associated with using a proprietary RPC mechanism. Some day, it is hoped, there will be a standard RPC protocol and API. Standardization of RPC is covered in Chapter 9.

1.4 History of Sun's RPC Mechanism

The idea of remote procedure calls has been around for a long time. One of the first RPC mechanisms was developed by Jim

White while he was working at SRI during the 1970s [WHIT 76]. White later went to work at Xerox where he managed several network-related research projects. In the next few years, several RPC mechanisms were developed at Xerox, but only one, *Courier*, was released as a product in 1981 [XERO 81]. The Courier implementation was done by Alan Frieier. During this time, an engineer named Bob Lyon was working for White at Xerox. Although Lyon did not develop any of the Xerox RPC mechanisms, he left Xerox in 1983 to work for the startup company Sun Microsystems. Lyon developed Sun's version of the RPC mechanism in 1985. Another major accomplishment for Lyon, working with others, was the development of the Network File System (NFS). NFS uses the RPC mechanism to provide transparent file access in a distributed computing environment. NFS has become the industry de facto standard for distributed file systems.

Lyon's goal for RPC was to adapt the best features from Courier, yet keep his implementation flexible since the RPC mechanism was new to UNIX. He believed that the original RPC architecture was well conceived by Jim White almost a decade earlier. The flexibility of Lyon's implementation has been confirmed by the number of platforms to which the RPC Library has been ported.

2 eXternal Data Representation (XDR)

XDR is a standard for the description of data in a machine-independent format. This chapter covers XDR in detail and is provided to give you a complete reference to XDR. XDR is typically used to represent RPC arguments and results in a machine-independent format, although XDR has other uses as shown in the last section of this chapter. In depth knowledge of XDR is not required for RPC programming but can be useful. For an overview of XDR, it is recommended that you read the first two sections of this chapter.

The XDR standard has two aspects. The first addresses the issue of data representation; it defines a uniform way to represent data types. The second addresses data description; it defines a language that can describe data structures of arbitrary complexity in a standard way, hence the term XDR standard. The language can only describe data; it is not a programming language. XDR is a standard in the sense that it provides only one way to do data conversions. Both aspects of the standard are aimed at increasing the portability of data.

By following the XDR standard, you can represent data in a manner that is independent of computer architectures, programming languages, and compiler conventions—in other words, you can represent data that is portable. The XDR standard works effectively in any data interchange situation. For example, a program that observes the XDR standard can properly interpret XDR-format data read from a tape file, no matter what language or computer was used to create the tape. Even programs running on the same computer can use XDR to their advantage; for example, programs written in different languages can share the data in an XDR-format data structure, even if their compilers represent or align data differently. Moreover, future programs, written in any language, can also interpret such a structure by simply observing the XDR standard.

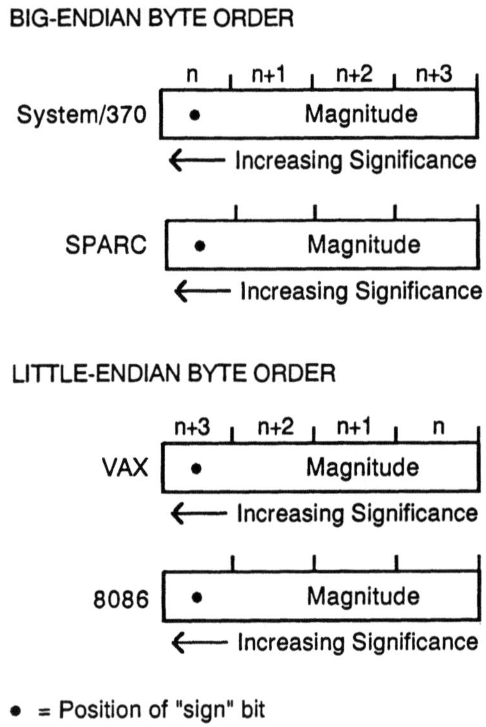

FIGURE 2.1. *Example 32-bit integer representations.*

XDR is necessary because of the diversity of computer architectures. By being innovative and independent, the designers of computers, programming languages, and compilers have substantially limited the portability of data. Because they were designed independently, different architectures often represent the same data types differently. For example, Figure 2.1 shows how four popular computer/microprocessor families represent 32-bit integers. All four architectures store integers in two's-complement notation with the sign bit adjacent to the most-significant-magnitude bit. In the representation used by the System/370 and the SPARC architectures, the most significant bit is in the byte with the lowest address. In contrast, in the 8086 and VAX representation, the most significant bit is in the byte with the highest address. The two byte orders are often called big-endian, the lowest memory address containing the high-order byte of the integer (System/370 and SPARC), and little-endian, the lowest memory address containing the low-order byte of the integer (8086 and VAX). The term big-endian comes from the two words "big" and "end". A big-endian integer "ends" with the high-order byte—or the "big" byte. The two words were combined and the "-ian" suffix was added to "end" as a memorization aid. The term little-endian similarly results because the integer ends with the low-order byte.

Although the issue is sometimes argued fervently, the point is not that one byte order is "right," but that integers are not portable between little-endian and big-endian computers. Suppose a program running on a SPARC sends the integer 1 over a network to a program running on a VAX, as shown in Figure 2.2. The SPARC transmits byte *n* first and the VAX reads the value into its byte *n* , and the remaining bytes are likewise transmitted and received in order of ascending addresses. Because of their opposite byte orders, however, what was the most significant byte of the SPARC integer becomes the least significant byte of the VAX integer, and vice versa. The VAX interprets the transferred integer not as 1 but as 2 ^ 24 because bit 0 of the SPARC integer has become bit 24 of the VAX integer. The result is the same when the value 1 is transferred from a VAX to a SPARC.

Byte ordering is not the only architectural incompatibility that leads to nonportable data. For example, some architectures represent integers in one's-complement notation rather than two's-complement notation. Floating point representations also vary between different computer architectures. Machine architectures are not the only source of nonportable data; languages and compilers are also sources. For example, strings defined in Pascal are represented as arrays of bytes, while C strings are terminated by an extra byte containing the null character (0). Also, compilers for the same language may align the members of a structure differently; even a given compiler may offer different alignment options for optimizing the use of space or time.

This chapter introduces you to XDR data encoding. The associated data description language is covered in the chapter on *rpcgen*. The actual XDR standard document is in Appendix 2.

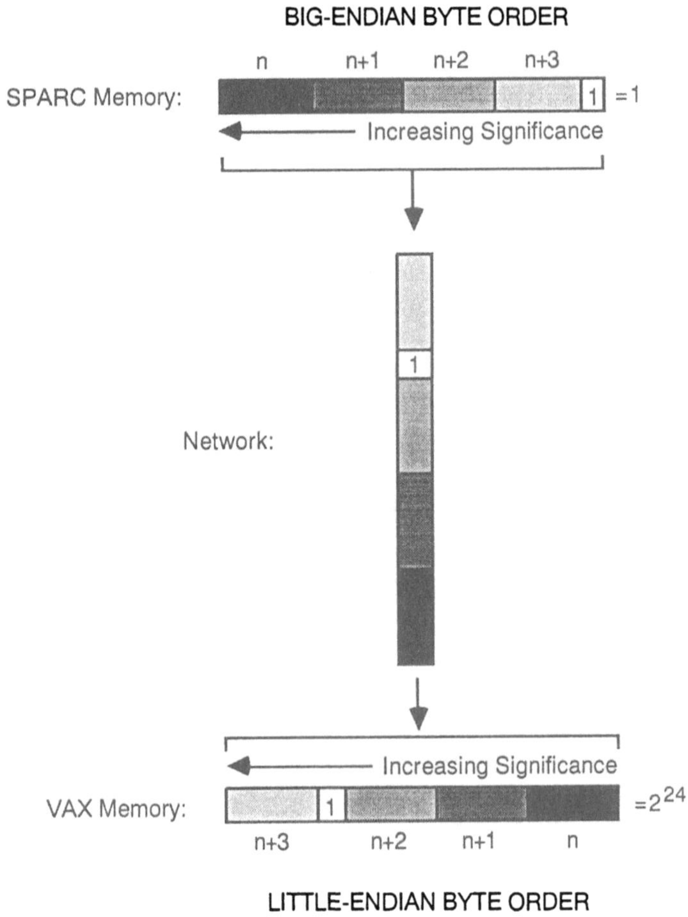

FIGURE 2.2. *SPARC-VAX integer transfer.*

2.1 XDR Definition

XDR is a standard for the description and encoding of data. It is useful for transferring data between different computer architectures and has been used to communicate data between computers as diverse as the Sun workstation, the VAX, the IBM-PC, and the Cray. The XDR standard assumes that bytes, or octets (see NOTE),

Note: An octet is an 8 bit quantity. The number of bits in a byte is dependent on the computer architecture, although in recent years, most computer architectures use 8 bit bytes. Throughout the book the term byte is used to denote an 8 bit quantity.

are portable. A given hardware device encodes the bytes onto the various media in such a way that other hardware devices may decode the bytes without loss of meaning. For example, the Ethernet standard specifies that bytes be encoded with the least significant bit first.

2.2 XDR Data Representation

The XDR approach to standardizing data-representations is canonical: the standard defines a single byte order (big-endian), a single floating-point representation (IEEE), and so on. Any program running on any computer creates portable data by translating its local representations into a machine-independent format referred to as the XDR representation of the data. The single standard completely decouples programs that create or send portable data from those that use or receive portable data. The advent of a new computer, a new language, or a new compiler has no effect on the community of existing portable data creators and users. A new computer joins this community by being "taught" how to convert between the standard representations and its local representations; the local representations of the other computers are irrelevant. Conversely, to existing programs running on other computers, the local representations of the new computer are also irrelevant; such programs can immediately read portable data produced by the new computer because such data conforms to the canonical standard the programs already understand.

Strong precedents exist for XDR's canonical approach. For example, TCP/IP, UDP/IP, XNS, Ethernet and all protocols below layer 5 of the OSI model are canonical protocols. The advantage of any canonical approach is simplicity; in the case of XDR, you write a single set of conversion routines once and never touch them again, no matter what new computers or languages appear in the future. The canonical approach has a small disadvantage. Suppose two little-endian computers are transferring integers according to the XDR standard. The sending computer converts the integers from the little-endian byte order to the big-endian (XDR) byte order; the receiving computer performs the reverse conversion. Because both computers observe the same byte order, their conversions are unnecessary. The point, however, is not necessity, but cost as compared to the alternative.

The time spent converting to and from a canonical representation is insignificant, especially in networking applications. In real-world applications, most of the time required to prepare a data structure for transfer is not spent in conversion but in traversing the elements of the data structure. To transmit a tree, for example, you must visit each leaf and copy each element in a leaf record to a buffer and align them there; storage for the leaf may have to be deallocated as well. Similarly, to receive a tree, you must allocate storage for each leaf, move and properly align data from the buffer to the leaf, and construct pointers to link the leaves together. Every computer pays the cost of traversing and copying data structures whether or not conversion is required. In networking applications, communication overhead—the time required to move the data down through the sender's protocol layers, across the network, and up through the receiver's protocol layers—dwarfs conversion overhead.

The alternative to a canonical standard is multiple standards plus a protocol that specifies which standard has been used to encode a particular piece of data. In this approach, called "receiver makes it right," the sender precedes the data with a tag that describes the format of the data. The number of different data-representations used by computers today (not to mention future computers or future representations defined by languages) precludes supporting all of them in the protocol. A more practical alternative is to support a few of the most common representations. Multiple representation standards have their own problems, the first of which is the need to write a conversion library for every representation defined by the protocol. Note as well that supporting a few representations rather than one prevents unnecessary conversions between computers of a few types but is no improvement for computers that do not conform to one of the common representations; these computers must still convert all data transmitted and received.

The data types defined by XDR are a multiple of four bytes in length. Because XDR's block size is four, reading a sequence of XDR-encoded objects into a buffer results in all objects being aligned on four-byte boundaries provided that the buffer itself is so aligned. This automatic four-byte alignment of XDR types ensures that they can be accessed efficiently on almost all computers. Although a few computers, for example, Crays, have an alignment factor of eight, they can still use XDR by using two XDR blocks instead of one. An XDR block size of eight would exact a substantial storage penalty on most computers without improving performance. XDR's four-byte block size is thus a compromise that maximizes performance on almost all architectures without consuming excessive memory or transmission bandwidth.

Any bytes added to an XDR object to make its length a multiple of four bytes are called fill bytes; the XDR standard specifies that fill bytes contain binary zeros. For example, an XDR string of five characters is padded with three fill bytes to make it eight bytes long. Because fill bytes contain zeros, variable-length XDR data can be consistently compared by different computers.

The exact formats of the XDR representations are specified in the XDR standard in Appendix 2. Note that the decision to use big-endian byte ordering in the XDR standard was based not upon the 68000 microprocessor, but on the byte ordering already used by the Defense Advanced Projects Research Agency (DARPA) Internet.

2.3 XDR Library

The XDR Library is a collection of C functions that convert data between local and XDR representations—that is, between a machine-dependent format and a machine-independent format, respectively. The procedures in the library fall broadly into two groups: those that create and manipulate XDR streams, and those that convert and transfer data to and from these XDR streams. An XDR stream is a byte stream in which data exists in its XDR representation format. Data is converted, by the XDR Library routines, from a machine-dependent format into its XDR representation and then placed into the XDR stream. Bytes are read from the XDR stream and converted, by the XDR Library routines, from the XDR representation into machine-dependent format.

An XDR filter is a procedure that serializes and deserializes data objects of one type. Serializing (often called "encoding") means converting an object from its local representation into the XDR representation and writing the result to a stream. Conversely, deserializing (or "decoding") means reading an XDR-format object from an XDR stream and converting the object to its local representation. The library contains XDR filters for the XDR standard primitive and composite types. You can use these filters directly, and you can also use them to build custom filters that handle locally defined types, such as complex structures. The simplest way to create a custom filter is to use the *rpcgen* compiler described in Chapter 7. With *rpcgen*, you can concentrate on describing the complex data structures, leaving the implementation of the XDR filters to the compiler.

The design of the XDR Library is oriented toward the C language, but not toward the UNIX operating system. In particular, since XDR routines do not depend on the UNIX I/O system, they are portable. The following discussion refers to the values TRUE and FALSE, which are defined in the ⟨*rpc/types.h*⟩ header associated with the RPC/XDR implementation. On SunOS, the RPC include files are located in the directory */usr/include/rpc*.

2.3.1 XDR Streams

The XDR stream abstraction makes XDR filters media-independent. XDR filters read and write data from the XDR stream where this stream can reside on any type of media—for example; memory, disk drive, tape drive, ... A filter interacts only with a stream; the stream interacts with the actual data source or destination. The XDR Library has three kinds of streams: standard I/O, memory, and record streams. Although the streams supplied with the library cover many kinds of media, you can also create custom streams.

The XDR handle is the data type that supports the XDR stream abstraction. This handle is defined in the ⟨*rpc/xdr.h*⟩ header file and is type defined to *XDR*. You do not need to access the members of the XDR handle, but you do need to allocate space for the handle. The handle contains information about the operation that is being applied to the stream, an operations vector, and some private data fields. The valid operations on a stream are:

XDR_ENCODE - encodes the object into the stream
XDR_DECODE - decodes the object from the stream
XDR_FREE - releases the space allocated by an XDR_DECODE request.

The operations are defined in an enumeration, *xdr_op*, in the ⟨*rpc/xdr.h*⟩ header file. The XDR_FREE operation is discussed in more detail in the section on XDR filters. The operations vector contains the address of functions that actually read and write data to the stream, and the function that destroys the stream. Stream destruction involves deallocating resources associated with the stream. The functions used depend on the type of stream the XDR handle is associated with. The private data fields are provided for the stream implementor; one must never make any assumptions about their values.

To create your own custom stream, you would have to implement all the operation functions in the operation vector. The operation functions would interact with the media in which the XDR stream would reside. The difficulty of creating your own stream is dependent upon the given media, but the decoupling provided by the operation vector gives you a well defined interface into the XDR Library, thus increasing the ease of this task.

2.3.1.1 Standard I/O Streams A standard I/O stream connects the XDR stream to a file using the C standard I/O mechanism. When data is converted from its local format to its XDR representation, it is actually written into the file. When bytes are read from the XDR stream and converted to their local format, the bytes are actually read from the file. Using a standard I/O stream to create a file containing data in its XDR representation format is an easy way to make data portable across computers. An example at the end of this chapter shows you how to do this.

Here is the synopsis of the XDR Library routine used to create a standard I/O stream:

```
void
xdrstdio_create(xdr_handle, file, op)
XDR             *xdr_handle;
FILE            *file;
enum xdr_op     op;
```

This routine initializes the XDR handle pointed to by *xdr_handle*. Remember that you must allocate the space for the XDR handle as shown in the example below. The XDR stream data is written to, or read from, the standard I/O stream file. The argument *op* defines the type of operation being performed on the XDR stream. The standard I/O XDR stream is unidirectional, either an encoding stream or a decoding stream. Notice that this function returns the type *void*, meaning that no error checking is performed on the arguments. You should make sure the arguments are valid. For example, a call to an XDR filter using the XDR handle would fail if the *file* argument did not reference an open file. An important note about this function is that the destroy routine associated with this XDR stream calls *fflush()* on the file stream, but never *fclose()*. You should call *fclose()* to close the file when you are through with it.

Here is an example of the use of *xdrstdio_create()*:

```
        ...
XDR     xdr_handle;        /* Allocate space for XDR handle */
FILE    *fp;
        ...
if ((fp = fopen("portable", "w")) == NULL) {
        /* Process the error and exit this function*/
}
xdrstdio_create(&xdr_handle, fp, XDR_ENCODE);
        ...
fclose(fp);
        ...
```

The example opens a file named *portable* and then associates an XDR standard I/O stream with it. All subsequent calls to XDR filters using *xdr_handle* encode data into the file. Once the file has data, another process can open it up for reading and call *xdrstdio_create()* with an operation of XDR_DECODE to cause subsequent calls to XDR filters to read data from the file and decode it into a local representation format. The section on XDR filters demonstrates this procedure.

2.3.1.2 Memory Streams Whereas a standard I/O stream represents a connection to a file, a memory stream is a connection to a block of memory. Memory streams can access an XDR-format data structure located in memory. A common example is the XDR encoding/decoding of arguments to a remote procedure call. The arguments are passed through from the calling program to the RPC Library where they are encoded into an XDR memory stream and then passed on to the networking software for transmission to the remote procedure. The networking software receives the results and writes them into the XDR memory stream. The RPC Library then invokes XDR routines to decode the data from the stream into the storage allocated for the results. Other examples of the use of memory streams include the encoding/decoding of non-indexed data in a database, and the encoding/decoding of data in a distributed shared memory system.

Here is the synopsis of the XDR Library routine that creates a memory stream:

```
void
xdrmem_create(xdr_handle, addr, size, op)
XDR           *xdr_handle;
char          *addr;
u_int         size;
enum xdr_op   op;
```

This routine initializes the XDR handle pointed to by *xdr_handle*. The XDR stream data is written to, or read from, a block of memory at location *addr* whose length is *size* bytes long. The memory location in *addr* should be aligned on a XDR unit boundary, which is four bytes. The memory block should be large enough to hold the amount of data in XDR representation that you intend to encode into the stream. The argument *op* defines the type of operation being performed on the XDR stream. The memory XDR stream is also unidirectional—either an encoding stream or a decoding stream. This function returns type *void*, which indicates that no error checking is performed on the arguments. You should make sure that the arguments are valid. For example, a call to an XDR filter using the XDR handle would fail if the *addr* argument does not reference a valid memory location.

Here is an example of the use of *xdrmem_create()*:

```
        ...
XDR     xdr_handle;      /* Allocate space for XDR handle */
char    *mem;
u_int   size;

size = RNDUP(BUF_SIZE);
mem = malloc(size);
if (mem == NULL) {
        /* Process the error and exit this function*/
}
xdrmem_create(&xdr_handle, mem, size, XDR_ENCODE);
        ...
free(mem);
        ...
```

The example allocates BUF_SIZE number of bytes for the XDR stream. The macro *RNDUP*, defined in ⟨*rpc/xdr.h*⟩, was used to ensure that the size of the buffer used for the stream is a multiple of BYTES_PER_XDR_UNIT. This precaution ensures that the re-

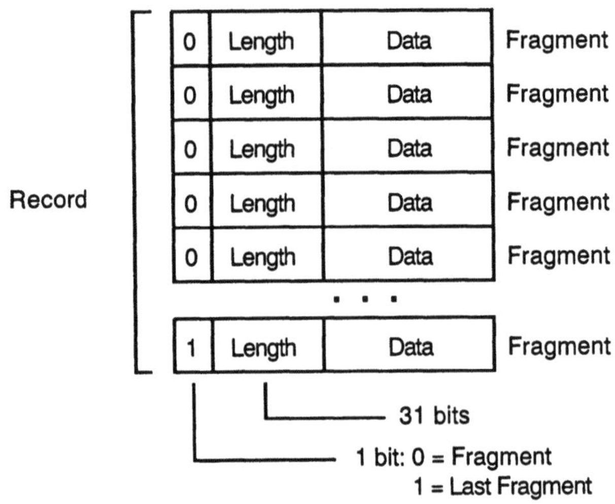

FIGURE 2.3. *Record marking.*

turned memory address is suitably aligned for use as an XDR stream. All subsequent calls to XDR filters using *xdr_handle* encode data into the memory buffer. Now another function can come along and associate an XDR_DECODE stream with the memory buffer to cause subsequent calls to XDR filters to read data from the memory buffer and decode it into a local representation format. The section on XDR filters shows you how to do this.

2.3.1.3 Record Streams Even when a medium is stream-oriented it is sometimes desirable to delimit records in the stream. For example, if an error is detected at the beginning of a record by the XDR filter, the remainder of the record can be skipped. To do this requires that the start and end of a record are marked, and are therefore discernible, in the stream. These record delineations require bytes in the stream (in addition to the XDR representation data) that provide record boundary information.

The records in a record stream are delimited as shown in Figure 2.3. A record is composed of one or more fragments. A fragment consists of a four-byte header followed by 0 to 2 ^ 31 - 1 bytes of data. A header contains two values: a bit that, when set, marks the last fragment of a record and 31 bits that, interpreted as an unsigned integer, specify the length of the fragment data. Note that headers conform to the XDR standard for byte ordering, but not for encoding. This design flaw is due to premature optimization; encoding the header as an XDR boolean and an XDR unsigned integer would have resulted in eight bytes of overhead for each fragment.

Here is the synopsis of the XDR Library routine used to create a record stream:

```
void
xdrrec_create(xdr_handle, sendsize, recvsize, iohandle, readit, writeit)
XDR            *xdr_handle;
u_int          sendsize, recvsize;
char           *iohandle;
int            (*readit)(), (*writeit)();
```

This routine initializes the XDR handle pointed to by *xdr_handle*. The XDR stream data is written to a buffer of size *sendsize*, and is read from a buffer of size *recvsize*. Space for both buffers is allocated by this routine. Because record streams provide buffering, it was felt that values less than 100 bytes were an unreasonable size for a buffer. Therefore, buffer size values of less than 100 result in a size of 4000 being used. The *iohandle* argument identifies the medium that supplies records to and accepts records from the XDR stream buffers (just as a file descriptor identifies the file being used). This argument is not used by *xdrrec_create()*, but is passed on to the *readit()* and *writeit()* routines. The last two arguments are the addresses of the *readit()* and *writeit()* routines. When a stream's input buffer is empty, *readit()* is called by the XDR filter to read data from the medium into the buffer. Similarly, when the XDR stream output buffer is full, *writeit()* is called by the XDR filter to write buffered data to the medium. The behavior of these two routines is similar to the system calls *read()* and *write()*, except that the *iohandle* argument is passed to the former routines as the first argument. Because the *iohandle* and the read and write procedures decouple the stream from the medium that is accepting or supplying records, a record stream can be associated with anything supporting read and write primitives.

Here is the synopsis of the *readit()* and *writeit()* routines which are the same:

```
int
func(iohandle, buf, nbytes)
char           *iohandle, *buf;
int            nbytes;
```

The *iohandle* argument is the same as the one specified in the *xdrrec_create()* call, and can be a pointer to a standard I/O FILE type (assuming that the size of the pointer to these objects is the same size as a pointer to a *char*). To ensure the portability of your code, one could do a mapping on the *iohandle;* this mapping could use a number guaranteed to fit in a *char* * to index a table that would return the proper type. The *buf* argument is the address of the buffer to read data into for the *readit()* function and is the address of the buffer to write data from for the *writeit()* function. The function returns the number of bytes transferred or -1 to indicate an error.

Here is an example of the use of *xdrrec_create().* A standard I/O stream is used for the medium.

```
example()
{
          ...
    FILE  *fp;
    XDR   xdr_handle;      /* Allocate space for XDR handle */
    char  *filename;
    u_int size;
    int   read_data();
    int   write_data();
          ...
    if ((fp = fopen(filename, file_type)) == NULL) {
          return (FAILURE);
    }
    xdrrec_create(&xdr_handle, (u_int)0, (u_int)0, (char *)fp,
                read_data, write_data);
          ...
}/* example */
int
read_data(fp, buf, cnt)
    FILE  *fp;
    char  *buf;
    int   cnt;
{
    int   nread;
    nread = fread(buf, 1, cnt, fp);
    if (nread == 0) {
          nread = -1;
    }
    return (nread);
}/* read_data */
int
```

```
write_data(fp, buf, cnt)
        FILE    *fp;
        char    *buf;
        int     cnt;
{
        int     nwrite;

        nwrite = fwrite(buf, 1, cnt, fp);
        if (nwrite == 0) {
                nwrite = -1;
        }
        return (nwrite);
}/* write_data */
```

The example creates an XDR record-based stream. The default size will be used for the send and receive buffer because the buffer size arguments are set to 0. A pointer to the *FILE* type is used as the I/O handle. Notice that this value is passed into the *read_data()* and *write_data()* routines. The *read_data()* routine reads *cnt* bytes from the standard I/O stream into the input buffer. The *write_data()* routine writes *cnt* bytes from the output buffer to the standard I/O stream.

Unlike standard I/O and memory streams, record streams can handle encoding and decoding in one stream; you select encoding or decoding by simply setting the *x_op* field in the XDR handle before calling a filter. For example, if *xdr_handle* is a pointer to an XDR handle, then the stream is set for encoding by the following statement:

```
xdr_handle->x_op = XDR_ENCODE;
```

In addition to XDR filters, three other XDR Library routines can be applied to record streams. The synopses for these routines follows:

```
bool_t
xdrrec_endofrecord(xdr_handle, sendnow)
XDR             *xdr_handle;
bool_t          sendnow;
```

This routine terminates a record being encoded and, optionally, flushes the write buffer. If the argument, *sendnow*, is set to TRUE, the stream's *writeit()* function is called; otherwise, *writeit()* is called by an XDR filter when the output buffer has been filled.

```
bool_t
xdrrec_skiprecord(xdr_handle)
XDR             *xdr_handle;
```

This routine skips to the beginning of the next record in a record stream that is being decoded. Before decoding data from the stream, you should always call this procedure to guarantee proper record alignment with the first record.

```
bool_t
xdrrec_eof(xdr_handle)
XDR             *xdr_handle;
```

This routine indicates whether more data, beyond the current record, is currently in the read buffer for a record stream that is being decoded. The routine does not indicate that the next call to the *readit()* routine will not return data, simply that no more data is in the read buffer.

A complete example of the use of record-based XDR streams is at the end of this chapter.

2.3.1.4 Stream Related Macros The header file ⟨*xdr.h*⟩ defines three XDR Library macros that manipulate XDR streams. Here are the synopses for each:

```
u_int
xdr_getpos(xdr_handle)
XDR             *xdr_handle;
```

This macro invokes the get-position routine associated with the XDR handle pointed to by *xdr_handle*. The routine returns an unsigned integer, which indicates the position of the XDR byte stream. This routine is useful for determining how many bytes were required to XDR-encode data objects. A desirable feature of XDR streams is that simple arithmetic works with this number, although the XDR stream need not guarantee it. Note that it may not be possible for an XDR stream to get the current position due to an error or because it is impossible to determine the current position in the medium. For those streams this macro returns the equivalent value of *((u_int)-1)*. It is possible to determine the current position for the standard I/O, memory, and record-based XDR streams.

```
bool_t
xdr_setpos(xdr_handle, pos)
XDR             *xdr_handle;
u_int           pos;
```

This macro invokes the set position routine associated with the XDR handle pointed to by *xdr_handle*. The argument *pos* should be a position value obtained from *xdr_getpos()*. This macro returns TRUE if the XDR stream could be repositioned; otherwise, it returns FALSE. Note that it might not be possible to reposition some types of XDR streams, so this routine may fail with one type of stream and succeed with another. It is possible to set the position for the standard I/O, memory, and record-based XDR streams.

```
void
xdr_destroy(xdr_handle)
XDR             *xdr_handle;
```

This is a macro that invokes the destroy routine associated with the XDR handle pointed to by *xdr_handle*. You should call this routine when you are finished with the XDR stream. Destruction usually involves freeing memory allocated for private data structures associated with the stream. Using *xdr_handle* after you invoke *xdr_destroy()* results in undefined behavior.

2.3.2 XDR Filters

XDR filters are trifunctional; one filter can encode and decode one data type, and it can also free memory that a filter may have allocated. The free operation is discussed in more detail in the section on managing memory. Localizing the code that deals with a data type into a single routine increases the likelihood that the encode and decode operations are perfectly symmetrical—that decoding exactly reproduces the data that was encoded, allowing for differences in local representations. This is not much of an issue for the relatively simple filters supplied in the XDR Library, but it becomes significant when you develop custom filters for complex data structures. Custom filters are described in Section 2.3.2.3. All filters return a value of type *bool_t*. They return TRUE if they complete successfully and return FALSE otherwise. A filter can return FALSE if it receives bad data, such as encoded data that exceeds a maximum-length argument, or if there is an XDR stream error, as when a write to the file fails for a standard I/O

C Type	Filter	XDR Type
char	xdr_char ()	int
short int	xdr_short ()	int
unsigned short int	xdr_u_short ()	unsigned int
int	xdr_int ()	int
unsigned int	xdr_u_int ()	unsigned int
long	xdr_long ()	int
unsigned long	xdr_u_long ()	unsigned int
float	xdr_float ()	float
double	xdr_double ()	double
void	xdr_void ()	void
enum	xdr_enum ()	int

TABLE 2.1. *Primitive filters.*

stream (because the file system was full, or because of a disk drive failure, etc.).

2.3.2.1 Primitive Filters The XDR Library's primitive filters are listed in Table 2.1. They correspond to the C programming language primitive types. The first two arguments of all filters are identical no matter what kind of data is being encoded or decoded; primitive filters define only these two arguments. The first argument is a pointer to an XDR stream handle. The second argument is the address of the data of interest, referred to as an object handle. The object handle references the encoding source, or the decoding destination. An object handle is simply a pointer to any possible data type. Because the second argument is the address of an object, the filter can either read data from it (for encoding) or write data to it (for decoding).

The use of most XDR primitive filters is intuitive. If you want to encode or decode a variable of type *long*, you would use the *xdr_long()* routine. The use of the *xdr_void()* routine is not intuitive; why would you want to encode nothing into an XDR stream? Why decode nothing from an XDR stream? The *xdr_void()* routine is useful for describing operations that neither input nor output any data. The routine is also useful in the definition of discriminated unions and linked lists which are described later in this chapter.

The XDR Library also provides macros for encoding and decoding primitive data types. These macros are referred to as the XDR In-line macros and can significantly reduce the amount of time that it takes to encode and decode data. The macros are not as robust as the primitive routines because they use single accesses to get the data from the underlying buffer, and will fail to operate properly if the data is not correctly aligned. The In-line macros that perform the actual conversions do not return any indication of an error. To use these macros you would first call *xdr_inline()* to obtain a contiguous piece of the XDR stream buffer, then you would call the desired In-line macros to perform the encodings or decodings. Here is the synopses for In-line macros followed by an example:

```
long *
xdr_inline(xdr_handle, len)
XDR             *xdr_handle;
int             len;
```

This macro invokes the in-line routine associated with the XDR stream handle, *xdr_handle*. The routine returns a pointer to a contiguous piece of the XDR stream buffer. The argument *len* specifies the byte length of the desired buffer.

Note: The routine will cast a *caddr_t* pointer into a pointer to a long type. Warning: *xdr_inline()* may return NULL if it cannot allocate a contiguous piece of a buffer. Therefore the behavior may vary among different stream types.

The following In-line macros decode data from the specified buffer and then increment the buffer pointer so that it points to the next object in the buffer.

```
long
IXDR_GET_LONG(buf)
long            *buf;

bool_t
IXDR_GET_BOOL(buf)
long            *buf;

type
IXDR_GET_ENUM(buf, type)
long            *buf;
type            type;
```

Note that this macro returns a value cast to the type specified as the second argument.

```
u_long
IXDR_GET_U_LONG(buf)
long            *buf;

short
IXDR_GET_SHORT(buf)
long            *buf;

u_short
IXDR_GET_U_SHORT(buf)
long            *buf;
```

The following In-line macros encode data into the specified buffer and then increment the buffer pointer so that it points to the next position in the buffer. Note that the argument, *value*, is ultimately cast to the *u_long* type.

```
void
IXDR_PUT_LONG(buf, value)
long            *buf;
long            value;

void
IXDR_PUT_BOOL(buf, value)
long            *buf;
bool_t          value;

void
IXDR_PUT_ENUM(buf, value)
long            *buf;
enum_t          value;

void
IXDR_PUT_U_LONG(buf, value)
long            *buf;
u_long          value;

void
IXDR_PUT_SHORT(buf, value)
long            *buf;
short           value;

void
IXDR_PUT_U_SHORT(buf, value)
long            *buf;
u_short         value;
```

The following example uses the In-line macros to decode 10 short integers from the file *portable*. The example uses a standard I/O XDR stream type.

```
...
FILE        *fp;
XDR         xdr_handle;
long        *buf;
int         i, count;
short       array[10];
...
if ((fp = fopen("portable", "w")) == NULL) {
        /* Process the error and exit this function*/
}

xdrstdio_create(&xdr_handle, fp, XDR_ENCODE);
...
count = BYTES_PER_XDR_UNIT * 10;
buf = XDR_INLINE(&xdr_handle, count);
if (buf == NULL)
        /* Process the error          */
for ( i = 0; i < 10 ; i++) {
        array[i] = IXDR_GET_SHORT(buf);
}
...
xdr_destroy(&xdr_handle);
fclose(fp);
...
```

2.3.2.2 Composite Filters In addition to the primitive filters, the XDR Library provides composite filters for commonly used data types. As with the primitive filters, the first two arguments of an XDR composite filter are a pointer to an XDR stream handle and a pointer to an object handle. The additional arguments are described in the synopses for the composite filters below:

```
bool_t
xdr_string(xdr_handle, strp, maxsize)
XDR         *xdr_handle;
char        **strp;
u_int       maxsize;
```

This filter translates between strings and their corresponding local representations. Strings are represented in C as pointers to character arrays with the end of a string marked by a null character. The passed in string, excluding null character, cannot be longer than *maxsize* characters. The filter returns FALSE if, on encoding or decoding, the actual string length exceeds the maximum length. Note that the argument *strp* is the address of a pointer to the string. This routine returns FALSE if the pointer passed to it for encoding is null (*strp == NULL). For decoding, *xdr_string()* decodes the string into the location referenced by the pointer. If this pointer is null, then the routine allocates memory for the object and returns the address in the pointer. Also, because XDR strings are defined to contain ASCII characters, an implementation of *xdr_string()* on an EBCDIC computer converts characters from EBCDIC to ASCII on encoding and from ASCII to EBCDIC on decoding. The difference between the two character representation standards is that they use different underlying values to represent characters. For example, the character 'A' is represented by the value 65 in US ASCII while it is represented by the value 193 in EBCDIC.

If you do not know the size of the string being received, you could use the maximum value of an unsigned integer, UINT_MAX, for *maxsize* or you could use the *xdr_wrapstring()* routine. This routine always calls *xdr_string()* with the *maxsize* argument set to the maximum value of an unsigned integer.

Two XDR Library routines handle bytes: the routine *xdr_opaque()* handles a fixed length array of bytes and the routine *xdr_bytes()* handles a variable length array of bytes. The synopses for both routines follows:

```
bool_t
xdr_opaque(xdr_handle, cp, cnt)
XDR             *xdr_handle;
char            *cp;
u_int           cnt;
```

Sometimes it is useful to pass fixed-length uninterpreted data through an XDR stream. This data is referred to as *opaque* because this filter does not know the type of data. This filter does not interpret the contents of the object referenced by the object handle since the contents are opaque, but it simply copies the bytes directly to the XDR stream on encoding. On decoding, it copies the bytes directly from the XDR stream to the byte array referenced by *cp*. The additional argument *cnt* is the size in bytes of the opaque data.

```
bool_t
xdr_bytes(xdr_handle, arrp, sizep, maxsize)
```

```
XDR            *xdr_handle;
char           **arrp;
u_int          *sizep, maxsize;
```

This filter translates between an array of bytes and the XDR variable length opaque type. The filter does not interpret the contents of the object referenced by the object handle, just as *xdr_opaque()* does not. Its additional arguments are a pointer to an actual-length specifier and a maximum length. For encoding, this filter reads the actual-length specifier; for decoding it sets the actual-length specifier. If the array length exceeds the maximum length, the filter returns FALSE. This routine returns FALSE if the pointer passed to it for encoding is null (*arrp == NULL). For decoding, *xdr_bytes()* decodes the objects into the location referenced by the pointer. If this pointer is null, then the routine allocates memory for the objects and returns the address in the pointer.

Two XDR Library routines handle an array of objects: the routine *xdr_vector()* handles a fixed length array of objects and the routine *xdr_array()* handles a variable length array of objects. The synopses for both routines follows:

```
bool_t
xdr_vector(xdr_handle, arrp, size, elsize, elproc)
XDR            *xdr_handle;
char           *arrp;
u_int          size, elsize;
xdrproc_t      elproc;
```

This filter translates between fixed-length arrays and their corresponding local representations. The argument *arrp* is a pointer to the array. The argument *size* is the element count of the array. The argument *elsize* is the size of each of the array's elements, and *elproc* is the address of an XDR filter that is called for each element of the array to translate between the array element's local representation and its XDR representation for encoding; the reverse holds for decoding. Note that any filter can be passed to *xdr_vector()*, including custom filters described in the next section.

```
bool_t
xdr_array(xdr_handle, arrp, sizep, maxsize, elsiz, elproc)
XDR            *xdr_handle;
char           **arrp;
u_int          *sizep, maxsize, elsize;
xdrproc_t      elproc;
```

This filter is the counterpart of *xdr_vector()*, except that it handles variable-length arrays. It takes the same arguments as *xdr_vector()*, except that it takes a pointer to the pointer of the array, a pointer to the element count of the array and also takes an argument, *maxsize*, to define the maximum possible size of the array. When encoding, it reads the actual-length specifier; for decoding it sets the actual-length specifier. If the array length exceeds the maximum length, the filter returns FALSE. This routine returns FALSE if the pointer passed to it for encoding is null (*arrp == NULL). For decoding, *xdr_array()* decodes the objects into the location referenced by the pointer. If this pointer is null, then the routine allocates memory for the objects and returns the address in the pointer.

In C, a *union* is used to hold objects of different types and sizes. The union can only hold one object at a time. XDR language defines a type similar to a union called a *discriminated union*. It uses a discriminate to identify the type of the object that is currently stored in the union so that the XDR Library knows the correct XDR routine to invoke to encode/decode the object stored in the union. Although the XDR Library simulates the discriminated union for C, some programming languages, such as Ada or Pascal, directly support this type of union. Here is the synopsis for the composite filter routine that handles unions:

```
bool_t
xdr_union(xdr_handle, dscmp, unp, choices, defaultarm)
XDR                    *xdr_handle;
enum_t                 *dscmp;
char                   *unp;
struct xdr_discrim     *choices;
xdrproc_t              defaultarm;
```

This filter translates between a discriminated union and its corresponding local representation. A discriminated union can be simulated in C by the combination of a union and an enumeration that acts as the union's discriminant: The member of the union used is dictated by the enumeration. Because each member of a union is a different type, each member needs its own filter. An array, consisting of one element per member, can act as a directory to the member filters. Each array element is a structure consisting of a discriminant value (one value of the associated enumeration), and a pointer to the XDR filter that corresponds to that value. Given these three elements, the enumeration, the member filter, and the member filter directory, you can encode and decode a C union by calling *xdr_union()* with the following arguments: a pointer to the XDR handle, *xdr_handle*, a pointer to the discriminant, *dscmp*, a pointer to the union, *unp*, the name of the member filter directory, *choices*, and a pointer to an XDR filter for the default member, *defaultarm*. Use a NULL value for the *defaultarm* argument if the union has no default member. An example follows:

```
        ...
enum disc_type { END = 0, ERROR, SINGLE, DOUBLE };
struct xdr_discrim filter_dir[] = {
        { ERROR,      xdr_int        },
        { SINGLE,     xdr_float      },
        { DOUBLE,     xdr_double     },
        { END,        NULL           },
};
XDR                   xdr_handle;
bool_t                rtn_code;
enum    disc_type     disc;
union {
        int     error;
        float   svalue;
        double  lvalue;
} real_num;
        ...
/*
 * XDR stream opened for encoding
 */
        ...
real_num.svalue = 2.4;
disc = SINGLE;
rtn_code = xdr_union(&xdr_handle, &disc, &real_num, filter_dir, NULL);
        ...
```

The example results in *xdr_union()* interpreting the data in the union, *real_num*, as a single-precision floating-point value. Note that a default member is not specified. If you were decoding, *xdr_union()* would set the value of *disc* to the enumeration value that corresponds to the type that was decoded from the XDR stream and written into the union, *real_num*.

Two XDR Library routines handle pointers: the routine *xdr_reference()* handles a reference to an object and the routine *xdr_pointer()* provides the ability to handle a linked list, i.e. it serializes the null pointer. The synopses for both routines follows:

```
bool_t
xdr_reference(xdr_handle, pp, size, proc)
XDR                    *xdr_handle;
char                   **pp;
u_int                  size;
xdrproc_t              proc;
```

This filter is useful for handling references to an object. Since the object passed in is a pointer to some data type, the object handle is the address of the pointer to this data type. This filter encodes a pointer by encoding what it points to by invoking the associated XDR filter, *proc*, to actually encode the object. The *xdr_reference()* filter returns FALSE if the pointer passed to it for encoding is null (*pp == NULL). For decoding, this filter decodes an object into the location referenced by the pointer, **pp*. If this pointer is null, then the routine allocates memory for the object and returns the address in the pointer. The *size* argument is the size of the referenced object.

It is useful to use XDR filters to encode and decode complex structures such as trees and linked lists. The only problem is that these structures contain pointers to the next object on the list. It is not useful to encode the values of these pointers into an XDR stream because the memory address would have no meaning to a decoding filter on another computer. The XDR Library uses the *xdr_pointer()* routine to handle encoding and decoding linked lists. It encodes linked lists onto the XDR stream by placing an XDR boolean on the stream. A value of TRUE indicates there are more members of the list in the stream—the pointer was non-null. A value of FALSE indicates the end of the linked list—the pointer was null. If the pointer was non-null, *xdr_pointer()* calls *xdr_reference()* to handle the object referenced by the pointer value. The synopsis follows:

```
bool_t
xdr_pointer(xdr_handle, objpp, objsize, objproc)
XDR                    *xdr_handle;
char                   **objpp;
u_int                  objsize;
xdrproc_t              objproc;
```

This routine provides pointer chasing within structures and allows the representation of binary trees and linked lists. The only difference between this routine and *xdr_reference()* is that this routine serializes a null pointer. The additional arguments of this function are the size of the object addressed by the pointer and the address of an XDR filter to encode and decode each object. Since this routine uses *xdr_reference()*, memory is allocated for the objects when decoding.

The use of this routine is demonstrated in the following example.

```
    ...
typedef struct window {
        long            window_data;
        int             count;
        struct window*nextp;
} window_list;
    ...
bool_t
xdr_window_list(xdr_handlep, windowp)
        XDR             *xdr_handlep;
        window_list     *windowp;
{
        if (xdr_pointer(xdr_handlep, (char **)&windowp->nextp,
          sizeof(window_list),
          xdr_window_list) == FALSE) {
                return (FALSE);
        }
        if (xdr_long(xdr_handlep, &windowp->window_data) == FALSE) {
                return (FALSE);
        }
        return(xdr_int(xdr_handlep, &windowp->count));
} /* xdr_window_list */
```

The caller to *xdr_window_list()* passes in the address of the first *window_list* structure on the list. If it is encoding, the call to *xdr_pointer()* writes a TRUE boolean value to the stream if the next pointer is non-NULL. The *xdr_pointer()* routine calls *xdr_reference()* to encode what is referenced by the pointer using the *xdr_window_list()* routine. Note that this results in a recursive call to *xdr_window_list()* which calls *xdr_pointer()* which writes a TRUE boolean value to the stream if the next pointer is non-NULL, and calls *xdr_reference()* again and the recursion continues until the next pointer is NULL. When this happens, *xdr_pointer()* outputs a FALSE boolean value to the stream and the call returns to *xdr_window_list()* which encodes the *window_data* and *count* members to the stream. All of the calls to *xdr_pointer()* return in this manner. After encoding the linked list, the XDR stream would appear as follows:

TRUE ... FALSE window_data count ... window_data count

If *xdr_window_list()* is decoding, the recursion occurs in a similar manner as described above and the routine allocates memory to store the list. Remember to call *xdr_free()* with the XDR procedure argument *proc* set to the address of *xdr_window_list()* and the object handle *objp* set to the address of *windowp* to free up any allocated memory (see Section 2.3.2.4).

2.3.2.3 Custom Filters You may have noticed that the XDR Library doesn't provide an *xdr_struct()* filter. It would be difficult to know in advance the data types of the members of the structures. You can use the filters provided in the XDR Library to construct filters for programmer-defined data types. These filters are referred to as custom filters. A custom filter is thus analogous to a procedure that is constructed from calls to more primitive procedures. Because, like a procedure, it encapsulates the details of the constructed data type, a custom filter is easier to use and more reliable than encoding and decoding a structure member by member (which is nonetheless possible). You can write a custom filter, or, as described in Chapter 7, you can use the *rpcgen* compiler to create a custom filter from an XDR data description.

An example of a custom filter follows:

```
struct netuser {
        char            *nu_hostname;
        int             nu_uid;
        u_int           nu_glen;
        int             *nu_gids;
};
#define NLEN 255                        /* host names <256 chars */
#define NGRPS 20                        /* user can't be in > 20 groups      */
bool_t
xdr_netuser(xdr_handlep, nup)
        XDR             *xdr_handlep;
        struct netuser  *nup;
{
        if (xdr_int(xdr_handlep, &nup->nu_uid) == FALSE)
              return (FALSE);
```

```
if (xdr_string(xdr_handlep, &nup->nu_hostname, NLEN) == FALSE)
  return (FALSE);
    if (xdr_u_int(xdr_handlep, &nup->nu_glen) == FALSE)
      return (FALSE);
    return (xdr_array(xdr_handlep, &nup->nu_gids, &nup->nu_glen,
      NGRPS, sizeof(int), xdr_int));
}/* xdr_netuser */
```

The example contains a filter for a *netuser* data type. A *netuser* structure consists of a host name, a user ID, and an array of groups to which the user belongs. Following the model of the XDR Library filters, the netuser filter's name is *xdr_netuser()*, and its arguments are a pointer to an XDR handle and a pointer to an object handle—a pointer to an object whose type is *netuser*. The filter is a series of calls to XDR filters that encode and decode members of the *netuser* structure. Note that the XDR filters for the structure members are not called in the same order as they were declared in the structure definition. The order of the encoding is not important, but it is important that the filters are called in the same order for encoding and for decoding. For this example, it is important that the *nu_glen* member be encoded/decoded before the *nu_gids* member because its value is used when encoding/decoding the *nu_gids* member.

2.3.2.4 Managing Memory Many composite and custom objects have variable lengths. A process that decodes variable-length objects usually does not know how long the object will be. One way to manage storage for variable-length objects is to provide enough for the longest possible object. Alternatively, memory allocation can be delegated to an XDR filter. Because a filter decodes a variable-length object's count field before the data proper, it knows how much storage the object requires and can dynamically allocate just enough memory for it. Filters allocate memory using the *malloc()* C Library call.

A filter dynamically allocates memory when it gets a pointer to an object handle whose value is null. Upon return from the filter call, the object handle points to the dynamically allocated object. The following XDR filters can allocate memory:

> *xdr_array()* , *xdr_bytes()* , *xdr_pointer()* , *xdr_reference()* , *xdr_string()*, *xdr_vector()* , and *xdr_wrapstring()*.

You can free memory dynamically allocated by a filter by calling the *xdr_free()* routine. The synopsis for this routine follows:

```
void
xdr_free(proc, objp)
xdrproc_t       proc;
char            *objp;
```

This is the XDR Library generic memory freeing routine. The first argument, *proc*, is the address of the XDR routine that actually frees the object. The second argument, *objp*, is a pointer to the object itself. Note that the pointer passed to this routine is not freed, but what it points to is freed.

Another way to free memory is to manually set the *x_op* member in the XDR handle to XDR_FREE before calling the XDR filter. It is important to remember to reset the *x_op* variable back to its original value before continuing decoding or encoding operations. Using the *xdr_free()* routine to free memory is the preferred choice because you do not have to explicitly set values in the XDR handle.

An example of freeing memory allocated by an XDR filter follows:

```
#include <stdio.h>
#include <rpc/rpc.h>

#define MAXSIZE        256

           ...
        XDR      xdr_handle;
        enum     xdrop;
        xdr_op
        bool_t   rtn_code;
        char     letters[MAXSIZE];
        char     *ltr_ptr;
           ...
        xdrstdio_create(&xdr_handle, stdin, XDR_DECODE);
        /*
         * Decode a string into dynamic memory. ltr_ptr points
         * to the decoded string after the xdr_string() call.
         */
        ltr_ptr = NULL;
        rtn_code = xdr_string(&xdr_handle, &ltr_ptr, MAXSIZE);

        /*
         * Free the string just decoded
         */
        xdr_free(xdr_string, &ltr_ptr)
        ...
```

Note that the code to allocate and free memory for a object is localized in the same routine that encodes and decodes the object. Also note that custom filters automatically inherit the ability to dynamically allocate memory from their primitive filter components. Regardless of how complex a structure is, if you can describe the structure in the XDR language, you can use the XDR Library routines to create a filter that not only encodes and decodes the object but also allocates and frees memory for it.

2.4 Examples

This section contains two complete examples that show how to use a standard I/O stream and a record-based stream. The standard I/O stream example creates a portable file containing plot data stored in the XDR representation. The file contains a magic number, a version number, and the number of coordinate pairs in the file followed by the coordinate pairs. The magic number allows the data file to be properly identified by the UNIX *file* command, provided you have entered in the magic number for your coordinate file into the file */etc/magic*.[1] Refer to your operating system manual for more information about the file command and the */etc/magic* file. The version number in the coordinate file identifies the version of the program that created the file and is used by the program to determine if it knows the format of the file. Both the magic number and version number allow the portable data file to be self-descriptive.

The coordinates in the file are single-precision floating-point numbers. Remember that the XDR representation for *float* is the same format as the IEEE standard for normalized single-precision floating point numbers. The data in the file can now be read by any program running on any computer that uses the routines below. The XDR Library must be available on the computer on which you are running the program. If it is not, you can always get the source code and port it to the computer. Note that the error handling in the examples is vague, but you can always improve it by determining the cause of the error and reporting it to the user.

The standard I/O stream example is shown in Figure 2.4.

---

[1] The magic number must first be converted from its XDR representation to its local representation before the *file* command can identify the file.

```
#include <stdio.h>
#include <rpc/rpc.h>

#define PLOT_FILE_MAGIC    0×13FFFFFF /* Coordinate file magic number */
#define PLOT_FILE_VERSION  1          /* Coordinate file version number */
#define SUCCESS            0
#define FAILURE            1
#define DATA_FILE          "portable"

enum io_ops     { READ, WRITE };

/*
 *The coordinates could come from a file, keyboard or other device
 *they do not have to be statically allocated.
 */
#define MAX_COORD_PAIRS  10
float   x[MAX_COORD_PAIRS] = { 1.9, 2.8, 3.7, 4.6, 5.5, 6.4, 7.3, 8.2, 9.1, 9.9 };
float   y[MAX_COORD_PAIRS] = { 1.8, 3.5, 6.1, 7.2, 4.8, 3.9, 5.3, 7.2, 8.8, 9.9 };

void    print_xy();

main(argc, argv)
        int             argc;
        char            *argv[];
{
        int             i;
        /*
         *Print out the data coordinates
         */
        print_xy(x, y, MAX_COORD_PAIRS);

        /*
         *Create the portable data file
         */
        printf("\nCreating the portable data file\n");
        if (rw_data(DATA_FILE, x, y, MAX_COORD_PAIRS, WRITE) ==
           FAILURE) {
                fprintf(stderr, "Error: during file encoding\n");
                return (FAILURE);
        }
```

FIGURE 2.4. *Standard I/O stream example.*

```
        /*
         *Zero out our X and Y array
         */
        for (i = 0; i < MAX_COORD_PAIRS; i++) {
                x[i] = y[i] = 0.0;
        }

        /*
         *Read the coordinates back in
         */
        printf("\nReading the portable data file\n");
        if (rw_data(DATA_FILE, x, y, MAX_COORD_PAIRS, READ) ==
           FAILURE) {
           fprintf(stderr, "Error: during file decoding\n");
                   return (FAILURE);
        }

        /*
         *Print out the data coordinates
         */
        print_xy(x, y, MAX_COORD_PAIRS);

        return (SUCCESS);
} /*main */

void
print_xy(x, y, cnt)
        float                   *x;
        float                   *y;
        int                     cnt;

{
        int                     i;
        printf("X - Y coordinate pairs\n");
        for (i = 0; i < cnt; i++, x++, y++) {
                printf("%f %f\n", *x, *y);
        }
} /* print_xy */

int
rw_data(filename, x, y, cnt, op)
```

FIGURE 2.4 Continued

```
        char                    *filename;
        float                   *x, *y;
        int                     cnt;            /* Number of coordinate pairs */
        enum io_ops             op;
{
        FILE                    *fp;
        XDR                     xdr_handle;
        enum xdr_op             xdrop;          /* XDR Stream Operation        */
        int                     pair_cnt;       /* Number of coordinate pairs in the
                                                   XDR stream */
        int                     magic;          /* Magic number of file        */
        int                     version;        /* Version number of file */
        char                    i, status;
                                *file_type;     /* Standard I/O file operation  */
        if (op == READ) {
                xdrop = XDR_DECODE;
                file_type = "r";
        } else {
                xdrop = XDR_ENCODE;
                file_type = "w+";
                pair_cnt = cnt;
                magic = PLOT_FILE_MAGIC;
                version = PLOT_FILE_VERSION;
        }
        if ((fp = fopen(filename, file_type)) == NULL) {
                return (FAILURE);
}

        xdrstdio_create(&xdr_handle, fp, xdrop);
        /*
        *If we are writing the file then write out the magic number,
        *version number, and pair count. If we are reading the file
        *then read in the magic number, version number, and pair count.
        *Then verify that we can interpret the contents of the file and
        *that the pair_cnt is within the bounds of our x and y arrays.
```

FIGURE 2.4 Continued

```
        */
        status = SUCCESS;
        if (xdr_int(&xdr_handle, &magic) == FALSE ||
          xdr_int(&xdr_handle, &version) == FALSE ||
          xdr_int(&xdr_handle, &pair_cnt) == FALSE ||
          pair_cnt > cnt || magic != PLOT_FILE_MAGIC || version !=
          PLOT_FILE_VERSION) {
                status = FAILURE;
        }
        for (i = 0; i < pair_cnt && status == SUCCESS; i++, x++, y++) {
                if (xdr_float(&xdr_handle, x) == FALSE ||
                xdr_float(&xdr_handle, y) == FALSE) }
                        status = FAILURE;
                }
        }
        xdr_destroy(&xdr_handle);
        fclose(fp);
        return (status);
} /* rw_data */
```

FIGURE 2.4. Continued

The record-based stream example handles the same plot dat as in the previous example except that the data file is in a record oriented format. The first record on the stream contains the magi number and the version number. The second record in the strean contains the number of coordinate pairs in the file followed by th coordinate pairs. The stream could conceivably contain severa different plots, each in its own record. Figure 2.5 lists the modifie *rw_data()* routine from the previous example and the two routine that read data from the stream and write data to the stream.

```
int
rw_data(filename, x, y, cnt, op)
        char            *filename;
        float           *x, *y;
        int             cnt;            /* Number of coordinate pairs */
        enum io_ops     op;
{
        FILE            *fp;
        XDR             xdr_handle;
        enum xdr_op     xdrop;          /* XDR Stream Operation */
        int             pair_cnt;       /* Number of coordinate pairs in the XDR
                                           stream */
        int             magic;          /* Magic number of file */
        int             version;        /* Version number of file */
        int             i, status;
        char            *file_type;     /* Standard I/O file operation */
        int             read_data();
        int             write_data();

        if (op == READ) {
                xdr_handle.x_op = XDR_DECODE;
                file_type = "r";
        } else {
                xdr_handle.x_op = XDR_ENCODE;
                file_type = "w+";
                pair_cnt = cnt;
                magic = PLOT_FILE_MAGIC;
                version = PLOT_FILE_VERSION;
        }
        if ((fp = fopen(filename, file_type)) == NULL) {
                return (FAILURE);
        }

        /*
         * Note: Assuming the "FILE *" type is the same size as the "char *"
         */
        status = SUCCESS;
        xdrrec_create(&xdr_handle, (u_int)0, (u_int)0, fp, read_data, write_data);
```

FIGURE 2.5. *Record-based stream example.*

```
/*
 * Skip to the first record.
 */
if (op == READ) {
        xdrrec_skiprecord(&xdr_handle);
}

/*
 * If we are writing the file then write out the magic number and
 * version number in the first record. If we are reading the file
 * then read in the magic number and version number, and verify
 * that we can handle this file.
 */
status = SUCCESS;
if (xdr_int(&xdr_handle, &magic) == TRUE &&
  xdr_int(&xdr_handle, &version) == TRUE &&
  magic == PLOT_FILE_MAGIC && version ==
        PLOT_FILE_VERSION) {

        /*
         * If writing, mark the end of a record in the XDR stream without
         * flushing the buffer. Otherwise, skip to the next record.
         */
        if (op == WRITE) {
                xdrrec_endofrecord(&xdr_handle, FALSE);
        } else {
                xdrrec_skiprecord(&xdr_handle);
        }

        /*
         * If we are writing the file then write out the pair count.
         * If we are reading the file then read in the pair count and
         * verify that the pair_cnt is within the bounds of our x and
         * y arrays.
         */
        if (xdr_int(&xdr_handle, &pair_cnt) == FALSE || pair_cnt > cnt) {
                status = FAILURE;
        }

        for (i = 0; i < pair_cnt && status == SUCCESS;
                i++, x++, y++) {
```

FIGURE 2.5 Continued

```
                if (xdr_float(&xdr_handle, x) == FALSE ||
                    xdr_float(&xdr_handle, y) == FALSE) {
                                status = FAILURE;
                }
                }

                /*
                 * Mark end of a record in the XDR stream and flush the buffer

                 */
                if (op == WRITE) {
                        xdrrec_endofrecord(&xdr_handle, TRUE);
                }
        } else {
                status = FAILURE;
        }

        xdr_destroy(&xdr_handle);
        fclose(fp);
        return (status);
} /* rw_data */

int
read_data(fp, buf, cnt)
        FILE    *fp;
        char    *buf;
        int     cnt;
{
        int     nread;
        nread = fread(buf, 1, cnt, fp);
        if (nread == 0) {
                nread = -1;
        }
        return (nread);
} /* read_data */

int
write_data(fp, buf, cnt)
```

FIGURE 2.5 Continued

```
        FILE    *fp;
        char    *buf;
        int     cnt;
{
        int     nwrite;
        nwrite = fwrite(buf, 1, cnt, fp);
        if (nwrite == 0) {
                nwrite = -1;
        }
        return (nwrite);
} /* write_data */
```

FIGURE 2.5 Continued

2.5 Exercises

1. Show the contents of the XDR stream for the following C structure:

```
struct example1 {
        int     a;
        float   b;
        char    c[2];
} = {
        10, 2.2, 'a', 'b'
};
```

You will need to refer to Appendix 2 to determine the format of the XDR-encoded data types.

2. Write a filter for the structure used in problem 1 above.
3. Write a filter for the following linked list C structure.

```
struct object {
        int             attributes[10];
        int             values[10];
        struct object   *nextp;
};
```

The list terminates when a null pointer value is in the *nextp* member.

4. Write the necessary stream routines that connect an XDR stream to a database file. The stream should allow keyed access to records in the XDR stream. All data in the database file should be XDR encoded.

5. LISP S-expressions are data structures that can be any of the following: (a) an integer; (b) a double-length floating point number; (c) a symbol, which is like a string except that two symbols "a" and "a" are the same symbol; (d) a string, where two strings "a" and "a" are different; (e) null, a distinguished value; or (f) a pair, composed of two distinct S-expressions.
   Write C data structures, support code, and XDR routines for S-expressions.
6. As described in Exercise 5, S-expressions are suited to holding program information: they are acyclic and (usually excepting only symbols) each node is unique. The same data structures are also used to hold data, and can then be cyclic. For example, each element of a pair could point to the pair itself.
   Extend your code for Exercise 5 so that it correctly serializes cyclic structures. (Hint: you must put markers in the data stream, and use a multi-pass algorithm so you can tell when to emit the markers.)
7. Implement an XDR stream that only counts the bytes of data that go into it. How many ways can you think of to do this?

RPC Protocol

3

This chapter introduces Sun's RPC protocol. The information in this chapter is not required for finishing the book. It is recommended that you read about the portmapper service at the end of this chapter, but you can skip the rest of the chapter if you wish. This chapter explains the RPC mechanism in detail and is intended as a supplement to the RPC protocol specification in Appendix 3. You may want to scan over the protocol specification before reading this chapter.

3.1 RPC Messages

The RPC Library uses a message-passing scheme to handle communication between the server and the client. For a client to ask a server to execute a remote procedure, the client must send a message across the network to the server; similarly, for a server to indicate that it has executed a requested procedure, it must send a message back to the requesting client. The RPC protocol defines these messages, of which there are two types, *call* messages and *reply* messages. Clients send call messages to servers; a call message requests execution of a particular remote procedure and contains the arguments for the procedure. After executing a remote procedure for a client, a server sends a reply message to the client; a reply message contains the results of the remote procedure's execution. The fields in call and reply messages are encoded according to the XDR standard allowing servers and clients to run on different computer architectures. Note that you can specify your own representation for arguments and results (see Chapter 4) but that other fields within the messages are always encoded using XDR. To simplify the discussion, this chapter assumes XDR encoding of arguments and results.

The protocol specifies only the format of call and reply messages and the interpretation of the fields (other than procedure arguments and results) in these messages. Implementors are free to:

- Transmit RPC messages via any transport: the protocol is free of transport dependencies.
- Provide any programming interface to client and server software. Client programs may or may not know they are executing remote procedures; they may be blocked until a remote procedure returns a result, or they may run in parallel. A remote procedure may or may not know it is being called from across the network, and remote procedures may be executed on a server by one process, by a fixed number of processes, or by processes created dynamically for each call message.
- Implement the RPC protocol inside or outside an operating system kernel or both.

Note that although the implementations of RPC on a given network might vary radically from one computer to another, they can all act as clients or as servers, or as both clients and servers, by simply observing the RPC protocol.

It is important to point out that the RPC protocol does not try to implement any kind of reliability and that the RPC Library or distributed application must be aware of the type of transport protocol being used. If it knows that it is running on top of a reliable transport then most of the work is already done for it. On the other hand, if it is running on top of an unreliable transport it must implement its own retransmission and time-out policy.

Because of transport independence, the RPC protocol does not attach specific semantics to the remote procedures or their execution. In other words, the semantics are borrowed from the transport. For example, consider a distributed application running on a unreliable transport such as UDP. If the application retransmits RPC messages after short time-outs, the only thing it can infer if it receives no reply is that the procedure was executed zero or more times. If it does receive a reply, then it can infer that the procedure was executed at least once.

On the other hand, if you are using a reliable transport such as TCP, then you can infer from a reply message that the procedure

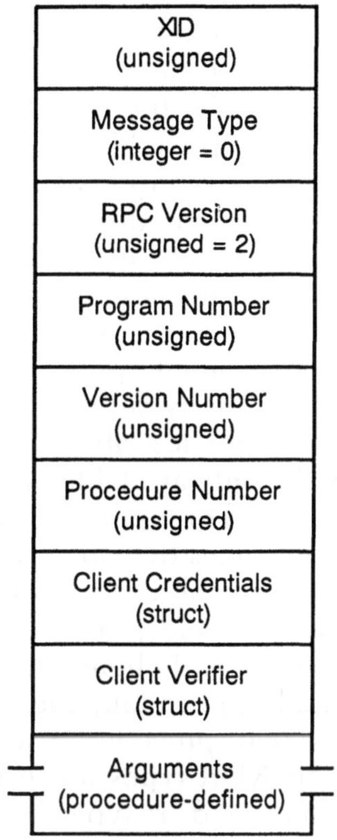

FIGURE 3.1. *Call message format.*

was executed exactly once, but if it receives no reply message, you still cannot assume that the remote procedure was not executed. Even if a reliable transport is used, you still need the ability to reconnect to the server after the server crashes.

3.1.1 Call Message

An RPC implementation can be conceptually divided into a client side and a server side. To execute a remote procedure call, the client side sends a call message to the server side; Figure 3.1 shows the format of the call message. All fields in the message are XDR standard types. A call message begins with a transaction identification (XID) field; the client side typically inserts a sequence number into this field. The XID field is mainly used to match reply messages to outstanding call messages; for example, if the client side has multiple outstanding call messages, replies can be matched to calls by their XID fields even if the replies arrive out of order. The XID field also allows the client and server sides to detect (and ignore) duplicate messages, which may occur if the protocol is implemented on an unreliable transport. The message type field distinguishes call messages from reply messages. Call messages set this field to zero. Following the message type comes an RPC version number. Just as the RPC protocol supports evolving distributed applications with remote program version numbers, it similarly supports the evolution of the RPC protocol itself; this chapter describes version 2 of the RPC protocol which is currently the only available version number. Note that a server side does not need to support all RPC protocol versions but it must reject call messages that specify a protocol version that it does not support. Following the RPC version number come the remote program, version and procedure numbers. Next are two fields, client credentials and client verifier, that identify a client user to a distributed application; these fields are described in Section 3.2. The remote procedure's arguments come next; the arguments and their XDR types are established by the remote procedure's developers and are typically described in documentation provided by them.

Because the RPC protocol is independent of the transport service on which it is implemented, the protocol cannot define the maximum length of call and reply messages. To define messages that are compatible with a group of transports, distributed application developers should ensure that their messages do not exceed the smallest maximum length specified by any of the transports.

3.1.2 Reply Message

Two kinds of reply messages are available: replies to successful calls and replies to unsuccessful calls.

"Success" is defined from the point of view of the RPC Library server side, not the remote procedure. An unsuccessful reply means that the server side has found something wrong with the

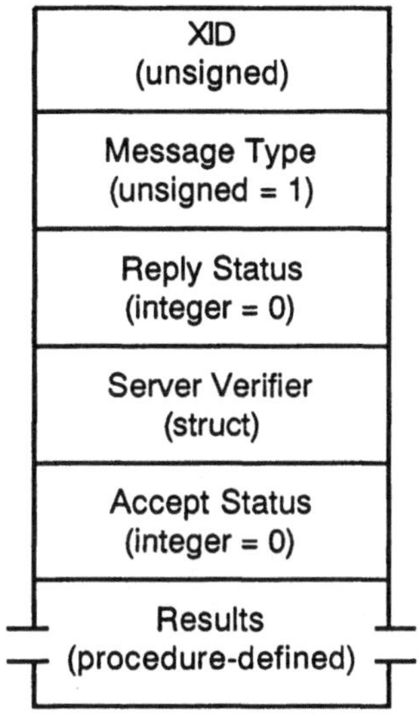

FIGURE 3.2. *Successful reply message format.*

call message. If a remote procedure rejects a call message, it returns a successful reply usually with an error code as the result of the remote procedure. Figure 3.2 shows the format of a successful reply message. A successful reply message begins with the transaction ID (XID) of its corresponding call message and a message type set to 1 identifying it as a reply. The reply status field and the accept status field together distinguish a successful reply from an unsuccessful one; both fields contain 0 in a successful reply. The server verifier field, described in Section 3.2, is used for server authentication. The final field in a successful reply contains the results returned by the remote procedure. The number and types of the results are defined by remote procedure developers, but all are encoded as XDR standard types.

The RPC server side is responsible for rejecting call messages that violate the RPC protocol. The RPC server side cannot detect bad arguments or inadequate credentials; detecting these conditions is the responsibility of remote procedures. Therefore, a successful reply message does not necessarily indicate that the remote procedure was executed. It could return the following conditions:

- The remote procedure executed successfully.
- The remote program, version, or procedure number specified in the call message is not available on the server; if the discrepancy is the version number, the reply contains the lowest and highest available version numbers.
- The remote procedure could not decode the arguments.

Unsuccessful reply messages have the same format as successful replies up to the reply status field, which is set to 1. The format of the remainder of the message depends on the condition that made the call unsuccessful. These conditions are described below:

- The RPC server side does not support the RPC protocol version specified in the call message; the reply contains the lowest and highest supported RPC version numbers.
- The client's credentials or verifier are improperly formed; the reply contains an *auth_stat* value that describes the problem.

3.2 Authentication Protocols

As previously stated, authentication parameters are opaque. This section describes the authentication types currently supported by the RPC Library. You are free to invent new authentication types, with the same rules of authentication type number assignment as there are for program number assignment. Refer to Appendix 1 for more information.

The credentials and verifiers are opaque to the RPC protocol. The credential and verifier fields in RPC messages (see Figures 3.1 and 3.2) are provided to allow a client process to identify the server and to allow the server to identify the client process. Specifically, a credential identifies, and a verifier authenticates, just as the name on an international passport identifies the bearer, while the photograph authenticates the bearer's identity. (Note that passport photographs are difficult to forge because they are embossed with a hard-to-duplicate stamp.) A call message contains a credential field and a verifier field. A reply message contains only a verifier; no credential is required in a reply because the client could not have made the call associated with the reply without knowing the server's identity (its credentials).

Credentials and verifiers share a common structure consisting of an XDR enumeration that defines the credential type, and the credential itself, whose format is type-specific. The RPC Library defines multiple credential types because no single type is adequate for all situations. Consider, for example, a diskless workstation that boots itself across a network. When booting, a workstation effectively has no operating system and has no user; it therefore has no way to create a credential. In this case, a null credential is appropriate, and, in fact, this is one of the types defined by the RPC Library. (A null credential has a null verifier.) New credential types can be added to the set of currently defined types. Whatever the type, the RPC Library server side implementation is responsible for authenticating the credential and passing it to the remote procedure. The remote procedure is responsible for interpreting the information contained in the credential. For example, the remote procedure might allow or prohibit a requested operation based on the information contained in the credential. As mentioned earlier, the remote procedure is also responsible for rejecting the credential if it is inappropriate.

In addition to the null credential, the RPC Library defines a UNIX-style credential type. A UNIX-style credential identifies a caller similar to the way the UNIX operating system identifies a user. The credential contains the caller's computer name, effective user ID, and a list of groups to which the caller belongs. A UNIX-style credential has a null verifier. Because they cannot be authenticated, UNIX-style credentials are appropriate for networks in which servers run the UNIX operating system, and in which users can be trusted not to forge credentials by assuming another user's ID.

The RPC Library provides an authentication type that is more secure than UNIX-style authentication. This type is based on the Data Encryption Standard (DES) [NATI 77] and is referred to as DES authentication, or secure RPC [TAYL 86]. The security of DES authentication is based on a sender's ability to encrypt the current time, which the receiver can then decrypt and check against its own clock. Two things are necessary for this scheme to work: (1) the client and server must agree on what the current time is and (2) the client and server must be using the same encryption key.

If a network has time synchronization, then client/server time

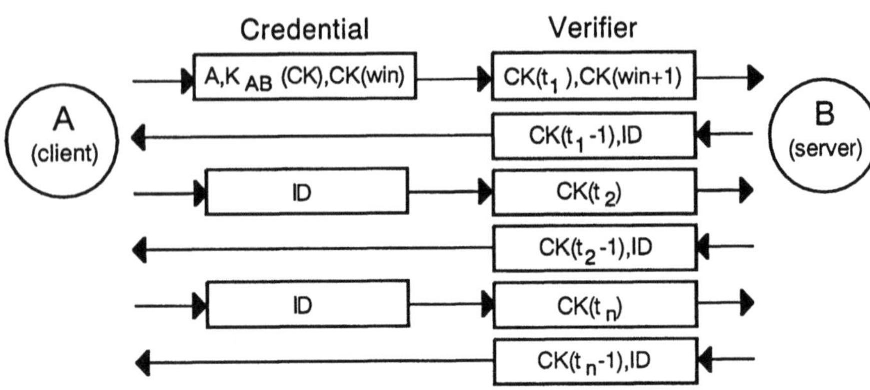

FIGURE 3.3. *Secure RPC authentication protocol.*

synchronization occurs automatically. If this is not available, you can compute timestamps by using the server's time instead of the network's time. In order to do this, the client asks the server what time it is, before starting the RPC session, and then computes the time difference between its own clock and the server's. This difference offsets the client's clock when the client is computing timestamps. If the client and server clocks get so out of sync that the server begins rejecting the client's requests, the authentication mechanism can resynchronize with the server.

The method for getting the server and client to use the same encryption key follows. When a client wishes to talk to a server, it generates at random a key to be used for encrypting the timestamps (among other things). This key is known as the conversation key, CK. The client encrypts the conversation key by using a public key scheme, and sends it to the server in its first transaction. This key is the only thing that is ever encrypted with public key cryptography. The particular scheme used is the Diffie-Hellman method [DIFF 76]. For now, assume that for any two agents, A and B, there is a DES key KAB that only A and B can deduce. This key is known as the common key, KAB.

Figure 3.3 illustrates the authentication protocol in more detail, describing client named A talking to server named B. A term of the form K(x) means x encrypted with the DES key K. Examining the figure, you can see that for its first request, the client's credential contains its name, A, the conversation key CK encrypted with the common key KAB, and win (window) encrypted with CK. The window specifies the life of a credential. It prevents somebody from listening to a client's conversation with the server and replaying it at some later time. The conversation key and the window are both encrypted to prevent somebody that is monitoring communications to easily determine the values.

For the following reasons, the client's verifier in the first request contains the encrypted timestamp and an encrypted verifier of the specified window, *win + 1*. Suppose somebody wants to impersonate A by writing a program that instead of filling in the encrypted fields of the credential and verifier just stuffs in random bits. The server decrypts CK into some random DES key and uses it to decrypt the window and the timestamp, which ends up as random numbers. After a few thousand trials, the random window/timestamp pair may pass the authentication system. The window verifier makes guessing the right credential much more difficult. The timestamp and verifier are both encrypted to prevent somebody that is monitoring communications from determining the values easily.

After authenticating the client, the server stores into a credential table the client's name, A; the conversation key, CK; the window; and the timestamp. The server stores the first three items because it needs them for future use. It stores the timestamp to protect against replays. The server only accepts timestamps that are chronologically greater than the last one it has seen, so any replayed transactions are rejected. In the reply message, the server returns as its verifier an index ID into its cached credential table, plus the client's timestamp minus one, encrypted by CK. The client knows that only the server could have sent such a verifier, because only the server knows what timestamp the client sent. The reason for subtracting 1 from it is to insure that it is invalid and cannot be reused as a client verifier. The index ID into the credential table is called the *nickname*. It is used in subsequent calls by the client to identify itself to the server. The nickname keeps the server from having to verify the clients's credentials on every call.

The first transaction is complicated, but in future transactions the client just sends its nickname and an encrypted timestamp to the server, and the server sends back the client's timestamp minus

1, encrypted by CK. This is shown in the last two transactions in Figure 3.3.

3.3 The Portmap Network Service Protocol

A client that needs to make a remote procedure call to a service must be able to obtain the transport address of the service. The process of translating a service name to its transport address is referred to as *binding* to the service. You could hard code the transport address of the service into the client program but a static binding approach is inflexible. It forces the service to have the same transport address every time it starts. A better approach would allow dynamic binding, providing some mechanism that translates a service name into its transport address. In distributed systems, the names and transport addresses of the currently available services are stored in a *name server* [COUL 88]. A service registers its name with the name server when it is first started. A client wishing to make an RPC presents the name of the service in a query to the name server. The name server looks up the name of the service in its internal tables and returns the transport address of the service, provided the service has registered itself with the name server. The rest of this section describes how binding is performed by the RPC mechanism.

A transport service provides process-to-process message transfers across a network. Each message contains a transport address that typically consists of a network number, a host number, and a port-number (the terminology can vary among transports). A port is a logical communication channel in a host—i.e., the transport address; by waiting on a port, a process receives messages from the network. How a process waits on a port varies from one operating system to the next, but most of them provide mechanisms that suspend a process until a message arrives at a port. A sending process does not send a message directly to a receiving process but to the port at which the process waits for messages. (Sometimes multiple processes wait at the same port, in which case a message sent to the port is implicitly addressed to any of the waiting processes.) Ports are valuable because they are the receiver of a message specified independently of the conventions of the receiving operating system. For example, in the context of distributed applications, a client program does not need to know anything about how a server's operating system identifies processes; it only needs to know the port-number associated with the remote program it wants to call. The *portmap* service is a network service that provides a standard way for a client to look up the port number of any remote server program which has been registered with the service. The *portmap* program is a binding service. Because it can be implemented on any transport that provides the equivalent of ports, the *portmap* service provides a single solution to a general problem that works for clients, servers, and most networks.

A portmap is a list of the port-to-program/version number correspondences on a computer. In other words, each different version of a remote program may use its own port. A *portmap* service, also referred to as the *portmapper*, maintains its host's portmap entries. Every computer that supports RPC-based services runs an implementation of the portmapper. The portmapper is typically started automatically when the computer is booted. As Figure 3.4 shows, both server programs and client programs call portmapper procedures. As part of its initialization, a server program calls its host's portmapper to create a portmap entry. Whereas server programs call portmappers to update portmap entries, clients call portmappers to obtain information about portmap entries. To find a remote program's port, a client program sends an RPC call message to the server's portmapper; if the remote program is registered on the server, the portmapper returns the relevant port-number in an RPC reply message. The client program can then send RPC call messages to the remote program's port. A client program can minimize its portmapper calls by caching the port-numbers of recently called remote programs.

The portmapper is the only network service that must have a well-known (dedicated) port—port-number 111. Other distributed applications can be assigned port-numbers statically or dynamically so long as they register their ports with their host's portmapper. For example, a server program based on the RPC Library typically gets a port number at runtime by calling an RPC Library procedure. Note that a given network service can be associated with port-number 256 on one server and with port-number 885 on another; on a given server, a service can be associated with a different port every time its server program starts. Delegating port-

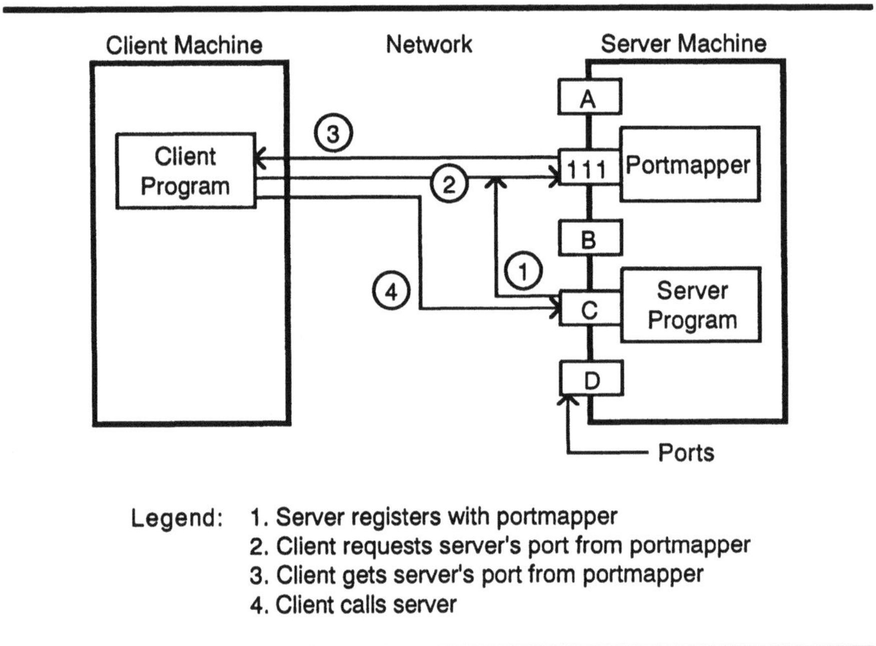

FIGURE 3.4. *Typical portmapping sequence.*

to-remote program mapping to portmappers also automates port-number administration. An alternative to the portmapper is to statically maintain the mapping of ports and remote programs in a file duplicated on each client. This requires updating all mapping files whenever a new remote program is introduced to a network. Another alternative is to place the port-to-program mappings in a shared file on a file server that is accessible to the client. This approach can cause severe headaches if the file server goes down.

It is important to note that the portmapper is specific to Sun's RPC Library implementation. The RPC protocol does not dictate the need for a portmapper. You are free to invent your own mechanism for binding a client to a server.

3.3.1 Portmapper Procedures

Clients and servers query and update a server's portmap by calling the portmapper procedures listed in Table 3.1. After obtaining a port, a server program calls the Unset and Set procedures

Remote Program Number 100000, Version 2		
Number	Name	Description
0	Null	Do nothing
1	Set	Add portmap entry
2	Unset	Remove portmap entry
3	Getport	Return port for remote program
4	Dump	Return all portmap entries
5	Callit	Call remote procedure

TABLE 3.1. *Portmapper remote procedures.*

its server's portmapper. Unset clears a portmap entry if there is one (as might be the case if the server program recently crashed). The Set procedure enters the server program's remote program number and port-number into the portmap. To find a remote program's port-number, a client program calls the Getport procedure of the server's portmapper. You can obtain a server's complete portmap by calling the Dump procedure.

The portmapper's *callit* procedure makes an indirect remote procedure call, as shown in Figure 3.5. A client program passes the target procedure's program number, version number, procedure number, and arguments in an RPC call message sent to *callit*. *Callit* looks up the target procedure's port-number in the portmap and sends an RPC call message to the target procedure, including in it the arguments received from the client. When the target procedure returns results to *callit*, it returns the results to the client program; also returned is the target procedure's port-number so the client can subsequently call the target procedure directly.

Because every instance of a remote program can be mapped to a different port on every server, a client has no way to send a RPC to all known servers of the remote procedure. This process is referred to as broadcast RPC and can be implemented using the portmapper since the *portmap* service receives requests on a well known port-number—111. The client can find a server running a remote program by broadcasting a call to *callit*, asking it to call the desired procedure for the remote program specified. *Callit* on each server either returns a successful reply if the procedure could be invoked or an error if the remote procedure could not be in-

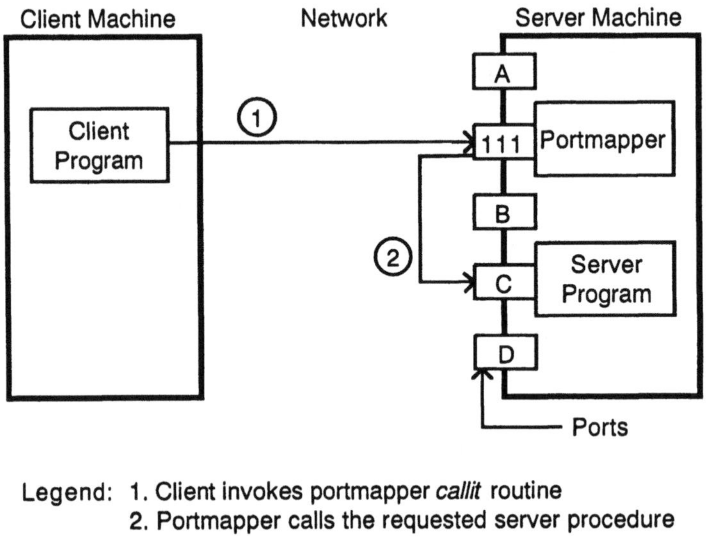

FIGURE 3.5. *Indirect remote procedure call.*

voked—typically indicating that the procedure is not available on the server. The successful replies would inform the client of the availability of the remote procedure. If this call is broadcast to all servers, the first reply received is likely to be from the server with the lightest workload. The mechanism used to broadcast the *callit* procedure call to all the portmappers is transport dependent.

The Sun RPC Library provides an interface to all portmapper procedures. Some of the RPC Library procedures also call portmappers automatically on behalf of client and server programs. Chapter 5 describes the interface to these library procedures.

RPC Programming

4

A program can use a remote procedure call to do a *jump subroutine* call to a procedure on another computer. A procedure is a routine or set of routines that take input arguments, perform processing, and return values to the caller. To invoke a remote procedure, the client program specifies the computer to invoke the procedure on, the procedure to invoke, the arguments to the procedure, and where the return value should be placed. To process remote procedure calls, the server program makes its service available to the network, waits for remote procedure calls to its service, dispatches requests to the appropriate procedures passing in the arguments to the procedure, and returns the results from the procedure to the client.

Remote-procedure-call programming uses the RPC mechanism to invoke procedures on computers. Before the procedure for making remote procedure calls can be discussed, it is necessary to examine the mechanisms for naming computers, for encoding and decoding RPC procedure arguments and return values, and for identifying remote procedures. Once you understand these concepts, you can explore the use of the RPC mechanism.

4.1 Computer Names

Before you can invoke a remote procedure on a remote computer, you must have some way to identify the remote computer. Computers have unique identifiers to distinguish them from other computers on the network. Typically, these identifiers allow people to easily reference computers. The computer names are referred to as host names, because they stand for the name of a computer host. A host name of *rpcsun* is easier for people to deal with than an Ethernet address of 08:99:88:44:55:26. The host name does not always indicate the purpose of the computer but in general is easier to remember than the network address of the computer.

4.2 RPC Procedure Argument Encoding and Decoding

A remote procedure can accept one argument and return one result. When you need to pass more than one argument, you would place all your arguments into a *argument* data structure. You then pass the data structure as the argument to the remote procedure. Similarly, when you need to return more than one result, you would place all your results into a *result* data structure. You then return the data structure as the result of the remote procedure.

As noted in Chapter 2, significant data representation differences can exist between the client computer and the server computer. The RPC Library allows you to specify the routines to use for encoding and decoding both the arguments and the results of the remote procedure. Typically, you use XDR filters for this purpose. The examples later in this chapter show you how to specify the filters for a remote procedure call.

You may have observed that XDR encoding and decoding always occurs, even between a client and server of the same architecture, adding unnecessary overhead to your network service. The overhead of the XDR routines is generally minimal. Even so, because of the flexibility of the RPC architecture, you are free to use your own routines to do the encoding and decoding. That is, you can write your own filters that verify that the architectures are the same and, if so, use the data without conversion. If they are not the same then the filter can invoke the correct XDR filter. The only restriction of this approach is that the RPC Library calls the filter with a pointer to an XDR handle and a pointer to the object handle of the object to encode/decode. The RPC Library expects a return value of TRUE to indicate success and FALSE to indicate failure. The data that is copied out or read in must be read from the stream, even though the data in the stream might not be in XDR representation. It is definitely up to you to ensure that the data is being consistently read from and written to the stream. In this case, the stream is not a true XDR stream.

4.3 Remote Procedure Identification

For identification purposes, remote procedures are organized as a four-level hierarchy as shown in Figure 4.1. A network service

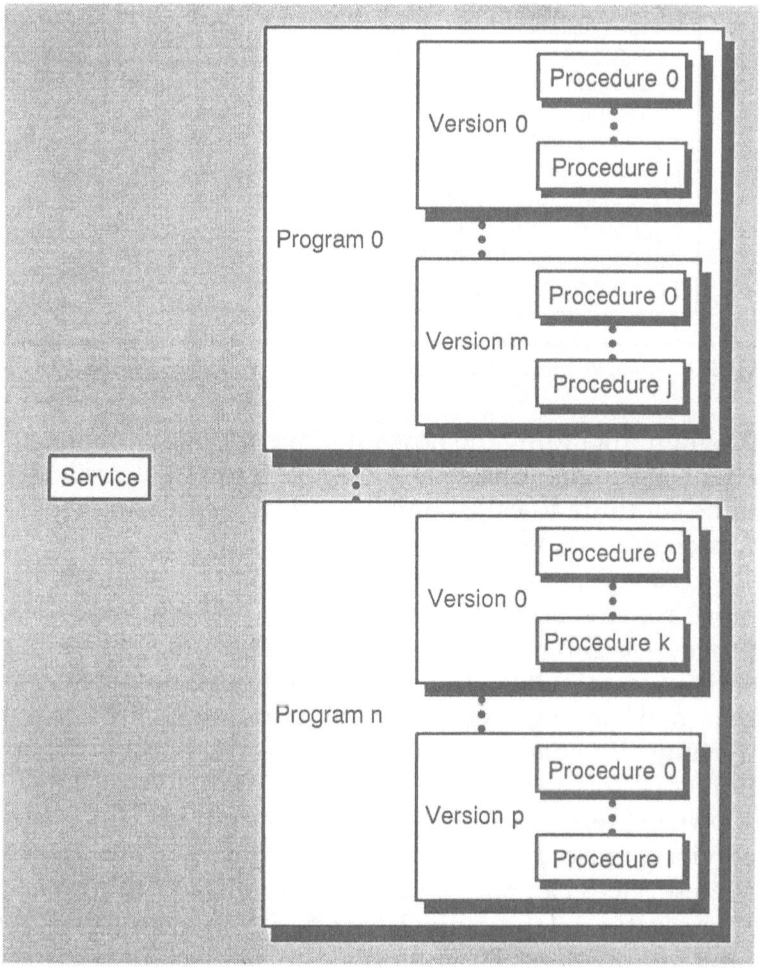

FIGURE 4.1. *Remote procedure identification hierarchy.*

consists of one or more remote programs; a remote program has one or more versions; a version has one or more procedures. One server process could support several remote programs. Because different versions of a remote program can exist simultaneously, network service developers can change a remote program's interface without disturbing client programs that rely on the old interface. For example, you could add a new procedure to the remote

Range (Hexadecimal	Administrator	Lifetime	Distribution
00000000 - 1FFFFFFF	Sun	Permanent	Public
20000000 - 3FFFFFFF	Local	Unknown	Local
40000000 - 5FFFFFFF	Developer	Transient	Local
60000000 - 7FFFFFFF	Reserved		
80000000 - 9FFFFFFF	Reserved		
A0000000 - BFFFFFFF	Reserved		
C0000000 - DFFFFFFF	Reserved		
E0000000 - FFFFFFFF	Reserved		

TABLE 4.1. *Remote program numbers.*

program. Including the new interface in a new version allows new client programs to use the new interface while existing applications continue to call the old interface. An example at the end of this chapter shows you how to do this.

Each version of a remote program is a collection of one or more remote procedures. A remote procedure is identified by program number, version number, and procedure number. You assign the procedure and version numbers. Remote program numbers may be assigned by developers, by Sun Microsystems, or dynamically generated by programs. To simplify the administration of remote program numbers, they are divided into the ranges shown in Table 4.1. The low range of numbers is for public network services, those that may be found on any network. Developers of such services can obtain program numbers in this range from Sun Microsystems. Appendix 1 covers the procedure for obtaining a program number. The numbers in the second range are locally administered; you can use these numbers to identify your own local network services or to test new services that will ultimately be assigned public numbers. The transient range is for applications that dynamically generate remote program numbers. The reserved ranges are for future definition and should not be used by network service developers.

Although you define procedure numbers, they usually start at 1, however, and are allocated sequentially. There is a convention of defining procedure number 0 of every remote program as a null procedure, a procedure that takes no arguments, returns no results, and performs no computation. When users follow this convention, they can determine if a service exists on a particular server by simply calling procedure 0. Calling the null procedure is also one way to measure the overhead of the RPC Library because this procedure takes essentially no time to execute. Chapter 8 describes this process in more detail.

Note that unlike remote programs and procedures, network services do not have identifying numbers. A network service has no embodiment in a piece of code, but is an umbrella term that describes a collection of one or more related remote programs. For example, a Distributed File Service could consist of a mount program, a lock manager program, a status monitor program, and a file access program.

The RPC Library provides routines that let you maintain an RPC program number database in the file */etc/rpc*. Each entry in this database contains the following information:

- The name of the distributed service.
- A list of alias names for the distributed service.
- The program number of the distributed service

The database allows you to specify the name of a distributed service instead of a program number. You can then call the routine *getrpcbyname()* to return the entry in the database that corresponds to the specified service name, thus providing the service's program number. Using the database in this manner allows you to change the program number of a distributed service without recompiling the service.

4.4 The RPC Library

As Figure 4.2 shows, the RPC Library is divided into a client side and a server side, each divided into an upper and lower level set of procedures. Note that only the major procedures are shown in Figure 4.2. The high-level procedures are easy to use, while those at the lower-level allow greater control over the generation, transmission, and receipt of RPC messages. The rest of this chapter focuses on high-level RPC programming, with low-level RPC programming being covered in the next chapter.

The include files associated with the RPC Library routines

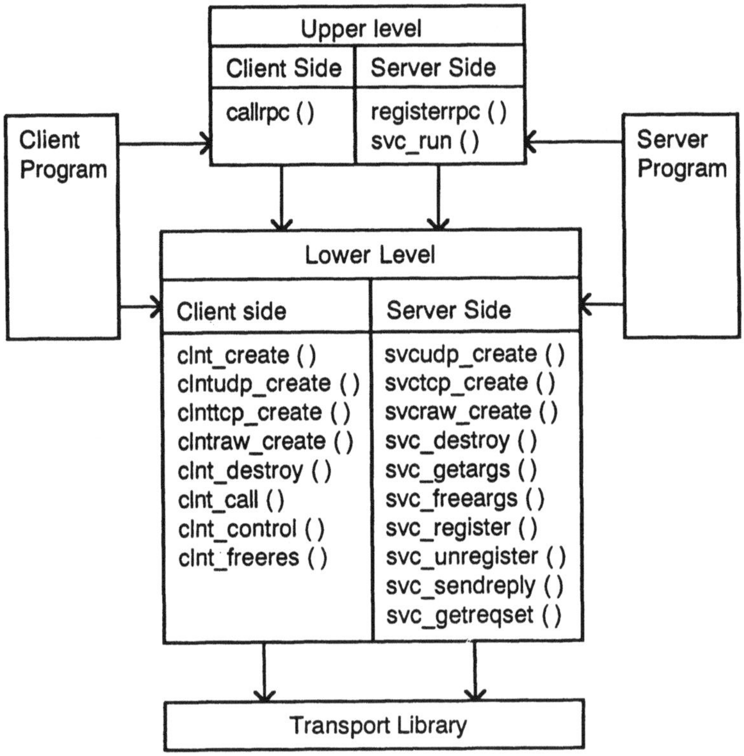

FIGURE 4.2. *RPC library organization.*

are typically found in the directory */usr/include/rpc*. Throughout this book, references to header files enclosed by angle brackets, ⟨ ⟩, are relative to the */usr/include* directory. References to header files that are not enclosed by angle brackets are relative to the current directory.

4.5 High-Level RPC Programming

High-level RPC programming refers to the simplest interface in the RPC Library that you can use to implement an RPC service. This interface is built on the low-level RPC programming interface discussed in Chapter 5. The high-level interface is the least flexible of the two. It consists of the *callrpc()*, *registerrpc()*, and *svc_run()*

12345	B
98765	C
67890	A
43210	B

FIGURE 4.3.

routines. These routines isolate almost all network dependencies from you; those dependencies that are not isolated are examined in Section 4.6. The *callrpc()* routine is used by the client of a service to call a remote procedure. The *registerrpc()* routine is used by a service to register a procedure with the RPC Library. After being registered, the procedure can be called by an application running on a remote computer. The *svc_run()* routine is used by a service to wait for procedure calls, dispatching the calls to the proper procedures when they arrive.

The rest of this section contains an example that uses the high-level routines and explores the specifics of the high-level RPC Library routines.

4.5.1 Grade Server Example

Typically a professor posts the results of an exam or final course grades in a location accessible by students. The list might look like Figure 4.3. The student's ID number is listed, followed by the grade. The professor can simply place the grades in a file and write a program that accepts a student ID number and returns a letter grade. Figure 4.4 lists the grade-reporter program. The grades are kept in a file called *grades* in the same format as the list in Figure 4.3.

The program expects the student ID number as the first argument. It opens the grade file and searches through it line by line looking for a student ID number that matches the one passed in. If it finds a match, it prints the corresponding grade. If it searches the entire file without finding a match, it informs you that the grade is not in the grade file.

The above program works fine as long as the student has access to the computer where the grade-reporter program and the grade file are located. The professor could improve access to his

```
/*
 * Grade-reporter program, given a student ID number, it reads
 * grades from the "grades" files
 */
#include <stdio.h>

#define GRADE_FILE   "grades"
#define NO           0
#define YES          1
#define ID_NUM_SIZE  5                    /* Doesn't include terminating NUL */
#define NO_GRADE     0

char    get_grade();
main(argc, argv)
        int     argc;
        char    *argv[];
{
        char            grade;
        int             ret_code;

        if (argc !=2) {
                fprintf(stderr, "usage: %s id#\n", argv[0]);
                return (1);
        }

        grade = get_grade(argv[1]);

        if (grade != NO_GRADE) {
                printf("Your grade is a %c\n", grade);
                ret_code = 0;
        } else {
                fprintf(stderr, "Could not find your grade in the grade file\n");
                ret_code = 1;
        }
        return (ret_code);
} /* main */

char
get_grade(id_num)
```

FIGURE 4.4.

```
        char            *id_num;
{
        FILE            *fp;
        char            grade, tmp_id_num[ID_NUM_SIZE + 1];
        int             done;

        done = NO;
        if ((fp = fopen(GRADE_FILE, "r")) != NULL) {
                while (done == NO && fscanf(fp,"%s %c", tmp_id_num, &grade)
                    != EOF) {
                        if (strncmp(id_num, tmp_id_num, ID_NUM_SIZE)
                            == 0) {
                                done = YES;
                        }
                }
                fclose(fp);
        } else {
                fprintf(stderr, "Error: cannot open file: %s\n", GRADE_FILE);
        }

        if (done == NO) {
                grade = NO_GRADE;
        }
        return (grade);
} /* get_grade */
```

FIGURE 4.4. Continued

grades by placing copies of the grade-reporter program and the grade file on several computers. This approach introduces a maintenance problem because the professor now needs to make sure that every computer has the latest copy of the grade file. Also, the professor could not change the format of the grade file without updating all the copies of the grade-reporter program. The students would be out of luck if their version of the grade-reporter program were incompatible with the grade file. It would be easier to have one copy of the grade file and let the students access it remotely. This can be done by converting the grade-reporter to a distributed application. Then the professor only has to post the grades on a computer known as the grade server. The client, or student, makes a request to the grade server supplying a student ID number and the server returns the grade to the client.

Converting the grade-reporter program into an RPC-based application requires little effort. All you need to do is divide it into a server program and a client program. The server program serves one procedure that does the work of getting the grade. The client program simply takes the input to the *get_grade* procedure and sends it to the server. Figure 4.5 shows the same program converted into an RPC-based service. Instead of one module, there are now three: one for the server side, *grade_svc.c,* one for the client side, *get_grade.c,* and one module that contains the custom XDR filters, *grade_xdr.c.*

The *grade_svc* program runs on the computer that holds the grades. The *registerrpc()* routine call simply informs the network service registration service, the portmapper discussed in Chapter 3, that the *get_grade_1()* procedure services requests to the GRADE_PROG, GRADE_VERS_1, and GET_GRADE_PROC combination. Remember that the program number, version number, and procedure number uniquely identify a remote procedure. The *svc_run()* routine is the service's remote procedure dispatcher. The routine waits until it receives a request. When it receives an RPC request for the procedure, it calls the *get_grade_1()* routine. The *_1* extension is a procedure-naming convention adopted to indicate the version number of the procedure. The *get_grade_1()* procedure hunts for the matching student ID number in the grades file, returning the corresponding letter grade if it gets a match. It returns NO_GRADE if it does not find the student ID number in the grades file. After *get_grade_1()* returns control to the dispatcher, it sends the results back to the client.

One change to the *get_grade()* procedure is that it now returns the address of the result of the function. Remote procedures that are used with the high-level library routines always take a pointer to the procedure arguments and always return a pointer to the results. Notice that the result, the grade, is stored in a static variable because you do not want a function returning the address of one of its automatic variables, a variable whose value becomes undefined when the function returns. Typically, high-level RPC procedures declare the results as a static within the scope of the actual procedure.

The *get_grade* program, i.e., the grade client, can run on any computer on the network, including the grade-server host. This program was easy to construct. It only required taking the original

The Header File - get_grade.h

```
/*
 * The program number was chosen from the locally administered program number
 * range. The version number and procedure numbers typically start from 1.
 */
#define GRADE_PROG          ((u_long)0x20000000)
#define GRADE_VERS_1        ((u_long)1)
#define GET_GRADE_PROC      ((u_long)1)

#define ID_NUM_SIZE         5         /* Doesn't include terminating NUL */
#define NO_GRADE            0

extern  bool_t  xrd_stu_id_num();
```

Grade Server - grade_svc.c

```
/*
 * Grade server program, invokes the get_grade() remote procedure.
 */
#include <stdio.h>
#include <rpc/rpc.h>
#include "get_grade.h"

#define GRADE_FILE  "grades"
#define NO          0
#define YES         1

main()
{
        char    *get_grade_1();

        if (registerrpc(GRADE_PROG, GRADE_VERS_1, GET_GRADE_PROC,
            get_grade_1, xdr_stu_id_num, xdr_char) == -1) {
                fprintf(stderr, "Error: cannot register service\n");
                return(1);
```

FIGURE 4.5.

```
        }
        svc_run();
} /* main */

char *
get_grade_1(id_num)
        char    *id_num;
{

        static char     grade;          /* Note the static declaration */
        FILE            *fp;
        char            tmp_id_num[ID_NUM_SIZE + 1];
        int             done;

        done = NO;
        if ((fp = fopen(GRADE_FILE, "r")) != NULL) {
                while (done == NO && fscanf(fp, "%s %c", tmp_id_num, &grade)
                        != EOF) {
                        if (strncmp(id_num, tmp_id_num, ID_NUM_SIZE) == 0){
                                done = YES;
                        }
                }
                fclose(fp);
        } else {
                fprintf(stderr, "Error: cannot open file: %s\n", GRADE_FILE);
        }

        if (done == NO) {
                grade = NO_GRADE;
        }
        return (&grade);
} /* get_grade */
```

Grade Client - get_grade.c

```
/*
 * Grade server client, calls the get_grade() remote procedure and prints
 * the results.
 */
```

FIGURE4.5. Continued

```
#include <stdio.h>
#include <rpc/rpc.h>
#include "get_grade.h"

main(argc, argv)
        int             argc;
        char            *argv[];
{
        int             status, ret_code;
        char            grade;

        if (argc != 3) {
                fprintf(stderr, "usage: %s server_name id#\n", argv[0]);
                return (1);
        }

        status = callrpc(argv[1], GRADE_PROG, GRADE_VERS_1,
                        GET_GRADE_PROC, xdr_stu_id_num,
                        argv[2], xdr_char, &grade);
        if (status == 0) {
                if (grade != NO_GRADE) {
                        printf("Your grade is a %c\n", grade);
                        ret_code = 0;
                } else {
                        fprintf(stderr, "Could not find grade in grade file\n");
                        ret_code = 1;
                }
        } else {
                fprintf(stderr, "Error: callrpc(); %s\n",
                clnt_sperrno((enum clnt_stat)status));
                ret_code = 1;
        }
        return (ret_code);
} /* main */
```

FIGURE 4.5. Continued

Grade XDR Filters - grade_xdr.c

```
/*
 * XDR filters for get_grade network service
 */
#include <rpc/rpc.h>
#include "get_grade.h"

bool_t
xdr_stu_id_num(xdr_handlep, objp)
        XDR     *xdr_handlep;
        char    *objp;
{
        return (xdr_string(xdr_handlep, &objp, ID_NUM_SIZE));
} /* xdr_stu_id_num */
```

Compiling the Example

```
% cc -c grade_xdr.c
% cc -o grade_svc grade_svc.c grade_xdr.o
% cc -o grade_clnt grade_clnt.c grade_xdr.o
```

FIGURE 4.5. Continued

program and removing the code that searches the grades file and replacing it with a remote procedure call to the grade server. The RPC was done by adding a call to *callrpc()* passing in the host name of the grade server, the remote procedure identifier (program number, version number, and procedure number), the input and output arguments, and the address of the XDR filters that do the encoding and decoding of the arguments. The program now takes the host name of the grade server and the student ID number as arguments. The program calls the RPC Library routine *clnt_sperrno()* to obtain a canned error message that describes why the *callrpc()* routine failed.

The XDR filter, *xdr_stu_id_num()*, is used by both the server and the client. The client uses it to encode the student ID argument into its XDR representation. The server uses it to decode the XDR representation of the student ID number into its local representation. The XDR filter in this example is called a *wrapper*. Its purpose is to map an XDR filter routine that takes three arguments into one that takes two. This technique is necessary because the RPC Library interface to the encoding/decoding routines defines only two arguments. The first is the pointer to an XDR memory stream handle and the second is a pointer to the data object. The wrapper simply specifies the maximum length possible for a student ID number string in the call to *xdr_string()*. A routine, *xdr_wrapstring()*, in the XDR Library handles string wrapping by setting the *maxsize* argument of *xdr_string()* to the maximum value of an unsigned integer.

4.5.2 High-Level RPC Routines

Below is a more detailed explanation of the RPC Library routines used in the preceding example. The function synopsis is followed by an explanation of the arguments and return values.

The simplest way of registering a remote procedure call with the RPC Library is with the routine *registerrpc()*. Its synopsis follows:

```
int
registerrpc(prognum, versnum, procnum, inproc, outproc)
u_long          prognum, versnum, procnum;
char            *(*procname)();
xdrproc_t       inproc, outproc;
```

The first three arguments identify the program number, version number, and procedure number being registered. The *procname* argument is the address of the procedure being registered. The *inproc* argument is the address of the XDR filter that will decode the incoming arguments. The *outproc* argument is the address of the XDR filter that encodes the procedure result that is returned to the calling process. The routine returns 0 to indicate success and −1 to indicate failure. This routine writes error messages to *stderr*.

You would call *registerrpc()* to explicitly register each procedure with the RPC Library. The null procedure, procedure 0, is automatically handled by the high-level library routines; you do not have to register it yourself. For example, if you had four remote procedures in your server—three non-null procedures plus one null procedure—you would call *registerrpc()* three times to register the three non-null procedures. Note that your server process exits if a call was made by a client to a procedure number that has not been registered, but other procedures have been registered for the associated program number and version number. This behavior only occurs when you use *registerrpc()* to register your procedures.

The synopsis of the *svc_run()* RPC Library routine follows:

```
void
svc_run()
```

This routine never returns control to the calling function unless a fatal error is detected. It takes no arguments and never returns any results. After successfully registering the procedure, the server program calls the *svc_run()* routine to wait for requests. This routine is the RPC Library's remote procedure dispatcher. The routine waits until it receives a request and then dispatches the request to the appropriate procedure. Note that the dispatcher takes care of decoding procedure arguments and encoding results, using the XDR filters specified when the remote procedure was registered.

You should register all the RPC procedures that a service handles before calling the *svc_run()* routine.

The simplest way of making a remote procedure call is with the RPC Library routine *callrpc()*. Its synopsis follows:

```
int
callrpc(host, prognum, versnum, procnum, inproc, in, outproc, out)
char          *host;
u_long        prognum, versnum, procnum;
xdrproc_t     inproc;
char          *in;
xdrproc_t     outproc;
char          *out;
```

The *host* argument specifies the name of the computer offering the service. The next three arguments are the program, version, and procedure numbers. Together they uniquely identify the procedure to be called. The *inproc* argument is the address of an XDR filter that encodes the arguments. The *in* argument is the address of the input argument to the RPC procedure. The *outproc* argument is the address of an XDR filter to decode the return value from the RPC procedure. The *out* argument is the address of where to store the return value of the RPC procedure. This routine returns a value of type *int*. This value can be cast to the type *clnt_stat* defined in the ⟨*rpc/clnt.h*⟩ header and then passed to the *clnt_sperrno()* routine to obtain a canned message. The type *clnt_stat* is an enumeration of possible RPC Library call return values. These return values are discussed in more detail in Chapter 5.

The *callrpc()* routine retries the call to the remote procedure five times (every 5 seconds). If it has not received a response after 25 seconds, it returns the equivalent *clnt_stat* value of RPC_TIMEDOUT. The high-level RPC programming routines do not provide a mechanism to let you specify the time-out value or the number of times to retry the call. You must use the low-level RPC programming routines, discussed in Chapter 5.

4.5.3 Supporting Multiple Versions of a Service

It is inevitable in the course of distributed application programming that an application needs to be updated after a given version has been released. Whether the need is motivated by a bug which needs fixing or the need for added functionality, the problem remains of how to introduce the changes in such a way as to reduce disruption of the existing installed base. The RPC program version number can be used to allow old and new versions of a distributed application to coexist. Updated servers can be written to support requests from either old or new clients. Clients can try the new version first when contacting a server, and then try the old version if the new one is not supported. An example of a server that supports multiple versions follows.

Assume that the grade server and *get_grade* program from the previous example has been distributed to several universities around the country, and each university has several computers around campus that act as the grade server. An astute student at one of these universities has decided to make the grade server more flexible by taking the course number of the class as an argument and having it return, in addition to the grade, the number of students that took the test and the average grade for the test. The student wants to add these new improvements to the grade server but also doesn't want to alienate students who are still using the old grade server. To do this, the student adds a new remote procedure to the grade server and updates its version number. Figure 4.6 lists the new grade server.

New Header File

```
#define GRADE_PROG          ((u_long)0x20000000)
#define GRADE_VERS_1        ((u_long)1)
#define GRADE_VERS_2        ((u_long)2)
#define GET_GRADE_PROC      ((u_long)1)

#define ID_NUM_SIZE     5       /* Doesn't include terminating NUL */
#define CLASS_SIZE      8       /* Doesn't include terminating NUL */
#define NO_GRADE        0

/*
 * The service error codes
 */
enum error {
        NO_ERROR = 0,
        E_NO_GRADE_FILE,        /* Couldn't open the grade file     */
        E_NO_GRADE,             /* Couldn't find a grade for ID # */
};

typedef struct {
        char            class[CLASS_SIZE + 1];
        char            id_num[ID_NUM_SIZE + 1];
} grade_args;

typedef struct {
        char            grade;
        char            average;
        int             num_students;
        enum    error   error;
} grade_res;

extern  bool_t  xdr_stu_id_num();
extern  bool_t  xdr_grade_args();
extern  bool_t  xdr_grade_res();
```

FIGURE 4.6.

New Grade Server

```
/*
 * Version 2.0 Grade server program, invokes the get_grade() remote
 * procedure. Still supports Version 1.0.
 */
#include <stdio.h>
#include <rpc/rpc.h>
#include "get_grade2.h"

#define GRADE_FILE  "grades"
#define NO          0
#define YES         1

main()
{
        char            *get_grade_1();
        grade_res       *get_grade_2();
        int             failure = 0;

        if (registerrpc(GRADE_PROG, GRADE_VERS_1, GET_GRADE_PROC,
           get_grade_1, xrd_stu_id_num, xdr_char) == -1) {
                fprintf(stderr, "Cannot register version 1 of service\n");
                failure++;
        }

        if (registerrpc(GRADE_PROG, GRADE_VERS_2, GET_GRADE_PROC,
           get_grade_2, xdr_grade_args, xdr_grade_res) == -1) {
                fprintf(stderr, "Cannot register version 2 of service\n");
                failure++;
        }

        /*
         * Exit if both calls to registerrpc failed. Otherwise, continue
         * to run if one or both calls to registerrpc succeeded.
         */
        if (failure == 2) {
                return (1);
        }
        svc_run();
} /* main */

/*
```

FIGURE 4.6. Continued

```
 * The get_grade_1 routine is the exact same as in the previous example
 */
grade_res *
get_grade_2(argsp)
        grade_args      *argsp;
{
        static grade_res results;
        char            tmp_id_num[ID_NUM_SIZE + 1];
        FILE            *fp;
        int             done;

        done = NO;
        results.error = NO_ERROR;
        if ((fp = fopen(argsp->class, "r")) != NULL) {
                fscanf(fp, "%c %d", &results.average, &results.num_students);
                while (done == NO && fscanf(fp, "%s %c", tmp_id_num,
                        &results.grade) != EOF) {
                        if (strncmp(argsp->id_num, tmp_id_num,
                           ID_NUM_SIZE) == 0) {
                                done = YES;
                        }
                }
                fclose(fp);

                if (done == NO) {
                        results.error = E_NO_GRADE;
                }
        } else {
                results.error = E_NO_GRADE_FILE;
        }

        return (& results);
} /* get_grade_2 */
```

New Grade Client

```
/*
```

FIGURE 4.6. Continued

```
 * Grade server client, calls the get_grade() remote procedure and prints
 * the results.
 */
#include <stdio.h>
#include <rpc/rpc.h>
#include "get_grade2.h"

main(argc, argv)
        int     argc;
        char    *argv[];
{
        grade_args      args;
        grade_res       results;
        u_long          version;
        int             loop_cnt, ret_code, status;
        char            grade;

        if (argc != 4) {
                fprintf(stderr, "usage: %s server_name class# id#\n", argv[0]);
                return (1);
        }

        if (strlen(argv[2]) > CLASS_SIZE) {
                fprintf(stderr, "Error: class name length exceeds %d\n",
                        CLASS_SIZE);
                return (1);
        }

        if (strlen(argv[3]) > ID_NUM_SIZE) {
                fprintf(stderr,"Error: Student ID number length exceeds %d\n",
                        ID_NUM_SIZE);
                return (1);
        }

        strncpy(args.class, argv[2], CLASS_SIZE + 1);
        strncpy(args.id_num, argv[3], ID_NUM_SIZE + 1);
        version = GRADE_VERS_2;

        status = callrpc(argv[1], GRADE_PROG, version, GET_GRADE_PROC,
                        xdr_grade_args, &args, xdr_grade_res, &results);
        if ((enum clnt_stat)status == RPC_PROGVERSMISMATCH) {
```

FIGURE 4.6. Continued

```
            version = GRADE_VERS_1;
            status = callrpc(argv[1], GRADE_PROG, version,
                            GET_GRADE_PROC, xdr_stu_id_num, argv[3],
                            xdr_char, &grade);
    }
    if (status == 0) {
       if (version == GRADE_VERS_1) {
            if (grade != NO_GRADE) {
                    printf("Your grade is a %c\n", grade);
                    ret_code = 0;
            } else {
                    fprintf(stderr, "Could not find grade in grade file\n");
                    ret_code = 1;
            }
       } else {
              switch (results.error) {
            case NO_ERROR:
                    printf("Your grade is a %c\n", results.grade);
                    printf("Class average: %c Number of students: %d\n",
                                    results.average, results.num_students);
                    ret_code = 0;
                    break;

            case E_NO_GRADE_FILE:
                    fprintf(stderr, "Could not find your class grade file\n");
                    ret_code = 1;
                    break;

            case E_NO_GRADE:
                    fprintf(stderr, "Could not find grade in grade file\n");
                    ret_code = 1;
                    break;

            default:
                    fprintf(stderr, "Service returned undefined error code\n");
            }
       }
    } else {
            fprintf(stderr, "Error callrpc(): %s\n",
                    clnt_sperrno((enum clnt_stat)status));
            ret_code = 1;
```

FIGURE 4.6. Continued

```
        }
        return (ret_code);
} /* main */
```

New XDR Routines

```
/*
 * XDR filters for get_grade network service
 */
#include <rpc/rpc.h>
#include "get_grade2.h"

/*
 * xdr_stu_id_num routine is the same as in the previous example
 */

bool_t
xdr_grade_args(xdr_handlep, objp)
        XDR             *xdr_handlep;
        grade_args      *objp;
{
        char            *tmp = objp-<class;

        if (xdr_string(xdr_handlep, &tmp, CLASS_SIZE) == FALSE) {
                return (FALSE);
        }
        return (xdr_stu_id_num(xdr_handlep, objp->id_num));
} /* xdr_grade_args */

bool_t
xdr_grade_res(xdr_handlep, objp)
        XDR             (xdr_handlep;
        grade_res       *objp;
{
        if (xdr_char(xdr_handlep, &objp->grade) == FALSE ||
                xdr_char(xdr_handlep, &objp->average) == FALSE ||
                xdr_int(xdr_handlep, &objp->num_students) == FALSE ||
                xdr_enum(xdr_handlep, &objp->error) == FALSE) {
                return (FALSE);
        } else {
                return (TRUE);
        }
} /* xdr_grade_res */
```

FIGURE 4.6. Continued

The modification to the server was simple. Just add the new get grade procedure, *get_grade_2()*, and a *registerrpc()* call to register the new version of the procedure. Note that the server program does not exit as long as it can register one or more versions of the remote program. It is up to you if you want to do this. You could just as easily exit if one of the *registerrpc()* calls failed. The change to the client program might not be as obvious. First, the client makes an RPC to version 2 of the service. If you get the RPC_PROGVERSMISMATCH error, you know that although the server you are talking to supports the grade service, it does not support version 2. Next, try version 1 of the service. It is important to remember that the arguments of the remote procedure are now different between version 1 and version 2, so you need to process the return values differently depending on which version of the service replied.

The XDR filter was modified to handle the new argument to the grade procedure, *grade_args* structure, and the new return value, *grade_res* structure. Remember that the order of the calls to XDR filter primitives for structure members does not matter. What matters is that you do it consistently for both the server and client.

After writing the new version of the grade server, you would then propagate the new server to anyone that wanted to use it. The new server would still service requests from the *get_grade* program, and the new client program can still get grades from the old server programs. One would hope that the new version would eventually replace all the old servers, but experience has shown that someone out there will always be running the old version of the software. So it is best to maintain backward compatibility.

4.6 Advantages/Disadvantages of Using High-Level RPC Programming

As with most programming interfaces, there are some advantages to using it and some disadvantages. The advantages are that the routines make it easy to implement a network service because you do not have to worry about the details, and the routines provide a transport-independent interface. The disadvantages of using these routines are that you:

- cannot specify the type of authentication the server would perform on the client (the topic of authentication is covered in Chapter 5). The current implementation defaults to no authentication;
- cannot specify the type of transport to use. The current implementation defaults to User Datagram Protocol (UDP);
- cannot specify the amount of time the *callrpc()* routine waits for a reply from the service before returning an error. The current implementation defaults to 25 seconds.

Also, using the routines is less flexible because the details of the RPC implementation are hidden from you.

Sun's implementation of the high-level RPC programming interface uses UDP to transmit messages to and receive messages from the remote procedure. The size of these messages is restricted to less than the maximum UDP packet size for both computers. A *packet* is a unit of data information consisting of a header, data information, and a trailer. A constant, UDPMSGSIZE, is defined in ⟨*rpc/clnt.h*⟩ that specifies the maximum amount of data that can be sent between the client and server or vice a versa. In SunOS 4.0 RPC, this size is 8800 bytes, and includes any overhead of UDP message headers, the overhead of XDR encoded RPC message headers, the overhead of the authentication type used, and the overhead of the argument or the result of a remote procedure in its XDR representation format. A rule of thumb is to keep the size of the XDR encoded arguments or results under 8192 bytes. Using UDP involves other considerations that you need to evaluate when you implement a network service. Chapter 5 covers transports in more detail and Chapter 8 covers the considerations in using the transports, including how to calculate the size of the XDR-encoded arguments and results.

Another important thing to remember is that you are not restricted to using Sun's high-level RPC programming interface. You can write your own high-level routines based on the low-level interface. You can then choose the transport, time-out values, authentication, and any other defaults that you wish to assign to the routines. Your new high-level interface will work on any computers that support Sun's RPC Library.

4.7 Exercises

1. Implement a distributed application that allows you to send messages to another user anywhere in the network.
2. Implement a network service that maintains a schedule for lab machine usage.
3. Implement your own XDR-encoding short circuit mechanism for XDR-encoding arguments and results between two computers of the same architecture (discussed in Section 4.2).
4. Implement a network service that provides your application with a list of available resources. How can other distributed applications use this information?

Low-Level RPC Programming

5

Low-level RPC programming refers to the lowest layer of the RPC programming interface. This layer gives you the most control over the RPC mechanism and is the most flexible layer. In particular it allows:

- selection and manipulation of the transport interface that lies below the RPC Library;
- the ability to use your own network service registration service instead of the portmapper;
- specification of RPC time-out values and retries;
- specification of the authentication mechanism used;
- explicitly freeing memory allocated by XDR filters.

This chapter discusses transport related issues, the use of the low-level routines, processing errors detected by the RPC mechanism, and the use of the authentication mechanism.

5.1 Transport Interface

Several popular transport protocols are currently in use, and the number will likely increase. Each of these protocols may have several implementations, each of which, while observing the transport protocol, may present a different programming interface. The RPC Library uses two techniques to maximize its independence from network transports. To allow connection of new or alternate transports, the RPC Library interacts with transports indirectly via sockets. A socket is a transient object used for interprocess communications. Sockets were introduced in the 4.2BSD UNIX release from the University of California at Berkeley [LEFF 89].

For more information on sockets, refer to the operating-system manual for your computer. The RPC Library dependencies on sockets have been isolated in the implementation, making it easy to port to an operating system that doesn't support sockets. In fact the AT&T UNIX System V Release 4 RPC Library implementation has replaced the use of sockets with the use of the Transport Interface Library that uses the STREAMS input/output architecture.

The RPC Library uses two types of sockets: datagram sockets and stream sockets. A datagram socket provides an interface to what is generally known as a datagram transport service. Datagram sockets behave like block devices. A block of data is written to a datagram socket with the *sendto()* operation, and a block is read from a datagram socket with the *recvfrom()* operation. The RPC Library uses an XDR memory stream to encode/decode data objects to/from a datagram socket. In SunOS 4.0, the datagram transport service is the User Datagram Protocol (UDP) running on the Internet Protocol (IP). Little effort is required to add or substitute other datagram-style transports.

A stream socket provides an interface to a virtual circuit transport service. A stream socket behaves like a UNIX byte stream; bytes are read from and written to a stream socket with the usual *read()* and *write()* operations. The RPC Library encodes/decodes data to/from a stream socket via an XDR record stream. Stream sockets are currently implemented by the Transmission Control Protocol (TCP) running on the Internet Protocol, but additional or different virtual circuit transports can be "plugged into" the socket interface without much difficulty and with no effect on the rest of the RPC Library.

Datagram and stream transports represent different tradeoffs between reliability and speed. Datagram transports are fast but, in principle, unreliable; datagram packets may not arrive at their destinations, may be duplicated, or may arrive out of order. Stream transports are reliable but are slower than datagram transports. Stream transports can use up system resources even when data is not being transmitted because the connection to the other computer must be maintained. The upshot is that remote services built on datagram transports are fast, but the services must be prepared to handle errors (which, in practice, occur infrequently). In contrast, although stream transports typically provide slower performance than datagram transports, stream transports relieve service developers from a good deal of error handling. Also, stream transports are very unlikely to suffer from the inherent size limitations of datagram transports. Chapter 8 covers the differences between the two transports. Note that the RPC Library makes it easy to build a server program that communicates via both datagram and stream transports.

Two data abstractions in the RPC Library isolate you from the details of the transport. On the server side, is the transport handle. The associated structure is of type *SVCXPRT* and is defined in ⟨*rpc/svc.h*⟩ . On the client side, is the client handle. The associated structure is of type *CLIENT* and is defined in ⟨*rpc/clnt.h*⟩. Both handles contain operation vectors that allow the RPC Library code to multiplex to the correct routine for the transport being used. In almost all cases, you do not need to directly access the values inside these handles. Instead, they are passed as an argument to some of the RPC Library routines.

5.2 Grade Server Example Revisited

The grade server example from the previous chapter was modified to use the low-level RPC Library routines to demonstrate their use. Your approach to writing an RPC-based application is more detailed when you use the low-level routines. You need to do the following on the server side:

1. Get a transport handle.
2. Register the service with the portmapper.
3. Call the library routine to dispatch RPCs.
4. Implement the dispatch routine.

On the client side, you need to do the following:

1. Get a client handle.
2. Call the remote procedure.
3. Destroy the client handle when you are done.

Figure 5.1 lists the low-level implementation of the grade service. Note that comments in the code tie low-level procedure calls with the steps listed above. The example is followed by a brief explanation highlighting the differences between the two approaches. The next section covers the specifics of the low-level routines.

The *grade.h* and the *grade_xdr.c* modules are not shown in Figure 5.1 because they are exactly the same as in the previous chapter. The *grade_svc.c* and *get_grade.c* modules now contain the functional decomposition of the high-level routines into their low-level routines.

In the server module, the call to *svcudp_create()* creates the transport handle. The call to *pmap_unset()* ensures that the service, if previously registered, is unregistered with the portmapper. (An instance of the service could have still been registered if it crashed before calling *svc_unregister()*.) The call to *svc_register()* registers the service with the portmapper and specifies the function to use for dispatching remote procedure calls to this service. The call to *svc_run()* is the same as in the example in the previous chapter. Note that although it is a high-level routine, it can still be used with the low-level routines. Calls to *svc_unregister()* and *svc_destroy()* were placed after the call to *svc_run()* to ensure that the service is unregistered and resources associated with the transport handle deallocated if *svc_run()* ever returns due to the detection of a fatal error. The function *dispatch()* is new to the server. The high-level routines took care of dispatching, but you need to write your own dispatch routine when you use the low-level routines—a fairly simple task, or use *rpcgen* which is covered in Chapter 7. The first few lines are the null procedure short circuit which uses *svc_sendreply()* to send a null reply to the client. The switch statement transfers control to the called procedure. The example has only one procedure, GET_GRADE_PROC, which calls *svc_getargs()* to decode the arguments to the procedure. Then it calls *get_grade_1()* to get the grade and *svc_sendreply()* to send the reply back to the client. The *get_grade_1()* procedure is the same as in the previous chapter. Note that the *registerrpc()* high-level routine has been replaced by calls to *svcudp_create()*, *svc_register()* and the new dispatch routine.

On the client side, the *callrpc()* high-level routine has been replaced by calls to *clnt_create()*, *clnt_call()* and *clnt_destroy()*.

Grade Server - grade_svc.c

```
/*
 *Grade server program, invokes the get_grade() remote procedure.
 */
#include <stdio.h>
#include <rpc/rpc.h>
#include "get_grade.h"

#define GRADE_FILE  "grades"
#define NO          0
#define YES         1

main()
{
        SVCXPRT         *transp;
        void            dispatch();

        /*
         * 1) Get a transport handle
         */
        transp = svcudp_create(RPC_ANYSOCK);
        if (transp == NULL) {
                fprintf(stderr, "Error: svcudp_create() call failed\n");
                return (1);
        }

        /*
         * 2) Register the service with the portmapper
         */
        (void) pmap_unset(GRADE_PROG, GRADE_VERS_1);
        if (svc_register(transp, GRADE_PROG, GRADE_VERS_1,
           dispatch, IPPROTO_UDP) == FALSE) {
                fprintf(stderr, "Error: unable to register grade service\n");
                svc_destroy(transp);
                return(1);
        }

        /*
         * 3) Call the library routine to dispatch RPCs
         */
```

FIGURE 5.1

```
        svc_run();
        fprintf(stderr, "Error: svc_run() shouldn't return\n");
        svc_unregister(GRADE_PROG, GRADE_VERS_1);
        svc_destroy(transp);
        return (1);
}/* main */

/*
 * 4) Implement the dispatch routine
 */
void
dispatch(rqstp, transp)
        struct svc_req      *rqstp;
        SVCXPRT             *transp;

        char                id_num[ID_NUM_SIZE + 1], *gradep;
        char                *get_grade_1();

        if (rqstp->rq_proc == NULLPROC) {
                svc_sendreply(transp, xdr_void, 0);
                return;
        }

        switch(rqstp->rq_proc)
        {
        case GET_GRADE_PROC:
                if (svc_getargs(transp, xdr_stu_id_num, id_num) == FALSE) {
                        svcerr_decode(transp);
                        return;
                }

                gradep = get_grade_1(id_num);
                if (svc_sendreply(transp, xdr_char, gradep) == FALSE) {
                        svcerr_systemerr(transp);
                }
                break;

        default:
                svcerr_noproc(transp);
                break;
        }
} /* dispatch */
```

FIGURE 5.1 Continued

```
/*
 * The get_grade_1() routine is the same as in the previous chapter.
 */
```

Grade Client - get_grade.c

```
/*
 * Grade server client, calls the get_grade() remote procedure and prints
 * the results.
 */
#include <stdio.h>
#include <rpc/rpc.h>
#include "get_grade.h"

struct   timeval timeout = { 25, 0 };
main(argc, argv)
         int      argc;
         char     *argv[];
{
         CLIENT              *clnt_handlep;
         enum                clnt_stat status;
         char                grade;
         int                 ret_code;

         if (argc != 3) {
                  fprintf(stderr, "usage: %s server_name id#\n", argv[0]);
                  return (1);
         }

         /*
          * 1) Get a client handle
          */
         clnt_handlep = clnt_create(argv[1], GRADE_PROG, GRADE_VERS_1,
                                     "udp");
         if (clnt_handlep == NULL) {
                  clnt_pcreateerror(argv[1]);
                  return (1);
         }

         /*
          * 2) Call the remote procedure
          */
         status = clnt_call(clnt_handlep, GET_GRADE_PROC, xdr_stu_id_num,
                           argv[2], xdr_char, &grade, timeout);
```

FIGURE 5.1 Continued

```
        if (status == RPC_SUCCESS) {
                if (grade != NO_GRADE) {
                        printf("Your grade is a %c\n", grade);
                        ret_code = 0;
                } else {
                        fprintf(stderr, "Could not find grade in grade file\n");
                        ret_code = 1;
                }
        } else {
                clnt_perror(clnt_handlep, argv[1]);
        }

        /*
         * 3) Destroy the client handle when done
         */
        clnt_destroy(clnt_handlep);
        return (ret_code);
} /* main */
```

FIGURE 5.1 Continued

The routine *clnt_create()* gets a client handle for the transport specified. The routine *clnt_call()* actually makes the remote procedure call to the service. Note that you can now specify a time-out when making a RPC. Time-outs are discussed in the next section. The routine *clnt_destroy()* simply deallocates any memory associated with the client handle. The changes to the client side were not as extensive as the ones to the server side.

5.3 Fundamental Low-Level RPC Routines

More than 30 low-level RPC routines exist. This section covers the details of these low-level routines. Typically, server side routine names start with *svc* and client side routine names start with *clnt*.

5.3.1 Server Side Low-Level RPC Routines

Three routines create a transport handle. The function, *svcudp_create()*, gets a transport handle for the UDP transport.

The function, *svctcp_create()*, gets a transport handle for the TCP transport. The function, *svcraw_create()*, gets a transport handle for the Raw transport which is discussed in Chapter 8. The synopses of the other two functions follows:

```
SVCXPRT *
svcudp_create(sock)
int     sock;
```

This routine creates a UDP-based RPC service transport handle and returns a pointer to it. The routine returns NULL if it fails. The transport is associated with the socket specified by the *sock* argument. The value of *sock* may be RPC_ANYSOCK, in which case a new socket is created. Otherwise, *sock* is assumed to be an open socket descriptor. If the socket is not bound to a local UDP port, then this routine binds it to an arbitrary port.

```
SVCXPRT *
svctcp_create(sock, sendsz, recvsz)
int     sock;
u_int   sendsz, recvsz;
```

This routine creates a TCP-based RPC service transport handle and returns a pointer to it. If the routine fails, it returns NULL. The transport is associated with the socket specified by the *sock* argument. The value of *sock* may be RPC_ANYSOCK, in which case a new socket is created. Otherwise, *sock* is assumed to be an open socket descriptor. If the socket is not bound to a local TCP port, then this routine binds it to an arbitrary port. The routine then starts a TCP listener on the socket's associated port. The *sendsz* argument specifies the size in bytes of the buffer used to return data to the calling process. The *recvsz* argument specifies the size in bytes of the buffer used to receive data from the calling process. Buffer size values of less than 100 result in a size of 4000 being used. (Remember that stream transports use XDR record streams. The buffer size parameters are simply passed on to the *xdrrec_create()* routine.)

```
void
svc_destroy(xprt)
SVCXPRT         *xprt;
```

This routine takes a pointer to a transport handle as its argument. The routine deallocates memory used for private data structures and the transport handle. Use of the transport handle is undefined after you call this routine. If the RPC Library opened the socket associated with the transport handle then it will close the socket. Otherwise, the socket remains open. You should call this routine when you are through with the transport handle.

Once you have a transport handle, the next step is to register the service by using the *svc_register()* routine. The synopsis follows:

```
bool_t
svc_register(xprt, prognum, versnum, dispatch, protocol)
SVCXPRT        *xprt;
u_long         prognum, versnum;
void           (*dispatch) ();
u_long         protocol;
```

This routine associates the program number, *prognum,* and the version number, *versnum,* with the service dispatch procedure, *dispatch().* The service is not registered with the portmapper if the argument *protocol* is zero. If *protocol* is nonzero, a mapping of the triple (prognum , versnum , protocol) to *xprt->xp_port* is established with the local portmapper. Currently, this routine supports the following protocol values: zero, IPPROTO_UDP, and IPPROTO_TCP. The *svc_register()* routine returns TRUE if it succeeds, and FALSE otherwise.

You should call *pmap_unset()* before calling *svc_register()* to ensure that the service, if previously registered, is unregistered with the portmapper. An instance of the service could have still been registered if it crashed before calling *svc_unregister().*

The synopsis for the dispatch procedure follows:

```
void
dispatch(request, xprt)
struct svc_req   *request;
SVCXPRT          *xprt;
```

The argument, *request,* points to the service request structure. This structure contains the program number, version number and procedure number that is associated with the incoming RPC request. This structure also contains authentication information that is discussed in Section 5.6. The dispatch procedure is invoked by the RPC Library when a request has been received for the program number and version number associated with the dispatch routine (the association is done via *svc_register()*). You should return from the dispatch routine after sending a reply to the client. Section 5.4 shows you how to implement the dispatch routine.

```
void
svc_unregister(prognum, versnum)
u_long  prognum, versnum;
```

This routine removes the mapping of the program number, *prognum*, and version number, *versnum*, to the dispatch routines, and removes the mapping of all procedure numbers associated with the program number and version number to the port number (via *pmap_unset()*). Note that this includes mappings for both the UDP and TCP transport. You should always call this routine to unregister your service before exiting the application.

You may have a problem calling *svc_unregister()* if you have one server process for the UDP transport and another server process for the TCP transport, because the routine removes all mappings of the program number and version number with the local portmapper. You would have to develop a scheme where only one process called *svc_unregister()*, or the process would re-register itself with the portmapper after the other process called *svc_unregister()*.

The following routines are typically used in a service dispatch routine to decode the arguments to a procedure, free any memory allocated while decoding the arguments, and to send a reply to the client. Later on in this chapter is a discussion on implementing your own dispatch routine. Here are the synopses:

```
bool_t
svc_getargs(xprt, inproc, in)
SVCXPRT       *xprt;
xdrproc_t     inproc;
char          *in;
```

This routine decodes the arguments of an RPC request associated with the transport handle, *xprt*. The argument *in* is the address where the decoded RPC arguments are placed; *inproc* is the address of the XDR routine used to decode the arguments. This routine returns TRUE if decoding succeeds, and FALSE otherwise. You should call this routine after you know the procedure number of the call and the associated XDR decoding routine.

```
bool_t
svc_freeargs(xprt, inproc, in)
```

```
SVCXPRT      *xprt;
xdrproc_t    inproc;
char         *in;
```

This routine frees any memory allocated by the XDR filters used to decode the arguments to a service procedure. You should call this routine when you are through with the arguments, typically after the reply to a RPC has been sent back to the client. This routine returns TRUE if the results were successfully freed, and FALSE otherwise.

```
bool_t
svc_sendreply(xprt, outproc, out)
SVCXPRT      *xprt;
xdrproc_t    outproc;
char         *out;
```

This routine sends the results of a RPC to the client. The argument *xprt* is a pointer to the transport handle associated with the request. The argument *outproc* is the address of the XDR routine which is used to encode the results; and *out* is the address of the results. This routine returns TRUE if it succeeds, FALSE otherwise.

5.3.2 Client Side Low-Level RPC Routines

There are four routines which can be used to create a client handle. The function *clntudp_create()* gets a client handle for the UDP transport. The function *clnttcp_create()* gets a client handle for the TCP transport. The function *clnt_create()* provides a generic interface to the other two client handle creation routines. The function *clntraw_create()* gets a client handle for the Raw transport which is discussed in Chapter 8. The routines *clntudp_create()* and *clnttcp_create()* require an Internet address as the first argument. You can obtain this address by calling the routine *gethostbyname()*. This routine is usually included in networking libraries on operating systems that support sockets. The routine takes the host name as an argument and returns a pointer to a structure that contains, among other items, an array of addresses. The examples at the end of this chapter demonstrate how to use this routine.

Here are the synopses for the client handle creation routines:

```
CLIENT *
clnt_create(host, prognum, versnum, protocol)
char    *host;
```

```
u_long  prognum, versnum;
char    *protocol;
```

This routine provides a generic interface to the *clntudp_create()* and the *clnttcp_create()* routines. The *host* argument identifies the name of the remote host where the service is located. The service is identified by the program number, *prognum*, and the version number, *versnum*. The *protocol* argument indicates which kind of transport protocol to use. Currently the valid values for this field are "udp" and "tcp". Default time-outs are set but can be modified using the *clnt_control()* routine (discussed later in this section). The retry time-out for the datagram transport is 5 seconds and the total time-out is 25 seconds. The retry time-out is the amount of time that the RPC Library waits for the server to reply before retransmitting the request. The total time-out is the amount of time that the RPC Library waits before timing-out the RPC call and returning a time-out error.

The routine returns a valid client handle or the NULL value to indicate an error. Even if the requested version number is not registered with the *portmap* service on *host*, it still returns a pointer to a client handle if some version of the given program number is registered. The version mismatch is discovered when you do a *clnt_call()* later (see note on the next page).

```
CLIENT *
clntudp_create(addr, prognum, versnum, wait, sockp)
struct sockaddr_in     *addr;
u_long                 prognum, versnum;
struct timeval         wait;
int                    *sockp;
```

This routine creates a UDP-based RPC client handle for the argument *prognum* and *versnum*. The remote program is located at Internet address referenced by *addr*, which is the address of the computer that the service is running on. If the port number of the RPC service, *addr->sin_port*, is zero, then *clntudp_create()* consults the portmapper on the remote computer to obtain the port number that the service is running on. If *addr->sin_port* is non-zero, then it is assumed to contain the port number of the service. The UDP transport resends the call message in intervals of *wait* time until it receives a response or until the call times out. The total time for the call to time-out is specified as an argument to *clnt_call()* when the RPC is made. The argument *sockp* is a pointer to a socket descriptor; if the socket descriptor is set to RPC_ANYSOCK, this routine opens a new socket descriptor and sets *sockp* to point to it. Otherwise, if you pass in an open socket descriptor, you need to close the socket after you are through with the client handle. The authentication credentials associated with the client handle are set to no authentication, but you are free to set the authentication handle to the type of authentication desired. (Authentication is explained in more detail in Section 5.6.)

This routine returns a pointer to a client handle if it succeeds, otherwise it returns NULL. If *addr->sin_port* is zero and the requested version number is not registered with the remote *portmap* service, it still returns a pointer to a client handle if some version of the given program number is registered. The version mismatch will be discovered when you do a *clnt_call()* later (see note below).

```
CLIENT *
clnttcp_create(addr, prognum, versnum, sockp, sendsz, recvsz)
struct sockaddr_in      *addr;
u_long                  prognum, versnum;
int                     *sockp;
u_int                   sendsz, recvsz;
```

This routine creates a TCP-based RPC client handle for *prognum* and *versnum*. The semantics of the *addr* and the *sockp* arguments are the same as for the *clntudp_create()* routine. Since TCP-based RPC uses buffered I/O, the user may specify the size of the send and receive buffers with the arguments *sendsz* and *recvsz;* values less than 100 result in a size of 4000 being used. The authentication credentials associated with the client handle are set to no authentication. You are free to set the authentication handle to the type of authentication desired. Authentication is explained in more detail in Section 5.6. This routine returns a pointer to a client handle if it succeeds, otherwise it returns NULL. If *addr->sin_port* is zero and the requested version number is not registered with the remote *portmap* service, it still returns a pointer to a client handle if some version of the given program number is registered. The version mismatch will be discovered when you do a *clnt_call()* later (see note below).

Note: You may be wondering why the client handle creation routine would succeed even if the requested version number were not available on the specified computer. This occurs because differences between versions of your service are only known to your service. The portmapper does not know which version of the service is closest to the version requested (except when the requested version is available). Therefore, it will bind you to one of the versions of the service, inform you that the remote program is available, and let you determine which version of the service can be used by the client. This approach gives you the greatest amount of flexibility in determining which version of the service is appropriate.

```
void
clnt_destroy(clnt_handlep)
CLIENT *clnt_handlep;
```

This routine takes a pointer to a client handle as its argument. The routine deallocates memory used for private data structures and the client handle. Use of the client handle is undefined after you call this routine. If the RPC Library opened the socket associated with the client handle then it will close the socket. Otherwise, the socket remains open. You should call this routine when you are through with the client handle.

The *clnt_call()* routine initiates a RPC. The synopsis of this function follows:

```
enum clnt_stat
clnt_call(clnt_handlep, procnum, inproc, in, outproc, out, timeout)
CLIENT          *clnt_handlep;
u_long          procnum;
xdrproc_t       inproc;
char            *in;
xdrproc_t       outproc;
char            *out;
struct timeval  timeout;
```

This routine calls the remote procedure *procnum* associated with the client handle pointer, *clnt_handlep*. Remember that a client handle contains the port number of a service for the program and version number that was specified in the call to the client handle creation routine. The argument *in* is the address of the procedure's argument, and *out* is the address of where to place the result; the argument *inproc* encodes the procedure's arguments, and the argument *outproc* decodes the procedure's results. The argument *timeout* is the total time allowed for results to come back. The RPC Library may retransmit the call to the service before timing-out, depending on the type of transport used. Refer to the synopsis of the client handle creation routine used for more information. This routine returns a value of type *clnt_stat*, an enumeration of return values, defined in the ⟨*rpc/clnt.h*⟩ header. The *clnt_stat* values are discussed in more detail in Section 5.5.

```
bool_t
clnt_control(clnt_handlep, request, info)
CLIENT *clnt_handlep;
int     request;
char    *info;
```

This routine is used to change or retrieve various information associated with a client handle. The argument *request* indicates the type of operation, and *info* is a generic pointer to the information associated with the request. The supported values of *request* and the associated argument types for *info* and what the request does follows:

CLSET_TIMEOUT	struct timeval	set total time-out
CLGET_TIMEOUT	struct timeval	get total time-out

The total time-out is the amount of time that the RPC Library waits before timing-out the RPC call and returning a time-out error. If you set the time-out using *clnt_control()*, then the time-out argument passed to *clnt_call()* is ignored in all future calls.

CLGET_SERVER_ADDR	struct sockaddr	get server's Internet address

The following operations are valid for the UDP transport only:

CLSET_RETRY_TIMEOUT	struct timeval	set the retry time-out
CLGET_RETRY_TIMEOUT	struct timeval	get the retry time-out

The retry time-out is the amount of time that the RPC Library waits for the server to reply before retransmitting the request.

```
bool_t
clnt_freeres(clnt_handlep, outproc, out)
CLIENT       *clnt_handlep;
xdrproc_t    outproc;
char         *out;
```

This routine frees any memory that was allocated by the XDR routines when they decoded the results of a RPC. The argument *out* is the address of the results, and *outproc* is the XDR routine used to decode the results. This routine returns TRUE if the results were successfully freed, and FALSE otherwise.

5.4 Server Dispatch Routine

The server dispatch routine, as its name implies, dispatches an incoming RPC to the correct procedure. Typically, the dispatch routine decodes the incoming arguments, calls the appropriate procedure with the arguments, and takes the reply from the procedure and sends it off to the client. You can also add code to support multiple versions of a server and to authenticate the client in your dispatch routine. Of course, you are free to write your dispatch routine as you like. You could even do argument decoding and authentication inside the individual routines. The problem with this approach is that you are intermixing RPC Library routine calls all through your code. It is better to isolate the RPC Library routine calls in one layer. That way you are free to plug your remote procedures into the client for testing purposes. Testing is discussed in more detail in Chapter 8.

The dispatch routine takes two arguments. The first is the service request structure listed in Figure 5.2. The second argument is a pointer to the transport handle. The dispatch routine does not return a value. The service request structure identifies the program number, version number and procedure number associated with the incoming RPC. It also contains client authentication information which is discussed at the end of this chapter. The transport handle is provided to allow the dispatch routine to send information back to the client. Note that a copy of the pointer to the transport handle is also located in the service request structure. You should use the one that is explicitly passed in as the argument to the dispatch routine.

```
Service Request Structure
struct svc_req {
        u_long          rq_prog;          /* service program number */
        u_long          rq_vers;          /* service protocol version */
        u_long          rq_proc;          /* procedure number */
        struct opaque_auth rq_cred;       /* raw credentials from the wire */
        caddr_t         rq_clntcred;      /* read only cooked credentials */
        SVCXPRT         *rq_xprt;         /* associated transport handle */
    };
```

FIGURE 5.2

The following example shows you how to implement a dispatch routine for the remote procedures that have the following declarations:

```
int     resolve_int(int)
float   resolve_float(float)
double  resolve_double(double)
```

There are a lot of ways to implement a dispatch routine. The most common form is shown in the example in Figure 5.3. This form is similar to the dispatch routines generated by *rpcgen* (covered in Chapter 7).

This approach provides a generic mechanism that assigns the address of the XDR routine to decode the arguments to the *xdr_argument* variable, and assigns the address of the XDR routine to encode the results into the *xdr_result* variable. The variable *local* is a generic pointer that contains the address of the procedure to be invoked. The variable *results* is a generic pointer that contains the address of the results from the procedure invocation.

```
static void
resolver_1(rqstp, transp)
        struct svc_req *rqstp;
        SVCXPRT *transp;
{
        union {
                int     resolve_int_arg;
                float   resolve_float_arg;
                double  resolve_double_arg;
        } argument;
        char            *result;
        xdrproc_t       xdr_argument, xdr_result;
        char            *(*local)();

        switch (rqstp->rq_proc) {
        case NULLPROC:
                (void)svc_sendreply(transp, xdr_void, (char *)NULL);
                return;
```

FIGURE 5.3

```
        case RESOLVE_INT:
                xdr_argument = xdr_int;
                xdr_result = xdr_int;
                local = (char *(*)()) resolve_int_1;
                break;

        case RESOLVE_FLOAT:
                xdr_argument = xdr_float;
                xdr_result = xdr_float;
                local = (char *(*)()) resolve_float_1;
                break;

        case RESOLVE_DOUBLE:
                xdr_argument = xdr_double;
                xdr_result = xdr_float;
                local = (char *(*)()) resolve_double_1;
                break;

        default:
                svcerr_noproc(transp);
                return;
        }
        if (svc_getargs(transp, xdr_argument, &argument) == FALSE) {
                svcerr_decode(transp);
                return;
        }

        result = (*local)(&argument);

        if (svc_sendreply(transp, xdr_result, result) == FALSE) {
                svcerr_systemerr(transp);
        }
}/* resolver_1 */
```

FIGURE 5.3 Continued

These variables are then used in the call to *svc_getargs()*, in the call to the procedure, and in the call to *svc_sendreply()*. The switch on the procedure number invokes the case associated with the procedure being called. The NULLPROC case simply sends a *void* reply back to the client and the dispatch routine returns. The other cases assign values to the *xdr_argument* , *xdr_result,* and the *local* variables.

If you wanted to support multiple versions of a remote program, you would typically implement one dispatch routine for each version, appending an underscore and the version number to the name of each dispatch routine. You would then use *svc_register()* to associate the dispatch routine with the version supported. Of course, you could support multiple versions from one dispatch routine by adding some type of switch on the *rq_vers* member of the service request structure.

5.5 Processing RPC Library Errors

The RPC Library has several routines that process errors detected by the RPC mechanism. Client-side error routines print canned error messages to *stderr,* or they return strings containing error messages. This flexibility allows you to choose the mechanism for reporting the error to the user. The server-side routines typically send a reply message back to the client, indicating the detected failure.

The synopses for the server side error routines follows:

```
void
svcerr_auth(xprt, why)
SVCXPRT         *xprt;
enum auth_stat  why;
```

Called by a service that refuses to perform a RPC due to an authentication error specified by the *why* argument. The enumeration *auth_stat* is defined in ⟨*rpc/auth.h*⟩.

```
void
svcerr_decode(xprt)
SVCXPRT         *xprt;
```

Called by a service that cannot successfully decode its arguments.

```
void
svcerr_noproc(xprt)
SVCXPRT         *xprt;
```

Called by a service that does not implement the procedure number that the caller requests.

```
void
svcerr_noprog(xprt)
SVCXPRT        *xprt;
```

Called when the desired program is not registered with the RPC Library. You would typically not use this routine. You would only call this routine if you are not using the portmapper, but instead have implemented some other mechanism for determining the port number associated with a service (i.e. you have modified the RPC Library).

```
void
svcerr_progvers(xprt)
SVCXPRT     *xprt;
```

Called when the desired version of a program is not registered with the RPC Library. You would typically not use this routine. You only call this routine if you are not using the portmapper, but instead have implemented some other mechanism for determining the port number associated with a service (i.e. you have modified the RPC Library).

```
void
svcerr_systemerr(xprt)
SVCXPRT        *xprt;
```

Called by a service when it detects a system error not covered by any particular protocol. For example, if a service can no longer allocate storage, it may call this routine.

```
void
svcerr_weakauth(xprt)
SVCXPRT        *xprt;
```

Called by a service that refuses to perform a RPC due to insufficient, but correct, authentication arguments. The routine calls *svcerr_auth()* with the *why* argument set to AUTH_TOOWEAK, indicating to the client that the RPC was rejected due to security reasons. As you will see in Section 5.6, you are free to define your own reasons for rejecting requests.

The synopses for the client-side error routines follows:

```
void
clnt_pcreateerror(str)
char     *str;
```

This routine prints a message to *stderr* indicating why a client handle could not be created. The message is prepended with string, *str*, and a colon. This routine is used when a *clnt_create()*, *clntraw_create()*, *clnttcp_create()*, or *clntudp_create()* call fails.

```
void
clnt_perrno(stat)
enum clnt_stat   stat;
```

This routine prints a message to *stderr* corresponding to the condition indicated by *stat*.

```
void
clnt_perror(clnt_handlep, str)
CLIENT *clnt_handlep;
char       *str;
```

This routine prints a message to *stderr* indicating why a RPC failed; the argument *clnt_handlep* is a pointer to the client handle that was used in the call. The message is prepended with a string referenced by *str* and a colon. This routine is used after a *clnt_call()* call fails.

```
char *
clnt_spcreateerror(str)
char     *str;
```

This routine is like *clnt_pcreateerror()*, except that it returns a string instead of printing to *stderr*. Note that the pointer returned references static data that is overwritten on each call to this routine.

```
char *
clnt_sperrno(stat)
enum clnt_stat   stat;
```

This routine takes the same arguments as *clnt_perrno()*, but instead of printing the message to *stderr*, it returns a pointer to a string that contains the message. The string ends with a NEWLINE character. Note that unlike *clnt_sperror()* and *clnt_spcreaterror()*, the routine *clnt_sperrno()* does not return a pointer to static data so the result does not get overwritten on each call.

```
char *
clnt_sperror(clnt_handlep, str)
CLIENT *clnt_handlep;
char      *str;
```

This routine is like *clnt_perror()*, except that it returns a string instead of printing to *stderr*. Note that the pointer returned references static data that is overwritten on each call to this routine.

The *clnt_stat* values are listed in Figure 5.4 with an explanation associated with each value.

RPC_SUCCESS
: The RPC succeeded.

RPC_CANTENCODEARGS
: The encoding of the request to the service has failed. This means that the encoding of the RPC message header or the arguments to the remote procedure failed.

RPC_CANTDECODERES
: The decoding of the response from the service has failed. This means that the decoding of the RPC reply header or the results of the remote procedure failed.

RPC_CANTSEND
: Transport error detected while sending the request to the service.

RPC_CANTRECV
: Transport error detected when receiving a response from the service.

RPC_TIMEDOUT
: The RPC has timed out.

FIGURE 5.4

RPC_VERSMISMATCH
The service and client are not using the same version of the RPC protocol.

RPC_AUTHERROR
An authentication error has been detected.

RPC_PROGUNAVAIL
The requested program is not available. This error is sent to the client from the server using the *svcerr_noprog()* routine.

RPC_PROGVERSMISMATCH
The program and version are not properly matched. This error is sent to the client from the server using the *svcerr_progvers()* routine.

RPC_PROCUNAVAIL
The requested remote procedure is not available. This error is sent to the client from the server using the *svcerr_noproc()* routine.

RPC_CANTDECODEARGS
The service could not decode the arguments to the procedure. This error could be propagated to the client from the server using the *svcerr_decode()* routine.

RPC_SYSTEMERROR
The service has detected an error. This error is sent to the client from the server using the *svcerr_systemerr()* routine.

RPC_UNKNOWNHOST
The specified host name is unknown.

RPC_UNKNOWNPROTO
The specified protocol is not supported.

RPC_PMAPFAILURE
A call by the RPC Library to a portmapper function failed.

FIGURE 5.4 Continued

RPC_PROGNOTREGISTERED
The program is not registered with the portmapper on the specified host.

RPC_FAILED
An error that does not map to one of the above values was detected.

FIGURE 5.4 Continued

5.6 Authentication

The authentication mechanism used in the RPC Library is open-ended; a variety of authentication types may be plugged into it and may coexist on the network. Every RPC is authenticated on the server, and similarly, the client generates and sends authentication arguments for every RPC. Two terms are important for any RPC authentication system: credentials and verifiers. Using ID badges as an example, the credential is what identifies a person: it contains a name, address, birth date, etc. The verifier is the photo attached to the badge. You can verify that the credentials were not stolen by checking the picture on the person's badge against the person wearing it. In RPC, the process is similar. The client sends both a credential and a verifier to the server with each RPC request. The server sends back only a verifier, since the client could not have made the RPC to the server without knowing the server's credentials.

Currently, the RPC Library supports three types of authentication. The authentication types are often referred to as "flavors". The first is no authentication, the second is UNIX-style authentication that uses UNIX credentials, and the third is based on the Data Encryption Standard (DES). The third flavor of authentication is also referred to as secure RPC. You are free to invent new authentication types. The authentication type is identified by a unique number with the same rules for authentication type number assignment as there are for program number assignment. Refer to Appendix 1 for more information on authentication numbers.

An important note about the relationship between the RPC authentication and the network services that use them is that the

RPC Library deals only with authentication and not with the network service's access control. The services themselves must implement their own access-control policies and reflect these policies as return status in their protocols. Going back to the example of the badge with the picture on it, the RPC Library simply verifies that the person wearing the badge is the same person that is in the picture on the badge—the Library verifies the credentials. Now that you know the credentials are good, you can restrict access to your building based on the person's credentials.

The client specifies the type of authentication by setting the value of the pointer to the authentication handle in the client handle structure. When you create a client handle, by using one of the client-handle create functions, the authentication handle is set up for no authentication. The following sections show you how to set the authentication handle to the type of authentication that you want to use. Note that you can use a different authentication mechanism for different remote procedures within a distributed application by simply setting the authentication handle to the flavor desired before the RPC. When you are done with an authentication handle, you should call *auth_destroy()* to destroy the credentials and verifiers. The synopsis for this routine follows:

```
void
auth_destroy(auth)
AUTH   *auth;
```

This routine takes a pointer to an authentication handle as its argument. The routine deallocates memory used for private data structures and the authentication handle. Use of the authentication handle is undefined after calling this routine.

The following sections cover the use of each authentication flavor.

5.6.1 No Authentication

Some services might not require authentication of the client, in which case you would use the AUTH_NONE authentication flavor. Use of this flavor implies that the credentials and verifier sent to the server are null. The client-side would set the pointer to the authentication handle as follows:

```
clnt_handlep->cl_auth = authnone_create();
```

Nothing needs to be done on the server side because it gets null credentials and null verifiers. Any client on the network is allowed to use this service. Here is the synopsis for the *authnone_create()* routine:

*AUTH **
authnone_create()

This routine creates and returns an RPC authentication handle that passes nonusable authentication information with each RPC. This is the default authentication used by the RPC Library.

5.6.2 UNIX Authentication

Some services might want to restrict access to a certain set of users. They could do this by using UNIX-style authentication, which sets the credentials to the client's host name, user ID, group ID, and group-access-list. The verifier contains nothing. This means that a user of the service could generate the credentials of anybody on the network, and the service could not verify them. This mechanism is typically useful for restricting access to trusted users who do not have root privileges[1] on any computer in the network or those users that will not implement their own client to access the service.

Two routines are available for the client to use to build UNIX-style authentication handles. The synopses for the routines follows:

```
AUTH *
authunix_create(hostname, uid, gid, grouplen, gidlistp)
char    *hostname;
int     uid, gid, grouplen, *gidlistp;
```

This routine creates and returns a pointer to an authentication handle that contains UNIX authentication information. The argument *hostname* is the name of the computer on which the information was created; *uid* is the user's user ID; *gid* is the user's current group ID; *grouplen* is the number of groups in the group ID list *gidlistp,* which refers to an array of group IDs to which the user belongs.

---

[1] The UNIX operating system provides a special user name *root*. When you log in with this name, you become the most privileged user on the system, and can assume the user ID of any other user on your system.

*AUTH **
authunix_create_default()

Calls *authunix_create()* with the default values set for all the arguments.

On the server side, you can access the credentials of the client making the request through the *rq_cred* member of the service request structure that is passed into the dispatch routine. The *rq_cred* structure is defined as follows:

```
struct opaque_auth {
        enum_t oa_flavor;          /* flavor of auth */
        caddr_t oa_base;           /* address of more auth stuff */
        u_int   oa_length;         /* not to exceed MAX_AUTH_BYTES */
};
```

The structure above is also referred to as the "raw credentials". They are called this because the authentication information referenced by the *oa_base* member has not been processed, or "cooked". Typically, you only use *rq_cred* to access authentication information when your service does not support the flavor specified in *oa_flavor* . Normally you would use the *rq_clntcred* member of the service request structure that is passed into the dispatch routine. This member references credentials that have been processed, also referred to as the "cooked credentials". To access the cooked credentials, you simply cast the address in *rq_clntcred* to a pointer that references a known authentication structure and access the credentials through the pointer. An example below shows you how to do this.

The RPC Library guarantees the following to the service dispatch routine:

1. That the request's *rq_cred* structure contains valid data. You can inspect the request's *rq_cred.oa_flavor* to determine which type of authentication the caller used. You may wish to inspect the other fields of *rq_cred* if the style is not one of the styles that the service supports.
2. That the request's *rq_clntcred* field is either NULL or points to a structure that corresponds to a supported style of authentication credentials.

The code fragment in Figure 5.5 shows how, based on UNIX credentials, to restrict access to a client.

In Figure 5.5, access is denied to the client with a user ID of 99. The *authunix_parms* structure is defined in ⟨*rpc/auth_unix.h*⟩. The authentication check is usually short circuited for the null procedure as it is customary not to check the authentication arguments associated with a call to the null procedure. The routine *svcerr_weakauth()* sends a reply message to the client indicating that the request was rejected for security reasons. Note that the example does not distinguish between the case of an unsupported authentication flavor or the denial of access to the service because the client's user ID was 99. You could define your network service protocol to explicitly specify why access was denied. You do not have to put the authentication check into the dispatch routine, it

```
void
dispatch(rqstp, transp)
        struct    svc_req              *rqstp;
        SVCXPRT                        *transp;
{
        struct authunix_parms          *unix_cred;

        ...
        switch (rqstp->rq_cred.oa_flavor) {
        case AUTH_UNIX:
           unix_cred = (struct authunix_parms *)rqstp->rq_clntcred;
           if (unix_cred->aup_uid == 99) {
                 svcerr_weakauth(transp);
                 return;
           }
           break;

        default:
           svcerr_weakauth(transp);
           return;
        }
        ...
} /* dispatch */
```

FIGURE 5.5

can be done in the called procedure routine. The placement of the authentication check depends on the architecture of your service.

5.6.3 DES Authentication

UNIX authentication suffers from two major problems:

1. The naming is UNIX-system oriented, so other computers on the network that do not run UNIX may not be able to support this naming convention. Also, in a networking environment, there is a possibility of collisions in the user and group ID numbers assigned. A user ID on one computer may be used by a different user on a second computer. Even worse is the case of the super-user, user ID 0, where this user ID is the same for every UNIX system. You may not want the super-user of another computer to have super-user privileges on your computer.
2. There is no verifier, so credentials are easy to fake. The server has no means of verifying the client's credentials.

DES authentication rectifies these problems. It corrects the naming problem by basing naming on new names called *netnames*. A *netname* is merely a string of printable characters, and fundamentally, it is really these *netnames* that are authenticated. Thus the *netname* is the credential. DES authentication corrects the second problem of UNIX-style authentication by using a verifier.

Each user should have a globally unique *netname*, unique for all computers on all networks. Ideally, nobody else would have a *netname* that is the same as yours. Each operating system's implementation of DES authentication must generate *netnames* for its users that ensure this uniqueness when they call on remote servers. Operating systems already know how to distinguish local users and extending this mechanism to the network is easy. Library routines construct a *netname* by concatenating the operating system name, the user ID, and the domain name that the user is in. Refer to [COME 88] for more information on domains. For example, a UNIX user at Sun, domain *sun.com*, with a user ID of 515, would be assigned the following *netname: unix.515@sun.com.* Other non-SunOS environments may have other ways of generating *netnames,* but this does not preclude users of these non-SunOS environments from accessing the secure network services of the Sun environment.

DES authentication is recommended for people who want more security than UNIX authentication. The details of the DES authentication protocol are complicated and are explained in Chapter 3 for those who are interested. The remainder of this section deals with the user level interface to the DES authentication type.

For DES authentication to work, you have to do several things to your server computer and client computer. The *keyserv* daemon must be running on both computers. The users on these computers need public keys assigned by the network administrator. And, they need to have decrypted their secret keys by using their login password. This happens automatically when you log in, or you can do it manually by using the *keylogin* program. The "Secure Networking" chapter of the *Security Features Guide* explains how to set up secure networking in a SunOS environment.

The client uses the *authdes_create()* routine to build a DES authentication handle. The synopsis follows:

```
AUTH *
authdes_create(netname, window, syncaddr, deskeyp)
char               *netname;
u_int              window;
struct sockaddr    *syncaddr;
des_block          *deskeyp;
```

The *authdes_create()* routine creates and returns a pointer to an authentication handle that enables the use of the DES authentication system. The first argument *netname* is the network name of the server. This name is usually obtained by calling either *host2netname()* if the server is running as a root process or *user2netname()* if the server is not running as a root process. The *authdes_create()* routine calls *getnetname()* to get the client's *netname.* The routines that manipulate *netnames* are described below. The second argument, *window,* is a window on the validity of the client credential, given in seconds. A small window is more secure than a large one, but choosing too small a window increases the frequency of resynchronizations because of clock drift which can affect the performance of the RPC. The third argument, *syncaddr,* is optional. If it is NULL, the authentication system assumes that the local clock is always synchronized with the server's clock and will not attempt resynchronizations. If an address is supplied, however, the system uses the address for consulting the remote time service whenever resynchronization is required. This argument is usually the address of the server computer to which you are making requests, implying that the time service on the server computer is used for resynchronization. The final argument, *deskeyp,* is a pointer to a DES key and is optional. If it is NULL, the authentication system generates a random DES key for the encryption of credentials, otherwise the supplied DES key is used.

You should specify a sufficiently large value for the *window* parameter to ensure that your credentials do not keep timing out. A value of 300 seconds should be sufficient for most applications. Once your application is running and you are convinced that the DES authentication is working properly, then you can begin to reduce the time-out value if you need a smaller window. You will get the error RPC_AUTHERROR if your window value is too small and the credentials repetitiously time-out.

When allocating storage for *netnames,* you should allocate a character array of MAXNETNAMELEN + 1 length. The synopses for the library routines that manipulate *netnames* follow:

```
int
host2netname(netname, host, domain)
char    *netname, *host, *domain;
```

This routine converts a domain-specific host name, specified by the *host* and *domain* arguments, to an operating-system independent network name stored in the location referenced by the *netname* argument. It returns 1 if it succeeds and 0 if it fails. This routine is the inverse of *netname2host().*

```
int
netname2host(netname, host, hostlen)
char    *netname, *host;
int     hostlen;
```

This routine converts an operating-system independent network name specified by the *netname* argument to a domain-specific host name. The host name portion of the result is stored in the location referenced by the *host* argument. The number of bytes written into this location will not exceed *hostlen*. The host name is truncated if the *hostlen* argument is smaller than the actual number of bytes in the host name. This routine returns 1 if it succeeds and 0 if it fails. This routine is the inverse of *host2netname()*.

```
int
netname2user(netname, uidp, gidp, gidlenp, gidlistp)
char    *netname;
int     *uidp, *gidp, *gidlenp, *gidlistp;
```

This routine converts an operating-system independent *netname*, specified by the *netname* argument, to a domain-specific user ID. This ID consists of a user ID, stored in **uidp*, a group ID, stored in **gidp*, a group ID list length, stored in **gidlenp*, and a group ID list, stored in *gidlistp*. The group ID list should be large enough to hold the maximum number of group IDs that your operating system allows. This routine returns 1 if it succeeds and 0 if it fails. This routine is the inverse of *user2netname()*.

```
int
user2netname(netname, uid, domain)
char    *netname;
int     uid;
char    *domain;
```

This routine converts a domain-specific username, specified by the *uid* and *domain* arguments, to an operating-system independent netname. The network name is stored in the location referenced by the argument *netname*. This routine returns 1 if it succeeds and 0 if it fails. This routine is the inverse of *netname2user()*.

```
int
getnetname(netname)
char    *netname;
```

This routine places the unique, operating-system independent network name of the caller into the fixed-length array *netname*. The routine calls *host2netname()* if you are the root user. Otherwise, it calls *user2netname()*. This routine returns 1 if it succeeds and 0 if it fails.

Figure 5.6 shows a code fragment from the client side that sets up the DES authentication handle. The server is running as a root process.

The code segment shown in Figure 5.6 makes a call to *host2netname()* to create the server's *netname*. This *netname* is then passed to *authdes_create()* to create the authentication handle. The window for the credentials is 300 seconds. This means that the credentials have a lifetime of 300 seconds; if the server does not receive the credentials within 300 seconds they will have expired. A smaller window is more secure but results in a higher number of time resynchronizations between the time service and the client if you are using the time service. The NULL synchronization address argument indicates that you do not want to use a remote time service for time resynchronization and that the local clock is synchronized with the server's clock. The last NULL argument informs the library to generate a random DES key for the encryption of credentials.

On the server side, you can check client credentials in a manner similar to the previous example. The code fragment in

```
...
CLIENT          *clnt_handlep;
char            *server_name;
char            server_netname[MAXNETNAMELEN + 1];
...
if (host2netname(server_netname, server_name, NULL) == FALSE) {
        fprintf(stderr, "Couldn't create server's netname\n");
        return (1);
}

clnt_handlep->cl_auth = authdes_create(server_netname, 300, NULL, NULL);
if (clnt_handlep->cl_auth == NULL) {
        fprintf(stderr, "Couldn't create DES credentials - Is keyserv running?");
        return (1);
```

FIGURE 5.6

Figure 5.7 shows how to restrict access to a client based on the client's user ID.

In Figure 5.7, access is restricted to the client with user ID 99, just as in the UNIX authentication example. The *authdes_cred* structure is defined in ⟨*rpc/auth_des.h*⟩. The routine *netname2 user()* is called to map the client's netname into its user ID, group ID, number of groups, and list of groups that the client is a member of. The manifest constant NGROUPS is defined in ⟨*sys/param.h*⟩. You then weed out the client with user ID of 99. The calls to *svcerr_weakauth()* send a reply message to the client indicating that the server detected a security problem. You could move the check for user ID into the *get_grade* procedure and then have it

```
void
dispatch(rqstp, transp)
        struct   svc_req *rqstp;
        SVCXPRT         *transp;
{
        struct authdes_cred        *des_credp;
        int       uid, gid, gidnum, gids[NGROUPS];
        ...
        switch (rqstp->rq_cred.oa_flavor) {
        case AUTH_DES:
                des_credp = (struct authdes_cred *)rqstp->rq_clntcred;
                if (netname2user(des_credp->adc_fullname.name, &uid, &gid,
                   &gidnum, gids) == FALSE || uid == 99) {
                        /* Netname not found or unauthorized uid */
                        svcerr_weakauth(transp);
                        return;
                }

                break;

        default:
                svcerr_weakauth(transp);
                return;
        }
        ...
} /* dispatch */
```

FIGURE 5.7

return an application-specific error code to the calling client. It really depends on how you design the architecture of your service.

5.7 Example

This section contains a complete example that shows how to use the low-level routines to implement a network service based on the data base routines, *dbm,* provided in the *dbm* Library on SunOS. These routines maintain key/content pairs in a data base. Refer to your operating system manual for more information about *dbm*.

The DBM network service allows only one client to participate in a session at any time. The DES authentication type is used to ensure that the client has access to the database files, and to prevent another client from trying to access an already open database. To access a database, the client first connects to the service using the *dbm_connect()* routine and calls *dbminit()* to open the database. The client then proceeds to read data from or write data to the database. When the client is done it simply calls *dbmclose()* to close the database and *dbm_disconnect()* to end the session with the server. The listings for the example are in Figure 5.8.

The server *main()* routine creates a TCP transport handle and registers the service. The service dispatch routine, *dbm_prog_1(),* is typical for a dispatch routine. The exception is the verification that the client used the DES authentication type on the RPC call. Note that authentication is actually done in the service procedure routines. The routine *bzero()* is called to zero out the memory used to contain the decoded arguments for the RPC. The side effect of zeroing the memory is that the pointers in the arguments structures are set to zero. The XDR routines that are invoked via the *svc_getargs()* routine allocate storage for the values referenced by the pointers in the argument structure. The call to *svc_freeargs()* frees this memory after the reply to the RPC has been made.

The DBM server procedures authenticate the caller and then call the corresponding DBM routine. The *dbminit_1()* routine verifies that the caller has access to the DBM file and that the file is readable and writable by the user. Note that a DBM database consists of two files; one with a *.dir* extension and the other with

Remote DBM Header File

```
#define MAX_FILENAME_LEN        256

/*
 * The maximum number of bytes that can be stored in one record in the
 * database.
 */
#define MAX_DATUM_SIZE          256

typedef char *filename;

/*
 * The argument wrapper for the STORE procedure
 */
typedef struct {
        datum key;
        datum content;
} store_args;

#define DBM_PROG     ((u_long)0x20000010)

#define DBM_VERS_1   ((u_long)1)

#define DBMINIT      ((u_long)1)
#define DBMCLOSE     ((u_long)2)
#define FETCH        ((u_long)3)
#define STORE        ((u_long)4)
#define DELETE       ((u_long)5)
#define FIRSTKEY     ((u_long)6)
#define NEXTKEY      ((u_long)7)

extern  int          *dbminit_1();
extern  int          *dbmclose_1();
extern  datum        *fetch_1();
extern  int          *store_1();
extern  int          *delete_1();
extern  datum        *firstkey_1();
extern  datum        *nextkey_1();
```

FIGURE 5.8

```
bool_t  xdr_datum();
bool_t  xdr_filename();
bool_t  xdr_store_args();
```

Remote DBM Server Main and Dispatch Routines

```
#include <stdio.h>
#include <dbm.h>
#include <rpc/rpc.h>
#include "dbm_remote.h"

static void dbm_prog_1();
static void dbm_prog_2();

/*
 * This service should be run with an effective user ID of 0, the root user,
 * on a UNIX system. This ensures that any database on the computer can be
 * accessed by this service. Note that the client's credentials are
 * authenticated using the DES authentication flavor.
 */
main()
{
        SVCXPRT                 *transp;

        transp = svctcp_create(RPC_ANYSOCK, 0, 0);
        if (transp == NULL) {
                fprintf(stderr, "Error: svctcp_create() call failed\n");
                return (1);
        }

        (void) pmap_unset(DBM_PROG, DBM_VERS_1);
        if (svc_register(transp, DBM_PROG, DBM_VERS_1, dbm_prog_1,
           IPPROTO_TCP) == FALSE) {
                fprintf(stderr, "Error: unable to register (DBM_PROG,
                DBM_VERS_1, tcp).\n");
                svc_destroy(transp);
                return (1);
        }
```

FIGURE 5.8 Continued

```
        svc_run();
        fprintf(stderr, "Error: svc_run() shouldn't return\n");
        svc_unregister(DBM_PROG, DBM_VERS_1);
        svc_destroy(transp);
        return (1);
} /* main */
static void
dbm_prog_1(rqstp, transp)
        struct svc_req       *rqtp;
        register SVCXPRT *transp;
{
        union {
                filename        dbminit_1_arg;
                datum           fetch_1_arg;
                store_args      store_1_arg;
                datum           delete_1_arg;
                datum           nextkey_1_arg;
        } argument;
        char                    *result;
        xdrproc_t               xdr_argument, xdr_result;
        char                    *(*local)();

        switch (rqstp->rq_proc) {
        case NULLPROC:
                (void) svc_sendreply(transp, xdr_void, (char *)NULL);
                return;

        case DBMINIT:
                xdr_argument = xdr_filename;
                xdr_result = xdr_int;
                local = (char *(*)()) dbminit_1;
                break;

        case DBMCLOSE:
                xdr_argument = xdr_void;
                xdr_result = xdr_int;
                local = (char *(*)()) dmbclose_1;
                break;
```

FIGURE 5.8 Continued

```
case FETCH:
        xdr_argument = xdr_datum;
        xdr_result = xdr_datum;
        local = (char *(*)()) fetch _1;
        break;

case STORE:
        xdr_argument = xdr_store_args;
        xdr_result = xdr_int;
        local = (char *(*)()) store_1;
        break;

case DELETE:
        xdr_argument = xdr_datum;
        xdr_result = xdr_int;
        local = (char *(*)()) delete_1;
        break;

case FIRSTKEY:
        xdr_argument = xdr_void;
        xdr_result = xdr_datum;
        local = (char *(*)()) firstkey_1;
        break;

case NEXTKEY:
        xdr_argument = xdr_datum;
        xdr_result = xdr_datum;
        local = (char *(*)()) nextkey_1;
        break;

default:
        svcerr_noproc(transp);
        return;
}

/*
 * Make sure caller used DES credentials
 */
if (rqstp->rq_cred.oa_flavor != AUTH_DES) {
        svcerr_weakauth(transp);
        return;
}
```

FIGURE 5.8 Continued

```
        bzero((char *(&argument, sizeof(argument));

        if (svc_getargs(transp, xdr_argument, &argument) == FALSE) {
                svcerr_decode(transp);
                return;
        }

        result = (*local)(&argument, rqstp);

        if (svc_sendreply(transp, xdr_result, result) == FALSE) {
                svcerr_systemerr(transp);
        }

        if (svc_freeargs(transp, xdr_argument, &argument) == FALSE) {
                fprintf(stderr, "Error: unable to free arguments\n");
                exit(1);
        }
} /* dbm_prog_1 */
```

Remote DBM Server Procedures

```
#include <sys/types.h>
#include <sys/param.h>
#include <sys/stat.h>
#include <stdio.h>
#include <dbm.h>
#include <rpc/rpc.h>
#include "dbm_remote.h"

#define UID_NOT_SET -1

/*
 * Save callers user ID between calls and only allow this user to operate
 * on the database until they close it. In essence, this is a "stateful"
 * service.
 */
int             uid = UID_NOT_SET;
struct  stat    stat_buf;
```

FIGURE 5.8 Continued

```
/*
 * Get the user's ID from the cooked DES credentials.
 */
int
get_uid(des_credp)
        struct  authdes_cred    *des_credp;
{
        int                     tmp_uid, gid, gidnum, gids[NGROUPS];

        if (netname2user(des_credp->adc_fullname.name, &tmp_uid, &gid,
        &gidnum, gids) == FALSE) {
        tmp_uid = UID_NOT_SET;
        }
        return (tmp_uid);
} /* get_uid */

int *
dbminit_1(argp, rqstp)
        filename *argp;
        struct  svc_req *rqstp;
{
        static int      result;
        char            file[MAX_FILENAME_LEN];

        if (strlen(*argp) > MAX_FILENAME_LEN - 5) {
                result = -1;
                return (&result);
        }

        strncpy(file, *argp, MAX_FILENAME_LEN - 5);
        strcat(file, ".dir"):

        /*
         * Make sure that nobody is currently using this service and that
         * the specified database file exists.
         */
        if (uid != UID_NOT_SET || stat(file, &stat_buf) == -1) {
                result = -1;
                return (&result);
        }
```

FIGURE 5.8 Continued

```
	/*
	 * Verify that the user has read/write access to the database before
	 * calling dbminit().
	 */
	uid = get_uid(rqstp->rq_clntcred);
	if (stat_buf.st_uid == uid && (stat_buf.st_mode & S_IFREG) ==
	   S_IFREG && (stat_buf.st_mode & (S_IREAD | S_IWRITE)) ==
	   (S_IREAD | S_IWRITE)) {
		result = dbminit(*argp);
	} else {
		result = -1;
	}
	return (&result);
} /* dbminit_1 */

int *
dbmclose_1(argp, rqstp)
	void			*argp;
	struct svc_req	*rqstp;
{
	static int		result;
	int			tmp_uid;

	tmp_uid = get_uid(rqstp->rq_clntcred);
	if (tmp_uid == uid) {
		result = dbmclose();
		uid = UID_NOT_SET;
	} else {
		result = -1;
	}
	return (&result);
} /* dbmclose_1 */

datum *
fetch_1(argp, rqstp)
	datum			*argp;
	struct svc_req	*rqstp;
{
	static datum		result;
	int			tmp_uid;
```

FIGURE 5.8 Continued

```
        tmp_uid = get_uid(rqstp->rq_clntcred);
        if (tmp_uid == uid) {
                result = fetch(*argp);
        } else {
                result.dptr = NULL;
        }
        return (&result);
} /* fetch_1 */

int *
store_1(argp, rqstp)
        store_args          *argp;
        struct svc_req      *rqstp;
{
        static int          result;
        int                 tmp_uid;

        tmp_uid = get_uid(rqstp->rq_clntcred);
        if (tmp_uid == uid) {
                result = store(argp->key, argp->content);
        } else {
                result = -1;
        }
        return (&result);
} /* store_1 */

int *
delete1(argp, rqstp)
        datum               *argp;
        struct svc_req      *rqstp;
{
        static int          result;
        int                 tmp_uid;

        tmp_uid = get_uid(rqstp->rq_clntcred);
        if (tmp_uid == uid) {
                result = delete(*argp);
        } else {
                result = -1;
        }
        return (&result);
} /* delete_1 */
```

FIGURE 5.8 Continued

```
datum*
firstkey_1(argp, rqstp)
        void              *argp;
        struct svc_req    *rqstp;
{
        static datum      result;
        int               tmp_uid;

        tmp_uid = get_uid(rqstp->rq_clntcred);
        if (tmp_uid == uid) {
                result = firstkey();
        } else {
                result.dptr = NULL;
        }
        return (&result);
} /* firstkey_1 */

datum *
nextkey_1(argp, rqstp)
        datum             *argp;
        struct svc_req    *rqstp;
{
        static datum      result;
        int               tmp_uid;
        tmp_uid = get_uid(rqstp->rq_clntcred);
        if (tmp_uid == uid) {
                result = nextkey(*argp);
        } else {
                result.dptr = NULL;
        }
        return (&result);
} /* nextkey_1 */
```

Remote DBM Client Interface Routines

```
#include <rpc/rpc.h>
#include <dbm.h>
#include "dbm_remote.h"
```

FIGURE 5.8 Continued

```
/*
 * This module provides the interface from the client side, effectively
 * hiding the presence of the RPC layer. Ideally, the caller would never
 * know the difference between calling this routine and the same routine
 * in the C Library.
 */
int
dbminit(file)
        filename file;
{
        int      *result;

        result = dbminit_1(&file);
        return (*result);
} /* dbminit */

int
dbmclose()
{
        (void)dbmclose_1(NULL);
} /* dmbclose */

datum
fetch(key)
        datum   key;
{
        datum   *result;

        result = fetch_1(&key);
        return (*result);
} /* fetch */

int
store(key, content)
        datum   key;
        datum   content;
{
        store_args      tmp;
        int             *result;
```

FIGURE 5.8 Continued

```
        tmp.key = key;
        tmp.content = content;
        result = store_1(&tmp);
        return (*result);
} /* store */

int
delete(key)
        datum   key;
{
        int     *result;

        result = delete_1(key);
        return (*result);
} /* delete */

datum
firstkey()
{
        datum   *result;

        result = firstkey_1(NULL);
        return (*result);
} /* firstkey */

datum
nextkey(key)
        datum   key;
{
        datum   *result;

        result = nextkey_1(key);
        return (*result);
} /* nextkey */
```

FIGURE 5.8 Continued

Remote DBM Client RPC Routines

```
#include ⟨rpc/rpc.h⟩
#include ⟨sys/uio.h⟩
#include ⟨sys/socket.h⟩
#include ⟨sys/time.h⟩
#include ⟨dbm.h⟩
#include ⟨netdb.h⟩
#include ⟨memory.h⟩
#include "dbm_remote.h"
/*
 * Default timeout can be changed using clnt_conrol()
 */
static struct timeval      timeout = { 25, 0 };
static CLIENT              *clnt_handlep;

/*
 * Try to connect to the DBM service on the specified computer.
 * Return TRUE if we succeeded, FALSE otherwise
 */
bool_t
dmb_connect(hostname)
        char    *hostname;
{
        struct hostent    *hostent_p;
        struct sockaddr_in server_addr;
        int               socket, status;
        char              server_netname[MAXNETNAMELEN + 1];

        /*
         * Get the hosts IP address(es)
         */
        status = FALSE;
        if ((hostent_p = gethostbyname(hostname)) != NULL) {

                /*
                 * Initialize the socket address structure. Using the same
                 * address type that was returned by gethostbyname(). Set
                 * the port number to 0 so that clnttcp_create() will ask
                 * the portmapper for the port number of the service.
                 */
                server_addr.sin_family = hostent_p->h_addrtype;
                server_addr.sin_port = 0;
```

FIGURE 5.8 Continued

```
                /*
                 * Check to see if we can create a client handle for all the
                 * addresses returned by gethostbyname(). Stop trying after
                 * we get a client handle or after we tried all the addresses.
                 */
                socket = RPC_ANYSOCK;
                while (*hostent_p->h_addr_list != NULL) {
                        (void) memcpy((char *)(&server_addr.sin_addr),
                                *hostent_p->h_addr_list,
                                hostent_->h_length);
                        if ((clnt_handlep = clnttcp_create(&server_addr,
                           DBM_PROG, DBM_VERS_1, &socket, 0, 0)) != NULL)
                                break;          /* we got a handle */
                        hostent_p->h_addr_list++;
                }
                if (clnt_handlep != NULL) {
                        if (host2netname(server_netname, hostname, NULL) !=
                           FALSE) {
                                clnt_handlep->cl_auth = authdes_create(
                                   server_netname, 300, NULL, NULL);
                                   if (clnt_handlep->cl_auth != NULL) {
                                        status = TRUE;
                                   }
                        }

                        if (status == FALSE) {
                                clnt_destroy(clnt_handlep);
                                clnt_handlep = NULL;
                        }
                }
        }
        return (status);
} /* dbm_connect */

/*
 * Disconnect from the current server. Calls dbmclose_1() routine to ensure
 * that state kept by the server is properly reset.
 */
void
dbm_disconnect()
```

FIGURE 5.8 Continued

```
{
        (void)dbmclose_1(NULL);
        auth_destroy(clnt_handlep->cl_auth);
        clnt_destroy(clnt_handlep);
        clnt_handlep = NULL;
} /* dbm_disconnect */

int *
dbminit_1(argp)
        filename *argp;
{
        static int result;

        if (clnt_call(clnt_handlep, DBMINIT, xdr_filename, argp, xdr_int, &result,
           timeout) != RPC_success) {
                result = -1;
        }
        return (&result);
} /* dbminit_1 */

int *
dbmclose_1(argp)
        void     *argp;
{
        static int result;

        if (clnt_call(clnt_handlep, DBMCLOSE, xdr_void, argp, xdr_int, &result,
           timeout) != RPC_SUCCESS) {
                result = -1;
        }
        return (&result);
} /* dbmclose_1 */
datum *
fetch_1(argp)
        datum   *argp;
{
        static datum        result;
        static char         buffer [MAX_DATUM_SIZE];
```

FIGURE 5.8 Continued

```
        result.dptr = buffer;
        if (clnt_call(clnt_handlep, FETCH, xdr_datum, argp, xdr_datum, &result,
           timeout) != RPC_SUCCESS) {
                result.dptr = NULL;
        }
        return (&result);
} /* fetch_1 */

int *
store_1(argp)
        store_args        *argp;
{
        static int        result;

        if (clnt_call(clnt_handlep, STORE, xdr_store_args, argp, xdr_int, &result,
           timeout) != RPC_SUCCESS) {
                result = -1;
        }
        return (&result);
} /* store_1 */

int *
delete_1(argp)
        datum   *argp;
{
        static int result;

        if (clnt_call(clnt_handlep, DELETE, xdr_datum, argp, xdr_int, &result,
        timeout) != RPC_SUCCESS) {
                result = -1;
        }
        return (&result);
} /* delete_1 */

datum *
firstkey_1(argp)
        void    *argp;
{
        static datum      result;
        static char       buffer[MAX_DATUM_SIZE];
```

FIGURE 5.8 Continued

```
        result.dptr = buffer;
        if (clnt_call(clnt_handlep, FIRSTKEY, xdr_void, argp, xdr_datum, &result,
            timeout) != RPC_SUCCESS) {
                result.dptr = NULL;
        }
        return (&result);
} /* firstkey_1 */

datum *
nextkey_1(argp)
        datum   *argp;
{
        static datum        result;
        static char         buffer[MAX_DATUM_SIZE];

        result.dptr = buffer;
        if (clnt_call(clnt_handlep, NEXTKEY, xdr_datum, argp, xdr_datum, &result,
            timeout) != RPC_SUCCESS) {
                result.dptr = NULL;
        }
        return (&result);
} /* nextkey_1 */
```

Remote DBM XDR Routines

```
#include <dbm.h>
#include <rpc/rpc.h>
#include "dbm_remote.h"

bool_t
xdr_filename(xdrs, objp)
        XDR     *xdrs;
        filename*objp;
{
        return (xdr_string(xdrs, objp, MAX_FILENAME_LEN));
} /* xdr_filename */
```

FIGURE 5.8 Continued

```
bool_t
xdr_datum(xdrs, objp)
        XDR     *xdrs;
        datum   *objp;
{
        return (xdr_array(xdrs, (char **)&objp-)dptr, (u_int *)&objp-)dsize,
                MAX_DATUM_SIZE, sizeof(char), xdr_char));
) /* xdr_datum */

bool_t
xdr_store_args(xdrs, objp)
        XDR     *xdrs;
        store_args *objp;
{
        if (xdr_datum(xdrs, &objp-)key) == FALSE) {
                return (FALSE);
        }
        if (xdr_datum(xdrs, &objp-)content) == FALSE) {
                return (FALSE);
        }
        return (TRUE);
} /* xdr_store_args */
```

FIGURE 5.8 Continued

a *.pag* extension. The example only checks the *.dir* file and assumes that the *.pag* file has the same file modes. This service should be run with an effective user ID of 0 on a UNIX system. That way different users are guaranteed access to the database files. The service does not assume the user ID of the caller. The procedures only allow one user to access a database at a time by saving the user ID of the client that currently has a database open. The saved user ID and the open database file are considered to be state maintained by the server. Therefore, the DBM network service is a stateful service. The current user should call *dbmclose_1()* to inform the service that it is through accessing the database and that the server can discard any saved state. The service is now ready to accept requests from another client.

The DBM client interface routines simply provide the same programming interface as the DBM routines in the C Library. They map the calls to the corresponding client RPC layer. The fact that these routines use RPC is almost totally transparent to the user of the routine. RPC errors are not reported nor are they propagated back to the user. The client routines allow easy testing of the service by letting you link the DBM client interface layer with the server procedure layer directly, thus bypassing the RPC interface code. Testing techniques are discussed in more detail in Chapter 8.

The DBM client RPC layer actually invokes the RPC on the server. The routines *dbm_connect()* and *dbm_disconnect()* have been provided to allow the user to connect and disconnect to a server. Note the processing of the *hostent_p->h_addr_list* in the *dbm_connect()* routine. The routine *gethostbyname()* may return more than one IP address for the given host name. In this routine, every IP address on the list is tried until one succeeds.

5.8 Exercises

1. Modify the example in Section 5.7 to support access by more than one user concurrently. What state issues are involved?
2. The example in Section 5.7 does not recover from a server crash. If the service were stopped and restarted after the call to *dbm_connect()*, what error would the client see on the next RPC to the service? How can you modify the DBM client RPC layer to detect server crashes and recover from them?
3. The data stored in the example in Section 5.7 is not portable. How can you modify the example to ensure that the data is portable? Note that DBM databases are inherently non-portable due to the hashing algorithm used; you cannot take a DBM file created on a Sun386i and use it on a Sun-4. If you assume that the DBM file will always be resident on the same computer on which it was created, then you can ensure that the data contained in the database can be accessed by any client independent of the client's computer architecture.

4. Modify the example in Section 5.7 to support a new version of the DBM routines. These routines are the NDBM routines provided in the C Library. What do you have to do to support the DBM data type remotely?
5. What modifications would you make to the grade service in Figure 5.1? Will this service operate properly for all possible input values?

Additional RPC Library Features

6

The RPC Library provides users with several features in addition to those covered in Chapters 4 and 5. These features include asynchronous RPC, broadcast RPC, batch RPC, multiversion support for services, implementation of your own *svc_run()* routine, and routines to communicate with the portmapper. This chapter covers these features and provides examples demonstrating their use.

6.1 Asynchronous RPC

The RPC requests presented so far have a reply returned immediately by the server: The client sends an RPC request and then waits for the server's reply (or times out waiting for it). This characteristic is not always desirable. There are times when behavior closer to one-way message handling, or asynchronous RPC, is preferable.

Three facilities within the RPC Library handle asynchronous RPC: nonblocking RPC, callback RPC, and asynchronous broadcast RPC. Nonblocking RPC provides a one-way message facility from client to server but offers no path for replies from server to client. Callback RPC can be used with either normal request-reply RPC requests, or with nonblocking requests, to provide fully asynchronous two-way message handling between the client and one or more servers. Asynchronous broadcast RPC allows you to broadcast a RPC request but has no path for replies from the server to client. The next section describes broadcast RPC in detail.

6.1.1 Nonblocking RPC

Nonblocking RPC can be used in situations in which a simple one-way message-passing scheme is needed. If a reply is required, the client must either poll the server for the reply or make some other arrangements, such as callback RPC, to get the result.

You accomplish nonblocking RPC by setting the RPC time-out value to zero—either by setting the values in the *timeout* argument of *clnt_call()* to zero or by using *clnt_control()* to set the default time-out value to zero before making any RPC requests using the specified client handle. Here is an example:

```
...
struct timeval timeout;

...
timeout.tv_sec = 0;
timeout.tv_usec = 0;

if (clnt_control(clnt_handlep, CLSET_TIMEOUT, timeout) == FALSE) {
        /* Report an error */
}
...
```

Because the client doing a nonblocking RPC request does not wait for any reply from the server, it follows that the data type of the reply should be *void*, and the server should be written such that no reply is generated for the request. When you write server procedures to be used in conjunction with *rpcgen*, you can suppress the sending of a reply by returning a null value for the results pointer. This issue is discussed further in Chapter 7. A client call using the nonblocking RPC mechanism always returns the RPC_TIMEDOUT error, which can be ignored.

Another consequence that nonblocking RPC has on the semantics of the request is that the RPC Library no longer takes responsibility for retrying a request for which a reply has not been received. This means that if the RPC is sent over an unreliable datagram transport such as UDP, the message could be lost without the client's knowing it. Applications using nonblocking RPC must be prepared to handle this situation. Messages sent using a reliable connection-oriented transport such as TCP are delivered reliably; therefore, you do not have to worry about retransmitting the request.

Nonblocking RPCs over an unreliable transport can be useful for an update service. For example, you might want to send out time synchronization messages every X seconds, but you do not want to worry about RPC retransmissions, transport connections, and service acknowledgements. You can make nonblocking RPCs to the computers you wanted to update. The service can keep track of the last time it received an update to prevent it from missing too many updates. It can call the update host to explicitly get a reliable update after some maximum amount of time that it can be without updated information.

6.1.2 Callback RPC

Callback RPC is the most powerful of the asynchronous methods. It allows fully asynchronous RPC communication between clients and servers by enabling any application to be both a client and a server. Hence, it facilitates a peer-to-peer paradigm among the participating systems. It is also possible for a single client to initiate requests to different servers and then handle callbacks from each of them asynchronously. This arrangement is very useful in distributed applications. An example is remote debugging, in which the client is a window-system program and the server is a debugger running on the remote computer. Most of the time, the user enters commands at the debugging window which converts the users command into a debugger command, and then makes a RPC to the server (where the debugger is actually running), telling it to execute that command. When the debugger hits a breakpoint, however, the roles are reversed, and the debugger needs to make a RPC to the window program, so that it can inform the user that a breakpoint has been reached.

In order to initiate a RPC callback, the server needs a program number to call the client back on. Typically, a program number is dynamically selected from the transient RPC program number range, 0x40000000 to 0x5FFFFFFF. The client registers the callback service, using a transient program number, with the local *portmap* program (via *pmap_set()*) and registers the dispatch routine (via *svc_register()*). The program number is then sent as part of the RPC request to the server. The server initiates a normal RPC request to the client, using the given program number, when it is ready to do the callback RPC. The client must be waiting for the callback either explicitly via a call to *svc_run()* or via a call to a custom routine that processes incoming RPC requests.

Instead of having the client just send the server the program number, it could also send the server the port number that the callback service was registered on. You can obtain the port number using the routine *pmap_getport()* covered in Section 6.5. The port number could then be used by the server when it calls the client handle creation routine and would save a RPC to the client's portmapper to get the port number.

If the server had to constantly call back to the client, you might want to write the service to include both a server and a client process on both computers. The server and client on the same computer would communicate via an interprocess communication mechanism, which could be the RPC mechanism.

The following code segment provides an example of a routine that dynamically allocates a program number from the transient range and then registers the dispatch routine associated with the callback service.

```
#include <stdio.h>
#include <rpc/rpc.h>
#include <sys/socket.h>

u_long
svc_register_transient(transp, version, dispatch, protocol)
        SVCXPRT         *transp;
        u_long          version;
        void            (*dispatch)();
        u_long          protocol;
{
        static u_long prognum = 0x40000000;        /* The beginning of the tran-
                                                      sient range */

        /*
         *Get callback routine program number
         */
        while (pmap_set(prognum, version, protocol, transp->xp_port) == 0 &&
                prognum < 0x50000000) {
                prognum++;
        }
        if (prognum < 0x50000000) {
                /*
                 * protocol is 0 - pmap_set did registration with the portmapper
                 */
                if (svc_register(transp, prognum, version, dispatch, 0) == FALSE) {
                        svc_unregister(prognum, version);
                        return (0);
                }
```

```
    } else {
        prognum = 0x40000000;
        return (0);
    }
    /*
     * Post-increment the program number so the next call to this routine will start
     * searching after the program number just returned.
     */
    return (prognum++);
} /* svc_register_transient */
```

The *svc_register_transient()* routine takes as arguments a pointer to a transport handle, the version number of the service, the address of the service dispatch routine, and the protocol to be used. The routine loops, calling *pmap_set()* to register the service; if the call fails, the program number is in use. The routine then increments the program number and tries the call again. Once the call succeeds, *svc_register()* is called to register the dispatch routine. Note that a value of 0 is used for the protocol argument. This value informs the *svc_register()* routine that the program has already been registered with the portmapper. The *prognum* variable has been declared *static* to allow future calls to this routine to start the search for a program number where the last call stopped. Note that the search for program numbers stops at the end of the transient range instead of automatically wrapping back to the beginning of the transient range and continuing the search. You can add this capability to the routine if you so desire.

If the client calls *svc_run()* to wait for callback RPC requests from a service, it will not be able to do any other processing. If you need your client to continue doing work while waiting for callback RPC requests from a service, then you can spawn another process that calls *svc_run()* to wait for requests. The other alternative is to write your own *svc_run()* routine, which is discussed later in this chapter. Figure 6.1 contains the listing of an example service that uses callback RPC.

Header File - callback.h

```
#define EXAMPLE_PROG                 ((u_long)(0x20000020))
#define EXAMPLE_VERS                 ((u_long)(1))
#define EXAMPLE_PROC                 ((u_long)(1))
#define EXAMPLE_CALLBACK_VERS ((u_long)(1))
#define EXAMPLE_CALLBACK_PROC ((u_long)(1))

#define MAX_HOST_NAME_LEN      64      /* Includes terminating NUL      */

typedef struct {
        u_long prognum;
        u_long versnum;
        u_long procnum;
        char    hostname[MAX_HOST_NAME_LEN];
} call_info;

extern   bool_t   xdr_call_info();
```

Server Routines

```
#include <stdio.h>
#include <rpc/rpc.h>
#include "callback.h"

struct timeval timeout = { 25, 0};

main()
{
       SVCXPRT          *transp;
       void                dispatch();

       transp = svcudp_create(RPC_ANYSOCK);
       if (transp == NULL) {
```

FIGURE 6.1

```
            fprintf(stderr, "Error: svcudp_create() call failed\n");
            return (1);
      }

      (void) pmap_unset(EXAMPLE_PROG, EXAMPLE_VERS);
      if (svc_register(transp, EXAMPLE_PROG, EXAMPLE_VERS, dispatch,
         IPPROTO_UDP) == FALSE) {
            fprintf(stderr, "Error: Unable to register service\n");
            svc_destroy(transp);
            return(1);
      }

      printf("Server going into svc_run\n");
      svc_run();
      fprintf(stderr, "Error: svc_run() shouldn't return\n");
      svc_unregister(EXAMPLE_PROG, EXAMPLE_VERS);
      svc_destroy(transp);
      return (1);
} /* main */

void
dispatch(rqstp, transp)
      struct svc_req      *rqstp;
      SVCXPRT             *transp;

{
      call_info           callback_info;
      void                docallback();

      switch (rqstp->rq_proc) {
      case NULLPROC:
            if (svc_sendreply(transp, xdr_void, 0) == FALSE) {
                  fprintf(stderr, "Error: svc_sendreply() for NULLPROC failed\n");
            }
            break;

      case EXAMPLE_PROC:
            if (svc_getargs(transp, xdr_call_info, &callback_info) == FALSE) {
                  svcerr_decode(transp);
                  return;
            }
            if (svc_sendreply(transp, xdr_void, 0) == FALSE) {
```

FIGURE 6.1 Continued

```
                fprintf(stderr, "Error: svc_sendreply() for EXAMPLE_PROC
                        failed\n");
                return;
            }

            /*
             * Simulate a computation intensive task
             */
            printf("Performing computation intensive task\n");
            sleep (5);
            printf("Calling the client back with the results\n");
            docallback (&callback_info);
            break;
    }

}/* dispatch */

void
docallback(call_infop)
    call_info           *call_infop;
{
    CLIENT              *clnt_handlep;
    enum clnt_stat      status;

    clnt_handlep = clnt_create(call_infop->hostname, call_infop->prognum,
                               call_infop->versnum, "udp");
    if (clnt_handlep == NULL) {
        clnt_pcreateerror(call_infop->hostname);
        return;
    }

    status = clnt_call(clnt_handlep, call_infop->procnum, xdr_void,
                       NULL xdr_void, NULL, timeout);
    if (status != RPC_SUCCESS) {
        clnt_perror(clnt_handlep, call_infop->hostname);
    }

    clnt_destroy(clnt_handlep);
} /* docallback */
```

FIGURE 6.1 Continued

Client Routines

```
#include <stdio.h>
#include <rpc/rpc/rpc.h>
#include <sys/socket.h>
#include "callback.h"

main(argc, argv)
      int  argc;
      char **argv;
{
            SVCXPRT          *transp;
            call_info        callback_info;
            int              status;
            u_long           svc_register_transient();
            void             callback();

      if (argc != 2) {
            fprintf(stderr, "usage: %s hostname\n", argv[0]);
            return (1);
      }
      strncpy(callback_info.hostname, argv[1], MAX_HOST_NAME_LEN);

      if ((transp = svcudp_create(RPC_ANYSOCK)) == NULL) {
            fprintf(stderr, "Error: svcudp_create() call failed\n");
            return (1);
      }

      callback_info.prognum = svc_register_transient(transp,
                  EXAMPLE_CALLBACK_VERS, callback, IPPROTO_UDP);
      if (callback_info.prognum == 0) {
            fprintf(stderr, "Error: Couldn't register transient service\n");
            svc_destroy(transp);
            return (1);
```

FIGURE 6.1 Continued

```
    }

    printf("Using transient program number: %lu\n", callback_info.prognum);
    callback_info.versnum = EXAMPLE_CALLBACK_VERS;
    callback_info.procnum = EXAMPLE_CALLBACK_PROC;

    status = callrpc(callback_info.hostname, EXAMPLE_PROG,
            EXAMPLE_VERS, EXAMPLE_PROC, xdr_call_info, &callback_info,
            xdr_void, (xdrproc_t)0);
    if (status != 0) {
            fprintf(stderr, "Error callrpc(): %s\n",
            clnt_sperrno((enum clnt_stat)status));
            svc_unregister(callback_info.prognum, EXAMPLE_CALLBACK_VERS);
            svc_destroy(transp);
            return (1);
    }
    svc_run();
    fprintf(stderr, "Error: svc_run() shouldn't return\n");
    svc_unregister(callback_info.prognum, EXAMPLE_CALLBACK_VERS);
    svc_destroy(transp);
    return (1);
} /* main */
void
callback(rqstp, transp)
    struct svc_req      *rqstp;
    SVCXPRT             *transp;
{
    switch (rqstp->rq_proc) {
    case NULLPROC:
            if (svc_sendreply(transp, xdr_void, 0) == FALSE) {
                    fprintf(stderr, "Error: svc_sendreply() for NULLPROC failed\n");
            }
            break;
```

FIGURE 6.1 Continued

```
        case EXAMPLE_CALLBACK_PROC:
            if (svc_getargs(transp, xdr_void, 0) == TRUE) {
                printf("Client got callback from server\n");
                if (svc_sendreply(transp, xdr_void, 0) == FALSE) {
                    fprintf(stderr, "Error: exampleprog");
                }
            } else {
                svcerr_decode(transp);
                return;
            }
            svc_unregister(rqstp->rq_prog, rqstp->rq_vers);
            svc_destroy(transp);
            exit (0);
            break;
    }
} /* callback */
```

XDR Routine

```
#include <rpc/rpc.h>
#include "callback.h"

bool_t
xdr_call_info(xdrs, objp)
    XDR       *xdrs;
    call_info *objp;
{
    char            *tmp;

    tmp = objp->hostname;
    if (xdr_u_long(xdrs, &objp>prognum) == FALSE) {
        return (FALSE);
    }
```

FIGURE 6.1 Continued

```
    if (xdr_u_long(xdrs, &objp->versnum) == FALSE) {
        return (FALSE);
    }
    if (xdr_u_long(xdrs, &objp->procnum) == FALSE) {
        return (FALSE);
    }
    return (xdr_string(xdrs, &tmp, MAX_HOST_NAME_LEN));
} /* xdr_call_info */
```

FIGURE 6.1 Continued

The server *main()* routine simply gets a transport handle, registers the service and dispatch routine, and calls *svc_run()* to wait for RPC requests. The dispatch routine processes the EXAMPLE_PROC procedure call by getting the arguments and then automatically sending a reply back to the client. The arguments to this routine include the host name, program number, version number, and procedure number that identify the computer and remote program that the server should call back when the task is done. A computation intensive task is simulated by sleeping for 5 seconds. Finally, it calls the *docallback()* routine to notify the client that the task is complete.

The client gets a transport handle and registers a transient service by calling the *svc_register_transient()* routine. It then makes a RPC to the server. When this is done, it calls *svc_run()* to wait for the callback from the server. Typically you would perform processing while waiting for the callback. This can be done by creating a new process to wait for the callback from the server or you could write your own *svc_run()* routine. Note that the client side uses both high-level and low-level RPC Library routines.

6.2 Broadcast RPC

In Broadcast RPC, the client sends a broadcast packet for a remote procedure to the network and waits for numerous replies. Broadcast RPC uses unreliable, packet-based protocols. The amount of data broadcast is usually restricted by the type of network used. For example, the maximum transfer unit (MTU) of Ethernet is

1500 bytes. The current implementation uses the UDP transport and limits the size of the remote procedure call to 1400 bytes. The 1400 bytes include the size of the XDR-encoded RPC header and arguments. You cannot specify the authentication flavor for a broadcasted procedure call—the flavor defaults to AUTH_UNIX. The reply from the service can be the maximum size allowed by the UDP transport (8800 bytes). Broadcast RPC treats all unsuccessful responses as garbage by filtering them out, so if a version mismatch between the broadcaster and a remote service occurs, the user of broadcast RPC never knows. Remote procedures that support broadcast RPC typically respond only when the request is successfully processed and are silent if they detect an error. Because all broadcast RPC messages are sent to the portmapper, only services that register themselves with their portmapper are accessible via the broadcast RPC mechanism. (The reasons for broadcasting to the portmapper are discussed in Chapter 3.)

The number of computers that receive the broadcast depends on the configuration of your network. For example, your broadcast only goes out to your local network if you are using Ethernet and your routers to other networks do not forward broadcast packets.

The routine *clnt_broadcast()* is used to do broadcast RPC. Its synopsis follows:

```
enum clnt_stat
    _clnt_broadcast(prognum, versnum, procnum, inproc, in, outproc,
      out, eachresult)
u_long              prognum, versnum, procnum;
xdrproc_t           inproc;
char                *in;
xdrproc_t           outproc;
char                *out;
resultproc_t        eachresult;
```

This routine is like *callrpc()*, except the RPC is broadcast to the network instead of being sent to a specified host name. Currently, the RPC uses AUTH_UNIX credentials. Each time it receives a response from a remote procedure, this routine calls *eachresult()*. The synopsis for *eachresult()* follows:

```
eachresult(out, addr)
char                     *out;
struct sockaddr_in       *addr;
```

The argument *out* is the same as the out passed to *clnt_broadcast()*, except that the remote procedure's result is now XDR-decoded. The argument *addr* points to the socket address of the computer that sent the results. This is useful in case you want to contact the computer directly sometime in the future. If *eachresult()* returns zero, *clnt_broadcast()* waits for more replies; otherwise it returns with the RPC_SUCCESS status.

A value of zero can be passed in for the address of the *eachresult()* function. This occurrence results in the remote procedure call being broadcast, but the *clnt_broadcast()* routine does not wait for any replies and returns immediately. The remote procedure on the server side should not return any replies. This mechanism allows you to do asynchronous RPC broadcasts.

The time that it takes for *clnt_broadcast()* to return varies from computer to computer. If eachresult() always returns 0, *clnt_broadcast()* eventually times out and returns RPC_TIMEDOUT. For SunOS RPC Library implementation, the *clnt_broadcast()* routine transmits the broadcast and waits 4 seconds before retransmitting the request. It then waits 6 seconds before retransmitting the request and continues to increment the amount of time to wait by 2 until the timeout is greater than 14 seconds (wait intervals of 4, 6, 8, 10, 12, and 14 seconds for a total of 54 seconds). This scheme results in the request being broadcasted 6 times. The routine retransmits the broadcasts by default because an unreliable transport is being used. Increasing the amount of time between retransmissions is referred to as a back off algorithm. This type of algorithm applied to retransmission time-outs is a good idea because it reduces the load on the physical network and computers involved.

You can cause the routine to return sooner by having your *eachresult()* routine return a nonzero value. It is important to note that when *eachresult()* is executing, processing of incoming broadcast replies by the *clnt_broadcast()* routine is suspended. Typically, the *eachresult()* routine performs a minimum amount of processing to allow all replies to the broadcast to be processed. Otherwise, because of transport buffer size limitations, some of the responses may be dropped.

Broadcasting can locate a computer that has a remote service that you want to use. The following example shows how to use *clnt_broadcast()* to locate a grade server.

```
#include <sys/socket.h>
#include <netdb.h>
#include <strings.h>

static char grade_host[HOSTNAME_SIZE];

char *
findserver()
{
	enum clnt_stat	stat;
	int		proc_reply();

	grade_host[0] = ' ';
	stat = clnt_broadcast(GRADE_PROG, GRADE_VERS, NULLPROC,
			xdr_void, NULL, xdr_void, NULL, proc_reply);
	if (stat != RPC_SUCCESS) {
		fprintf(stderr, broadcast: %s\n, clnt_sperrno(stat));
		return (NULL);
	} else {
		return (grade_host);
	}
} /* findserver */
proc_reply(out, addr)
	void		*out;
	struct sockaddr_in *addr;
{
	struct hostent *hostentp;

	hostentp = gethostbyaddr(&addr->sin_addr.s_addr,
		sizeof(addr->sin_addr.s_addr), AF_INET);
	if (hostentp != NULL) {
		(void) strncpy(grade_host, hostentp->h_name, HOSTNAME_SIZE);
		return (1);
	} else {
		return (0);
	}
}/* proc_reply */
```

Some potential pitfalls are associated with using RPC broadcasts. You do not know who received the broadcasts; that depends on the physical layout of the network as discussed above. For example, suppose a network has two separate Ethernet networks, A and B, connected by a router that does not forward broadcast packets. Figure 6.2 shows the networks. If an application on network A uses broadcast RPC to locate RPC services, it will fail to get replies from any services on network B. Also, every time you

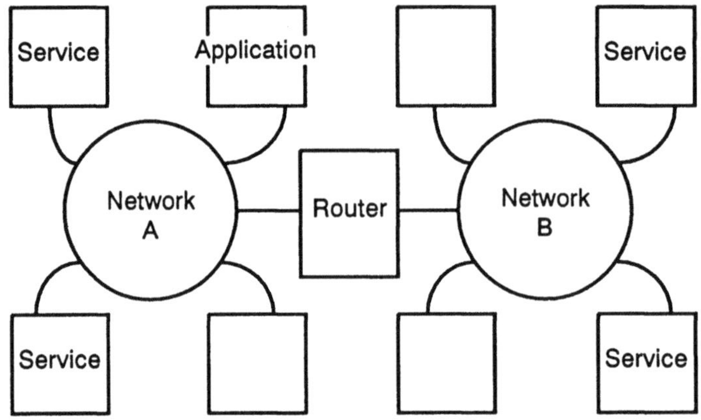

FIGURE 6.2 *Example network.*

send out a broadcast RPC request on your network, it activates the portmapper process on every computer on the network to process the broadcast request—even if the computer does not have the remote program registered on it. Although the broadcast RPC mechanism can be useful for locating services, it should not be abused.

6.3 Batching

The process of sending an RPC request to a server and waiting for a response requires some overhead. If a client has many requests to send but does not need a reply until the server has received all requests, then it is possible to reduce the overhead and speed up the overall throughput of the requests. Batch-mode RPC can be used to queue separate RPC requests on the client and then send them over the network in one batch to the server. This paradigm is suitable for streams of requests that are related but make more sense to structure as separate requests rather than one large one.

The RPC requests to be queued must not, themselves, expect any replies. Send them by setting the time-out value to zero, as with nonblocking RPC. In addition, the argument specifying the XDR function address to handle the reply must be NULL instead of the address of *xdr_void()*. When a nonqueuing RPC request is sent to the server, the entire queue of requests is flushed to the server. A nonqueuing RPC request has a nonzero time-out value and specifies a non-NULL address for the XDR function that handles the reply. From a programming standpoint, the semantics of this last request should be such that the server can distinguish it from the queued requests and send a reply to the client.

Since the sending of queued messages needs to be reliable, the batch-mode RPC mechanism exists only on reliable transports such as TCP. Note that when you use the TCP transport, buffers are used to buffer data sent and received. You can specify the size of these buffers in the *clnttcp_create()* and *svctcp_create()* routines. On the client side, the data in the buffer is flushed to the server to be processed if the amount of batched data exceeds the buffer size. This happens independent of a nonqueuing RPC request and is not noticeable by the client.

The example in Figure 6.3 demonstrates the use of the batching mechanism. This example is a simple interpreter service that provides the ability to add, subtract, multiply, and divide values that have been pushed onto the interpreter's stack. The server provides a PUSH procedure to push an integer onto the stack, an OPERATOR procedure to perform the specified operation using the top two values on the stack, and a POP procedure to return the top value off of the stack. The PUSH and OPERATOR procedures have been set up as batched procedures.

Header File

```
enum operator {
      ADD = 0,
      SUB = 1,
      MUL = 2,
      DIV = 3,
};
typedef enum operator operator;

#define INTERPRETER_PROG        ((u_long)0x20000030)
#define INTERPRETER_VERS_1 ((u_long)1)
#define PUSH                    ((u_long)1)
#define OPERATOR                ((u_long)2)
#define POP                     ((u_long)3)

bool_t xdr_operator();
```

FIGURE 6.3

Server Main and Dispatch Routines

```
#include <stdio.h>
#include <rpc/rpc.h>
#include "interp.h"

void     interpreter_prog_1();
void     *push_1();
void     *operator_1();
int      *pop_1();

main()
{
        register SVCXPRT*transp;

        transp = svctcp_create(RPC_ANYSOCK, 0, 0);
        if (transp == NULL) {
              fprintf(stderr, "Error: svctcp_create() call failed\n");
              return (1);
        }

        (void) pmap_unset(INTERPRETER_PROG, INTERPRETER_VERS_1);
        if (svc_register(transp, INTERPRETER_PROG, INTERPRETER_VERS_1,
           interpreter_prog_1, IPPROTO_TCP) == FALSE) {
              fprintf(stderr, "Error: cannot register INTERPRETER_PROG,
              INTERPRETER_VERS_1, tcp\n");
              svc_destroy(transp);
              return (1);
        }

        svc_run();
        fprintf(stderr, "Error: svc_run() shouldn't return\n");
        svc_unregister(INTERPRETER_PROG, INTERPRETER_VERS_1);
        svc_destroy(transp);
        return (1);
} /* main */

static void
interpreter_prog_1(rqstp, transp)
        struct svc_req *rqstp;
        SVCXPRT     *transp;
{
```

FIGURE 6.3 Continued

```
union {
        int            push_1_arg;
        operator       operator_1_arg;
} argument;
char                  *result;
xdrproc_t             xdr_argument, xdr_result;
char                  *(*local)();

switch (rqstp->rq_proc) {
case NULLPROC:
        (void) svc_sendreply(transp, xdr_void, (char*)NULL);
        return
case PUSH:
        xdr_argument = xdr_int;
        xdr_result = xdr_void;
        local = (char*(*)()) push_1;
        break;

case OPERATOR:
        xdr_argument = xdr_operator;
        xdr_result = xdr_void;
        local = (char*(*)()) operator_1;
        break;

case POP:
        xdr_argument = xdr_void;
        xdr_result = xdr_int;
        local = (char *(*)()) pop_1;
        break;

default:
        svcerr_noproc(transp);
        return;
}

if (svc_getargs(transp, xdr_argument, &argument) = = FALSE) {
        svcerr_decode(transp);
        return;
}

result = (*local)(&argument, rqstp);
```

FIGURE 6.3 Continued

```
        if (result != NULL && svc_sendreply(transp, xdr_result, result) == FALSE)
        {
                svcerr_systemerr(transp);
        }
} /* interpreter_prog_1 */
```

Server Procedures

```
#include <stdio.h>
#include <rpc/rpc.h>
#include "interp.h"
#define MAX_STACK_LEN      (8* 1024)

int     stack[MAX_STACK_LEN];
int     cur_index = 0;

void *
push_1(argp)
        int       *argp;
{
        if (cur_index <MAX_STACK_LEN) {
                stack[cur_index++] = *argp;
        } else {
                fprintf(stderr, "Error: PUSH stack overflow\n");
        }
        return(NULL);
} /* push_1 */

void *
operator_1(argp)
        operator *argp;
{
        int      a, b, c;

        if (cur_index > 1) {
                a = stack[cur_index - 2];
                b = stack[cur_index - 1];
                switch(*argp) {
                case ADD:
                        c = a + b;
                        break;
```

FIGURE 6.3 Continued

```
        case SUB:
                c = a - b;
                break;

        case MUL:
                c = a*b;
                break;

        case DIV:
                c = a/b;
                break;
        }
        push_1(&c);
        } else {
                fprintf(stderr, "Error: OPERATOR - must have 2 arguments on the
                stack\n");
        }
        return(NULL);
} /* operator_1 */

int *
pop_1(argp)
        void          *argp;
{
        static int results;

        if (cur_index > 0) {
                results = stack [--cur_index];
        } else {
                results = 0;
                fprintf(stderr, "Error: POP stack empty\n");
        }
        return (&results);
} /* pop_1 */
```

Client Routines

```
#include <stdio.h>
#include <rpc/rpc.h>
#include "interp.h"

static struct timeval timeout = { 25, 0 };
static struct timeval batch_timeout = { 0, 0};
```

FIGURE 6.3 Continued

```
void push_1();
void operator_1();
int  pop_1();
main(argc, argv)
        int         argc;
        char        **argv;
{
        CLIENT        *clnt_handlep;
        int           a, b, c;

        if (argc != 2) {
                fprintf(stderr, "usage: %s server_name\n", argv[0]);
                return (1);
        }

        clnt_handlep = clnt_create(argv[1], INTERPRETER_PROG,
                            INTERPRETER_VERS_1, "tcp");
        if (clnt_handlep == NULL) {
                clnt_pcreateerror(argv[1]);
                return (1);
        }

        /*
         * Print out the results of (c = a + b)
         */
        a = 5;
        b = 20;
        push_1(a, clnt_handlep);
        push_1(b, clnt_handlep);
        operator_1(ADD, clnt_handlep);
        c = pop_1(clnt_handlep);
        printf("%d = %d + %d\n", c, a, b);

        clnt_destroy(clnt_handlep);
        return (0);
} /* main */

void
push_1(argp, clnt_handlep)
        int         argp;
        CLIENT *clnt_handlep;
{
```

FIGURE 6.3 Continued

```
        if (clnt_call(clnt_handlep, PUSH, xdr_int, &argp, NULL, NULL,
            batch_timeout)
              != RPC_SUCCESS) {
              clnt_perror(clnt_handlep, "PUSH call failed");
              return;
}
} /* push_1 */

void
operator_1(argp, clnt_handlep)
        operator  argp;
        CLIENT *clnt_handlep;
{
        if (clnt_call(clnt_handlep, OPERATOR, xdr_operator, &argp, NULL, NULL,
            batch_timeout)
              != RPC_SUCCESS) {
                    clnt_perror(clnt_handlep, "OPERATOR call failed");
                    return;
        }
} /* operator_1 */

int
pop_1(clnt_handlep)
        CLIENT *clnt_handlep;
{
        int       results;

        if (clnt_call(clnt_handlep, POP, xdr_void, NULL, xdr_int, &results, timeout)
              != RPC_SUCCESS) {
                    clnt_perror(clnt_handlep, "POP call failed");
                    return (0);
        }
        return (results);
} /* pop_1 */
```

XDR Routine

```
#include <rpc/rpc.h>
#include "interp.h"
```

FIGURE 6.3 Continued

```
bool_t
xdr_operator(xdrs, objp)
	XDR		*xdrs;
	operator	*objp;
{
	return (xdr_enum(xdrs, (enum_t*)objp));
} /* xdr_operator */
```

FIGURE 6.3 Continued

The server main and dispatch routines are standard. The only thing to note is the bottom of the dispatch routine where a check has been added to see if the server procedure returns a NULL address; if so, then the dispatch routine will not send a reply to the client. The client routines follow the usual procedure of getting a client handle and calling the remote procedure. Note that the two batched procedure calls, PUSH and OPERATOR, have a timeout value of zero and specify a NULL address for the reply XDR routine.

Performance analysis was done between the service shown in the example in Figure 6.3 and one that does not batch the calls to the PUSH and OPERATOR procedures. There was a 15% improvement in performance for the batched version compared with the version without batching. Of course the performance difference between batched and non-batched can be dependent on the computer you are using, on its operating system, on the implementation of the RPC Library that you are using, and on the network service being implemented.

6.4 Writing Your Own svc_run() Routine

The current implementation of *svc_run()* does not return control to the calling application. If your application needs to do work while waiting for requests to an RPC service, you might consider creating a new process to handle the remote procedure requests. Your server would communicate with this process via an interprocess communications mechanism. This procedure may be inconvenient for the service that you are implementing, especially if you do not want to deal with multiple processes. For example, if your server needed to:

- process incoming RPC requests;
- perform callbacks;
- do application-specific tasks;

you would not want to call the *svc_run()* routine to process incoming RPC requests because it would not return. To get around this problem, you can implement your own *svc_run()* routine that processes incoming RPC requests, performs any required RPC callbacks, and does application specific tasks. Sun's RPC mechanism enables you to do this because the source code is publicly available. You should study the current implementation of *svc_run()* before writing your own. Once you are familiar with it, you can then design your own *svc_run()* routine to meet your needs. Also, because the RPC Library is written using the socket API, some familiarity with this mechanism is necessary.

When you implement your own *svc_run()*, do not do anything to decrease the portability of your application. You inhibit portability by establishing dependencies on the semantics of RPC Library internal variables. These internal semantics may be changed in a future release of the library. It is safe to make assumptions about documented external variables and routines as they are more likely to exist in future releases.

Figure 6.4 shows the actual code for the *svc_run()* routine. The routine simply loops forever, calling the *select()* system call to see if any of the relevant file descriptors have any data to be read—in other words, the call checks to see if one or more clients have made any RPC requests. Since a time-out value of 0 was used for the last parameter, the call to *select()* will not return until an RPC request has been received, or an error detected. The RPC Library defines the external variable *svc_fdset*, which contains the file descriptors from which the RPC service is accepting RPC requests. This variable should be treated as read-only: do not pass its address into the call to *select()*. This dynamic variable is updated by the RPC Library when services are registered or unregistered and also when TCP connections are accepted or closed by the server. You should declare another variable and then read in the

```
void
svc_run()
{
        fd_set          readfds;
        int             dtblsize = _rpc_dtablesize();
        extern int      errno;

        for (;;) {
                readfds = svc_fdset;
                switch (select(dtblsize, &readfds, (fd_set *)0, (fd_set *)0,
                        (struct timeval *) 0)) {
                case -1:
                        if (errno != EBADF) {
                                continue;
                        }
                        perror(svc_run: - select failed);
                        return;
                case 0:
                        continue;
                default:
                        svc_getreqset(&readfds);
                }
        }
}

/*
 * Cache the result of getdtablesize(), so we don't have to do an
 * expensive system call every time.
 */
int
_rpc_dtablesize()
{
        static int size;
        if (size == 0) {
                size = getdtablesize();
        }
        return (size);
}
```

FIGURE 6.4

value from *svc_fdset*, before each call to *select()*. More information on the *select()* system call can be obtained from the operating-system manual for your computer.

The routine *_rpc_dtablesize()* simply makes a call to a UNIX system call *getdtablesize()*, which returns the number of file descriptors that a given process can have. The routine caches this information so that *getdtablesize()* is only called once within a process. More information on the *getdtablesize()* system call can be obtained from the operating-system manual for your computer.

The *svc_run()* routine then does a switch on the return value from *select()*. If it returns an error, -1, the routine checks to see if it was because one of the file descriptors was invalid and, if not, proceeds to call *select()* again. If one of the file descriptors was invalid, it calls *perror()* to report an error, and the routine returns. A better approach would use the system error-logging mechanism, *syslog*, to report the error, as most services run as background processes and close the *stderr* file descriptor. If *stderr* is closed, the behavior of the *perror()* call would be undefined because it uses *stderr*. If *select()* returns 0, *svc_run()* calls *select()* again. The default case calls *svc_getreqset()* to process the incoming request. The synopsis for this routine follows:

```
void
svc_getreqset(rdfds)
fd_set      *rdfds;
```

The routine is called to process RPC requests on socket descriptors specified by the argument *rdfds*, the read-file-descriptor bit mask. You call *select()* to determine if any input is available to be processed. For each socket that needs to be processed, this routine reads in the request, authenticates the message, and calls the appropriate dispatch routine. It reads all the requests from one socket before proceeding to the next one. The routine returns when all sockets associated with the value of *rdfds* have been serviced.

Note that the *svc_run()* routine in Figure 6.4 is slightly different than the one distributed with the SunOS 4.0 version of the RPC Library. The difference is that the one in Figure 6.4 ignores all error codes returned from *select()* except for EBADF, whereas the *svc_run()* in the RPC Library ignores only the EINTR error code. This change was made because EBADF is the only error that should result in *svc_run()* returning. This change also makes *svc_run()* more tolerant of applications that handle signals and inadvertently modify the global variable *errno* inside their signal handling routine. The problem exists in *svc_run()* because the return from *select()* and the test of the errno variable is not an atomic operation and, in fact, control may be passed to a signal handling routine during this sequence of operations.

The example in Figure 6.5 presents a modified *svc_run()* routine that satisfies the example application requirements listed at the beginning of this section.

The new *svc_run()* calls *select()* with a time-out value set to TIMER_INTERVAL. The *select()* call now returns after

```
void
svc_run()
{
	fd_set			readfds;
	int			dtblsize = _rpc_dtablesize();
	struct timeval		timeout;
	extern int		errno;

	/*
	 * Setting the time-out value to TIMER_INTERVAL seconds causes select
	 * to return after the specified number of seconds if it doesn't
	 * have any incoming I/O on the specified file descriptors.
	 */
	timeout.tv_sec = TIMER_INTERVAL;
	timeout.tv_usec = 0;

	for (;;)
	{
		readfds = svc_fdset;
		switch (select(dtblsize, &readfds, (fd_set *)0, (fd_set *)0,
		&timeout)) {
		case -1:
			if (errno != EBADF) {
				continue;
			}
			perror("svc_run: - select failed");
			return;

		case 0:
			proc_callback_list();
			house_keeping();
			continue;
		default:
		   svc_getreqset(&readfds);
		}
	}
}
```

FIGURE 6.5

TIMER_INTERVAL number of seconds if it does not have any incoming data on one of the read file descriptors. If it returns a value of zero, indicating no activity, it calls *proc_callback_list()* to do callbacks, and then it calls the application's *house_keeping()* routine. Note that these application specific routines perform no processing of incoming RPC requests. Therefore, they should do a minimal amount of processing to ensure that RPC requests are processed in a timely manner.

6.5 Portmapper Routines

The RPC Library includes some routines that communicate with portmappers (see Chapter 3). Some communicate with any portmapper, and others communicate only with the one running on the same computer as the program making the call. The interface to the portmapper routines is tied to the socket API. The routines that communicate with other computers take the IP address of the computer in the form of a *sockaddr_in* data structure. You do not have to call these routines directly in order to implement an RPC service. They are only provided for those implementors who need more control over their environment at the expense of portability. More information on the socket API can be obtained from the operating-system manual for your computer.

The synopses for the portmapper routines are listed below:

```
struct pmaplist *
pmap_getmaps(addr)
struct sockaddr_in *addr;
```

This routine returns a list of the current RPC program-to-port mappings on the host located at the IP address referenced by the *addr* argument. This routine can return NULL, indicating that no information is being returned (i.e. no services have been registered with the remote portmapper). Errors are written to *stderr*. The data structure *pmaplist* is defined in ⟨*rpc/pmap_prot.h*⟩.

```
u_short
pmap_getport(addr, prognum, versnum, protocol)
struct sockaddr_in      *addr;
u_long                  prognum, versnum, protocol;
```

This routine returns the port number on which waits a service that supports the program number, *prognum*; version, *versnum*; and speaks the transport protocol associated with *protocol*. The value of *protocol* is IPPROTO_UDP or IPPROTO_TCP, defined in ⟨*netinet/in.h*⟩. In the case where the requested version number is not registered, but some version number is registered for the given program number, the call returns the port number of one of the registered versions. The port number returned is in the byte order of the computer that the call was made on. The value should be converted to network byte ordering format by using the *htons()* routine. Refer to your operating system manuals for more information on *htons()*. A return value of zero indicates that the mapping does not exist or that the RPC system failed to contact the remote portmap service. In the latter case, the global variable *rpc_createerr* contains the RPC status.

```
enum clnt_stat
pmap_rmtcall(addr, prognum, versnum, procnum, inproc, in, outproc,
out, timeout, portp)
struct sockaddr_in      *addr;
u_long                  prognum, versnum, procnum;
char                    *in, *out;
xdrproc_t               inproc, outproc;
struct timeval          timeout;
u_long                  *portp;
```

This routine instructs the portmapper on the host at IP address **addr* to make an RPC on your behalf to a procedure on that host. The argument **portp* is modified to contain the program's port number if the procedure succeeds. The definitions of other arguments and the return value are the same as for the *callrpc()* and *clnt_call()* routines. This procedure should be used to check whether a service is running on a computer, "pinging" the service, by sending a request to the null procedure and nothing else. The advantage of using this routine for pinging a service is that it does a port number lookup and a RPC in one step. The disadvantages of using this routine are that you cannot specify the authentication flavor—it defaults to none, and does not perform any error checking on the RPC.

```
bool_t
pmap_set(prognum, versnum, protocol, port)
u_long      prognum, versnum;
int         protocol;
u_short     port;
```

This routine establishes a mapping between the triple [*prognum, versnum, protocol*] and *port* on the computer's *portmap* service. Refer to Chapter 3 for more information on ports. The value of *protocol* is IPPROTO_UDP or IPPROTO_TCP. This routine returns TRUE if it succeeds, FALSE if it fails. One reason for failure is that the triple may have already been registered with the portmapper. If that is the case, then you should call *pmap_unset()* before calling *pmap_set()*. Note that the *pmap_set()* routine may be called by the *svc_register()* routine.

```
bool_t
pmap_unset(prognum, versnum)
u_long prognum, versnum;
```

This routine destroys all mapping between the triple [*prognum, versnum,* *] and ports on the computer's *portmap* service. Note that this includes mappings for both the UDP and TCP transport. This routine returns TRUE if it succeeds, FALSE otherwise. This routine is called by the *svc_unregister()* routine.

6.6 Exercises

1. Modify the callback RPC example in Figure 6.1 to allow the client to return the port number of its callback service to the server.
2. Modify the stack calculator network service example in Figure 6.3 so that it does not do batching. Compare the performance of the non-batched version versus the performance of the batched version.
3. Modify the stack calculator network service example in Figure 6.3 to have the server report internal errors to the client.
4. Modify the stack calculator network service example in Figure 6.3 to handle more than one client concurrently.
5. Add support for the *float* type to the stack calculator network service example in Figure 6.3.
6. Add support for matrix operations to the stack calculator network service example in Figure 6.3.
7. What is the relationship of the modifications made in Exercises 5 and 6 and "object oriented programming"?

Rpcgen

7

The program rpcgen assists in the implementation of RPC-based services. *Rpcgen* generates most of the code that interfaces with the RPC Library, enabling you to debug the main features of your application instead of spending time debugging and maintaining the code that interfaces to the RPC Library. *Rpcgen* is included with the RPC source distribution.

Rpcgen is a compiler that accepts a remote-program interface definition written in a language, called RPC Language (RPCL), which is similar to the C programming language. This definition, referred to as the "protocol specification" for the RPC service, includes a list of procedures and the data type of arguments and results for each procedure. From the protocol specification, *rpcgen* produces C-language output that includes client stub routines, a server skeleton, XDR filter routines for both arguments and results, and a header file that contains common definitions. The client stubs interface with the RPC Library routines and effectively hide the network from the user of the stub routines.

The interface to the client stub is very similar to the interface to the actual procedure on the server. The server skeleton similarly hides the network from the server procedures invoked by remote clients. The output files from *rpcgen* can be compiled and linked in the usual way: All you have to do is write the server procedures and link them with the server skeleton and XDR filter routines produced by *rpcgen* to get an executable server program. To use a remote service, you simply write an ordinary program that makes local procedure calls to the client stubs produced by *rpcgen*. Linking this program with the client stubs and XDR filter routines creates an executable program. *Rpcgen* options can suppress stub generation and can specify the transport used by the server skeleton. Figure 7.1 shows how a client program and a server program are constructed with the aid of *rpcgen*. You provide the top three modules—client application, remote-program protocol specification, and server procedures—*rpcgen* generates the rest.

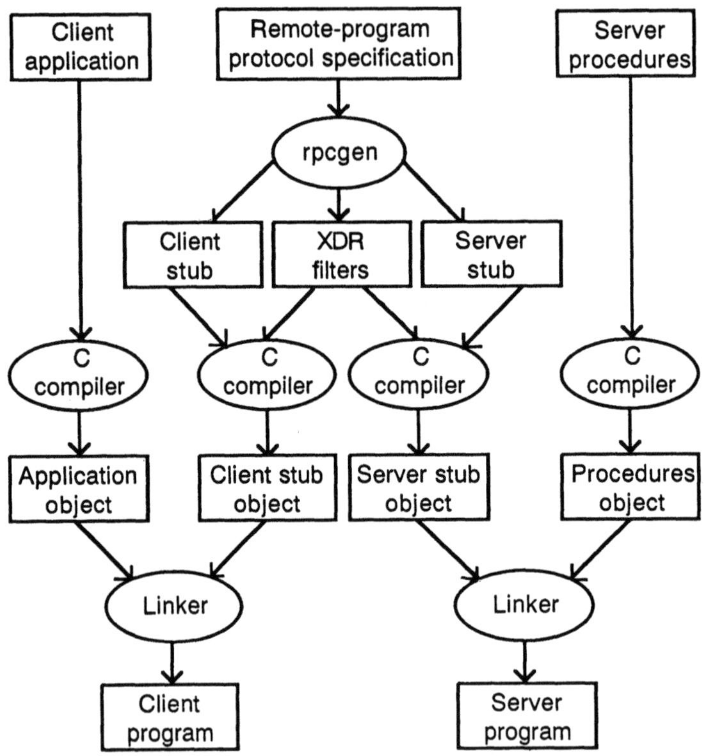

FIGURE 7.1. *Using rpcgen.*

Rpcgen reduces the amount of time you spend coding, debugging and maintaining RPC-related code by having *rpcgen* generate the code for you. The protocol specification in general is easier to modify and you are less prone to make a mistake than if you modified the individual C program modules. Like most compilers, *rpcgen* performs this task at a small cost in efficiency and flexibility. In speed-critical applications, hand-written routines can be linked with the *rpcgen* output without any difficulty. Also, you can proceed by using rpcgen output as a starting point and rewrite the generated code as necessary.

The protocol specification is not only used as input to *rpcgen* but is also used by other distributed application programmers who want to write clients for your servers or implement servers for your clients. Therefore, it is important to document your protocol specification using comments. This documentation should cover defined constants, defined data types, remote procedure semantics, any state maintained by the server, and any other information required to access your server. Another way to look at it is to imagine that somebody is going to write a tester for your server and the only documentation they have is the protocol specification.

You are not confined to using RPCL and *rpcgen* to define protocol specifications for distributed applications. You can define an input file for *rpcgen* that simply defines data types. *Rpcgen* would simply generate the header file and XDR routines that would handle XDR encoding and decoding of the data types defined in the input file. This process is useful for applications that run in a non-RPC environment and use XDR to maintain portable data. It is easier to write and modify the input file than it is to write and maintain the XDR routines used in your application. Refer to Chapter 2 for more information on XDR programming.

This chapter first presents a simple example showing how to use *rpcgen* to convert an existing application into a distributed application. It is followed by the *rpcgen* command line options and preprocessing directives. The chapter concludes with a discussion on the RPCL syntax and semantics.

7.1 Grade Server Example Revisited

By using *rpcgen,* you can convert the original *grade-reporter* program from Chapter 4 into a distributed application. Remember that the program takes a student ID number as an argument, searches the grade file for the corresponding grade and returns a grade. The grades are kept in a file called *grades.* To convert this program into a network service, you need to write a protocol specification, and separate the *main()* routine and the *get_grade()* routine into two different modules. The protocol specification is listed in Figure 7.2.

This protocol specification defines one procedure, GET_GRADE_PROC, for a version, GRADE_VERS_1, of the remote program, GRADE_PROG. These three values uniquely identify the remote procedure. The GET_GRADE_PROC declaration looks almost like a C function declaration. The procedure takes an argument of type *stu_id_num* and returns a value of type *char.* The type *stu_id_num* has been defined by the type definition above,

```
/*
 * Grade Service Protocol Specification
 *
 * Version 1 Remote Procedures
 *
 *      GET_GRADE
 *              This procedure accepts a student ID number and returns the
 *              corresponding grade. It returns the value NO_GRADE if a
 *              grade was not found.
 */
const   ID_NUM_SIZE = 5;     /* Doesn't include terminal NUL */
const   NO_GRADE = 0;

/*
 * Student ID number
 */
typedef string   stu_id_num<ID_NUM_SIZE>;

program GRADE_PROG {
        version GRADE_VERS_1 {
                char    GET_GRADE(stu_id_num) = 1;
        } = 1;
} = 0x20000000;
```

FIGURE 7.2

indicating that *stu_id_num* is of type *string* and has a maximum length of ID_NUM_SIZE. The syntax of the RPCL is explained in more detail in the following section. The GET_GRADE_PROC procedure was declared as procedure number 1; that is what the = *1* at the end of the declaration means in version 1 of the remote program. No null procedure (procedure 0) declaration is necessary because *rpcgen* generates it automatically for you. Notice that the program, version, and procedure numbers are declared in capital letters. Although the use of capital letters is not required, it is a good convention to follow.

Figure 7.3 shows how to compile the protocol specification located in the file *get_grade.x*, following the convention of using the *.x* extension on protocol-specification files.

The directory listing in Figure 7.3 shows the new files created by *rpcgen*. The files are listed in Figure 7.4.

```
% ls
get_grade.x
% rpcgen get_grade.x
% ls
get_grade.h     get_grade_clnt.c get_grade_xdr.c
get_grade.x     get_grade_svc.c
%
```

FIGURE 7.3

From the protocol-specification file *get_grade.x, rpcgen:*

1. Created a header file called *get_grade.h* that contains C preprocessor macros for GRADE_PROG, GRADE _VERS_1, GET_GRADE, and the two constants ID_NUM _SIZE and NO_GRADE. It contains the type definition for *stu_id_num.* Also, it contains external declarations for any generated XDR routines, in this case *xdr_stu_id_num().* The name of the created header file is formed by taking the basename of the input file to *rpcgen* and adding a *.h* suffix.
2. Created a client stub routine in the *get_grade_clnt.c* file. The name of the output file for client stub routines is formed by taking the basename of the input file to *rpcgen* and adding a *_clnt.c* suffix.
3. Created the server skeleton routines in the *get_grade_svc.c* file. The skeleton routines consist of the *main()* routine and the dispatch routine, *grade_prog_1().* The name used for the dispatch routine is constructed by mapping the program name to lowercase characters and appending an underscore followed by the version number that the dispatch routine serves. The main routine creates the transport handles and registers the service. The default is to register the program on both the UDP and TCP transports. You can select which transport to use with a command-line option to *rpcgen.* The dispatch routine dispatches incoming remote procedure calls to the appropriate procedure. This routine also handles calls to the null procedure. The name of the output file for the server skeleton is formed by taking the basename of the input file to *rpcgen* and adding a *_svc.c* suffix.

Grade Header File–get_grade.h

```
#define ID_NUM_SIZE 5
#define NO_GRADE 0

typedef char *stu_id_num;
bool_t xdr_stu_id_num();


#define GRADE_PROG ((u_long)0x20000000)
#define GRADE_VERS_1 ((u_long)1)
#define GET_GRADE ((u_long)1)
extern char *get_grade_1();
```

Grade Client Stud–get_grade_clnt.c

```
#include <rpc/rpc.h>
#include <sys/time.h>
#include "get_grade.h"

/* Default timeout can be changed using clnt_control() */
static struct timeval TIMEOUT = { 25,0 };

char *
get_grade_1(argp, clnt)
        stu_id_num      *argp;
        CLIENT          *clnt;
{
        static char res;

        bzero((char *)&res, sizeof(res));
        if (clnt_call(clnt, GET_GRADE, xdr_stu_id_num, argp, xdr_char,
                &res, TIMEOUT) != RPC_SUCCESS) {
                return (NULL);
        }
        return (&res);
}
```

FIGURE 7.4

Grade Server Skeleton–get_grade_svc.c

```
#include <stdio.h>
#include <rpc/rpc.h>
#include "get_grade.h"

static void grade_prog_1();

main()
{
        SVCXPRT *transp;

        (void)pmap_unset(GRADE_PROG, GRADE_VERS_1);

        transp = svcudp_create(RPC_ANYSOCK);
        if (transp == NULL) }
                (void)fprint(stderr, "cannot create udp service.\n");
                exit(1);
        }
        if (!svc_register(transp, GRADE_PROG, GRADE_VERS_1,
           grade_prog_1, IPPROTO UDP)) {
                (void)fprintf(stderr, "unable to register (GRADE_PROG,
                GRADE_VERS_1, udp).\n");
                exit(1);
        }

        transp = svctcp_create(RPC_ANYSOCK, 0, 0);
        if (transp == NULL) {
                (void)fprintf(stderr, "cannot create tcp service.\n");
                exit(1);
        }
        if (!svc_register(transp, GRADE_PROG, GRADE_VERS_1,
           grade_prog_1, IPPROTO_TCP)) {
                (void)fprintf(stderr, "unable to register (GRADE_PROG,
                GRADE_VERS_1, tcp).\n");
                exit(1);
        }

        svc_run();
        (void)fprintf(stderr, "svc_run returned\n");
        exit(1);
}
```

FIGURE 7.4 Continued

```
static void
grade_prog_1(rqstp, transp)
        struct svc_req    *rqstp;
        SVCXPRT           *transp;
{
        union {
                stu_id_num get_grade_1_arg;
        } argument;
        char *result;
        bool_t (*xdr_argument)(), (*xdr_result)();
        char *(*local)();

        switch (rqstp -> rq_proc) {
        case NULLPROC:
                (void)svc_sendreply(transp, xdr_void, (char *)NULL);
                return;

        case GET_GRADE:
                xdr_argument = xdr_stu_id_num;
                xdr_result = xdr_char;
                local = (char *(*)()) get_grade_1;
                break

        default:
                svcerr_noproc(transp);
                return;
        }
        bzero((char*)&argument, sizeof(argument));
        if (!svc_getargs(transp, xdr_argument, &argument)) {
                svcerr_decode(transp);
                return;
        }
        result = (*local)(&argument, rqstp);
        if (result != NULL && !svc_sendreply(transp, xdr_result, result)) {
                svcerr_systemerr(transp);
        }
        if (!svc_freeargs(transp, xdr_argument, &argument)) {
                (void)fprintf(stderr, "unable to free arguments\n");
                exit(1);
        }
}
```

FIGURE 7.4 Continued

Grade XDR Routines–get_grade_xdr.c

```
#include <rpc/rpc.h>
#include "get_grade.h"
bool_t
xdr_stu_id_num(xdrs,objp)
        XDR *xdrs;
        stu_id_num *objp;
{
        if (!xdr_string(xdrs, objp, ID_NUM_SIZE)) {
                return (FALSE);
        }
        return (TRUE);
}
```

FIGURE 7.4 Continued

4. Created the XDR routine for the *stu_id_num* type. The name of the output file for XDR routines is formed by taking the basename of the input file to *rpcgen* and adding a *_xdr.c* suffix. This routine is used by both the client and the server.

Note that *rpcgen* does not provide a mechanism to allow you to specify the type of authentication to use. The implementation of authentication varies depending on the application. Therefore, you choose and implement the security mechanism desired.

Now that you have seen the files generated by *rpcgen*, you can visualize the changes that need to be made to the *main()* routine on the client side and to the *get_grade()* routine on the server side. The modified routines are listed in Figure 7.5.

The client main has changed to accept the host name of the grade server as the first argument. It now gets a client handle before calling the *get_grade()* routine. A *_1* appended to the name of the *get_grade()* routine indicates that version 1 of the remote procedure is being called. In general, you name all remote procedures defined in the protocol specification by converting the identifier in the program definition (here GET_GRADE) to lowercase letters and then appending an underscore followed by the version

Grade Client Main–get_grade.c

```
/*
 * Grade server client, calls the get_grade() remote procedure and prints
 * the results.
 */
#include <stdio.h>
#include <rpc/rpc.h>
#include "get_grade.h"

main(argc, argv)
	int	argc;
	char	*argv[];
{
	CLIENT*clnt_handlep;
	char	*grade;
	int	ret_code;

	if (argc != 3) {
		fprintf(stderr, "usage: %s server_name id#\n", argv[0]);
		return (1);
	}

	clnt_handlep = clnt_create(argv[1], GRADE_PROG,
		GRADE_VERS_1, "udp");
	if (clnt_handlep == NULL) {
		clnt_pcreateerror(argv[1]);
		return (1);
	}

	grade = get_grade_1(&argv[2], clnt_handlep);
	if (grade != NULL) {
		if (*grade != NO_GRADE) {
			printf("Your grade is a %c\n", *grade);
			ret_code = 0;
		} else {
			fprintf(stderr, "Could not find your grade \n");
			ret_code = 1;
		}
	} else {
		fprintf(stderr, "Remote procedure call failed\n");
		ret_code = 1;
	}
```

FIGURE 7.5

```
        clnt_destroy(clnt_handlep);
        return (ret_code);
} /* main */
```

Grade Remote Procedures – grade_proc.c

```
#include <stdio.h>
#include <rpc/rpc.h>
#include "get_grade.h"

#define GRADE_FILE   "grades"
#define NO           0
#define YES          1

char *
get_grade_1(id_num)
        stu_id_num      *id_num;
{

        static char     grade;
        FILE            *fp;
        char            tmp_id_num[ID_NUM_SIZE + 1];
        int             done;

        done = NO;
        if ((fp = fopen(GRADE_FILE, "r")) != NULL) {
                while (done == NO && fscanf(fp, "%s %c", tmp_id_num,
                        &grade) != EOF) {
                        if (strncmp(*id_num, tmp_id_num,
                           ID_NUM_SIZE) == 0) {
                                done = YES;
                        }
                }
                fclose(fp);
        } else {
                fprintf(stderr, "Cannot open file %s\n", GRADE_FILE);
        }

        if (done == NO) {
                grade = NO_GRADE;
        }
        return (&grade);
} /* get_grade */
```

FIGURE 7.5 Continued

number. The *get_grade_1()* routine takes a pointer to the argument of the remote procedure and a pointer to a client handle as a second argument. If the remote procedure does not take an argument, i.e., argument type, then you still must pass in a NULL pointer for the argument to the remote procedure. The *get_grade_1()* routine returns a pointer to the grade. Also, the module includes the header files ⟨*rpc/rpc.h*⟩ and *get_grade.h.*

The *get_grade()* routine in the module *grade_proc.c* was modified to return a pointer to a character instead of returning a character. The declaration of the variable grade must be changed to static to ensure that you don't return a pointer to an automatic variable, a variable whose value becomes undefined when the function returns. A *_1* added to the name of the procedure indicates that it is version 1 of the procedure. Also, the module now includes the headers ⟨*rpc/rpc.h*⟩ and *get_grade.h.*

Figure 7.6 shows how to put all the modules together to generate a grade client. Figure 7.7 shows how to put all the modules together to generate a grade server.

You might be wondering why the constants ID_NUM_SIZE and NO_GRADE were put into the protocol-specification file and the constants GRADE_FILE, YES, and NO were not. The protocol-specification file should contain definitions that are necessary to describe the interaction between the client and the server. The ID_NUM_SIZE is important because it defines the maximum size of the argument to the GET_GRADE procedure. The NO_GRADE is required because it is necessary to define the semantics of the interpretation of the returned grade since the variable is overloaded. Not only does the grade returned contain a valid grade, it can also contain a special value, NO_GRADE, to indicate that the GET_GRADE procedure could not find a grade associated with the given student ID number. Instead of overloading the grade variable, you could have returned a structure that contained the grade and an error-code value. The error-code values would then be defined in the protocol specification. The constant GRADE _FILE was omitted because the client imposes no restrictions on which file the server uses to read grades from. The server could be changed to read grades from a file named *new_grades* without affecting the client's interaction with the service. Similarly, the constants YES and NO are not part of the protocol.

The routines that you write to interface with the client stubs

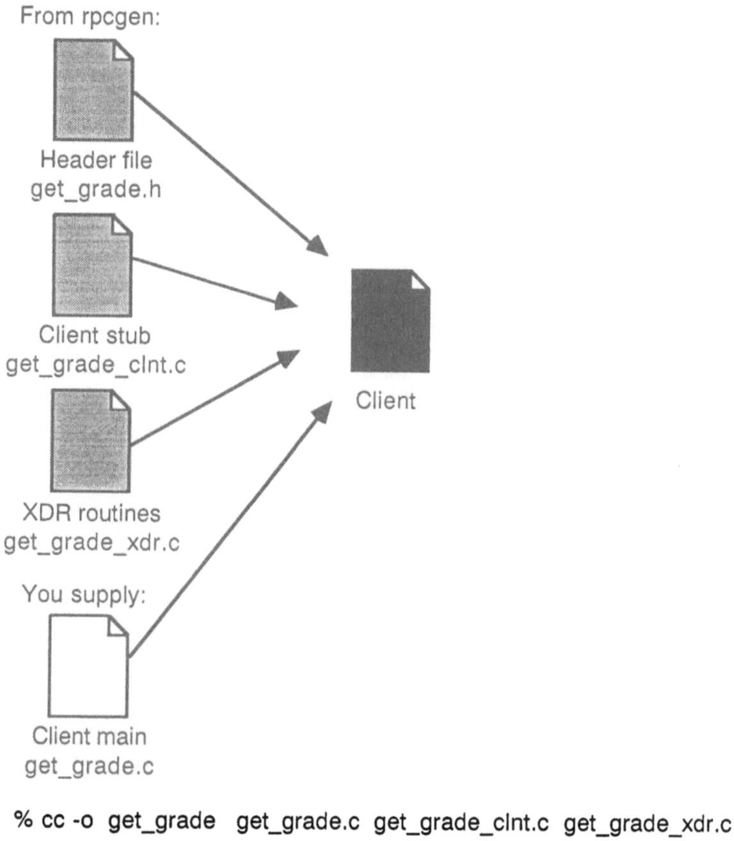

FIGURE 7.6. *Building the grade client.*

and server skeleton do not have to be written in the C programming language. You can use whatever language you desire provided the function linkage is compatible with C. You may have to adapt the header file generated by *rpcgen* to the language that you are using. For more information, refer to the reference manual for the language you want to use.

It is generally a good idea to make sure that your client program and the server procedures work before you link them with the client stubs and server skeleton, respectively. The example in this section converted a working application into a distributed application. When writing a new application, you write the proto-

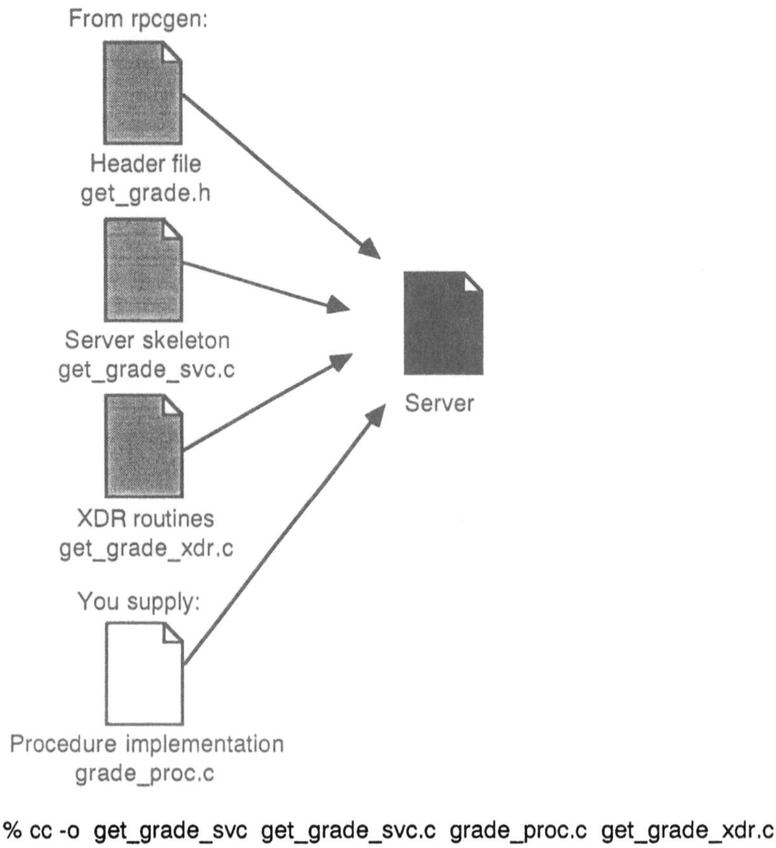

FIGURE 7.7. *Building the grade server.*

col specification first and then write the client application and server procedures. To test your application, you comment out any RPC Library calls in the client and then link the client to the server procedures. The procedure calls are executed as ordinary local procedure calls, and the program can be debugged with a local debugger. When the program is working, the client program can be linked to the client stub, and the server procedures can be linked to the server skeleton. Now the application can be tested as a distributed application. Chapter 8 examines testing methods in more detail.

Note that the server dispatch routine passes a pointer to a

svc_req structure to the invoked remote procedure. The server procedure, *get_grade_1()*, ignored this argument. A server procedure may want to know more about a RPC than just its arguments. For example, getting authentication information is important to procedures that implement some level of security. This extra information is actually supplied to the server procedure in the *svc_req* structure. Chapter 5 discusses the use of the information in the *svc_req* structure.

The client stubs generated by *rpcgen* always call *bzero()* to zero out the result value before making the RPC. If the result value contained pointers, they would be set to zero, indicating that the XDR filter invoked to decode results should allocate memory to the object referenced by the pointer and then set the pointer to the allocated memory. It is important to call *clnt_freeres()* to free the allocated memory when you are through with the results. The client stubs also return a NULL value if the call to *clnt_call()* fails. You can use *clnt_perror()* to print out the error message associated with the detected failure.

The server skeleton generated by *rpcgen* always calls *bzero()* to zero out the argument union before calling *svc_getargs()*. If the object used to hold the arguments for the RPC contains pointers, they would be set to zero, indicating that the XDR filter invoked to decode results should allocate memory to the object referenced by the pointer and then set the pointer to the allocated memory. Notice that *rpcgen* also generates a call to *svc_freeargs()* to free this memory when the dispatch routine is finished with the arguments. You are responsible for freeing any memory that may have been allocated when the results were XDR-encoded by the *svc _sendreply()* routine.

7.2 Command Line Options

The command line options to *rpcgen* are:

-c	Generates the XDR routines only.
-h	Generates the header file only.
-l	Generates the client-side stubs only.
-m	Generates the server-side skeleton only, but does not generate a *main()* routine. This option is useful for creating callback-routines or for writing your own *main()* routine.

Macro Name	Use
RPC_HDR	For header-file output
RPC_XDR	For XDR routine output
RPC_SVC	For server-skeleton output
RPC_CLNT	For client-stub output

FIGURE 7.8. *Rpcgen macros.*

-o outfile	Specifies the name for the output file. Be sure to specify an outfile name.
-s transport	Generates the server-side skeleton only, using the given transport. The current transports are udp and tcp.

Only one of the -c, -h, -l, -m, or -s options may be specified on the command line. The exception is the -s option: more than one -s option may be specified on the command line. The -o option can be used with any of the other options. Be sure to specify an output file name when you use the -o option. Failure to do so results in the truncation of your protocol-specification file. When the -c, -h, -l, or -s options are specified, the output is written to standard output unless the -o option is used.

7.3 Preprocessor Directives

The input file to *rpcgen* is run through the C-preprocessor before being compiled by *rpcgen*. Therefore, all preprocessor directives are legal within a protocol-specification file. *Rpcgen* reserves four preprocessor macro names listed in Figure 7.8.

The macro currently defined depends on which output file is being generated. The macros are useful for including comments and placing *#include* preprocessing directives into the generated files to ensure that they compile without modification.

Rpcgen has a percent-sign directive that is especially useful when used in conjunction with the predefined macros. Any line that begins with a percent sign is passed directly into the output file, without any interpretation of the line other than the removal of the percent sign. Figure 7.9 contains a simple example that demonstrates the preprocessing features.

Try the example to see if you get the results you expect. Note

```
/*
 * Remote Date Service Protocol Specification
 *
 *      GET_DATE
 *              This procedure returns the current date.
 */

%/*
% *    WARNING-DO NOT EDIT THIS FILE
% *    IT IS GENERATED BY RPCGEN-LOOK AT THE MAKEFILE
% */

#if     (RPC_CLNT | RPC_SVC)
%#include        "date_1.h"
%#include        "date_2.h"
#endif

typedef unsigned long   date_t;

program DATE_PROG {
        version DATE_VERS_1 {
                date_t  GET_DATE(void) = 1;
        } = 1;
} = 0x20000040;
```

FIGURE 7.9

that there is no guarantee that the compiler places the output passed through with the percent sign where you wanted it to. In general, lines with the percent-sign directive placed at the beginning of the protocol specification end up after the *#include* lines in the generated files. This behavior is not guaranteed in future releases of the *rpcgen* compiler.

7.4 RPC Language

RPCL is an extension of XDR language. The sole extension is the addition of the *program* type, meaning that RPCL is a data-description language that includes a mechanism for defining remote programs. RPCL is so close to the C programming language, however, that if you know C, you can pick up RPCL without

RPC Language Keywords		
bool	case	const
default	double	enum
float	hyper	opaque
program	string	struct
switch	typedef	union
unsigned	version	void

FIGURE 7.10

difficulty. The syntax of RPCL is described below, as are examples that show the corresponding code generated from the statements. The complete description of the XDR language syntax is in Appendix 2. For a description of the RPC extensions to the XDR language, see Appendix 3.

7.4.1 Comments

The comment delimiter is the same as the C language comment delimiter. The beginning of a comment is indicated by a /* and everything that falls between the /* and a matching */ is a comment. Comments can span multiple lines but they cannot be nested.

7.4.2 White Space

Blanks, tabs, and newlines are referred to as *white space.* White space separates items and is otherwise ignored.

7.4.3 Identifiers

An identifier can be composed of letters, digits, and the underscore character and must begin with a letter. Uppercase and lowercase letters are distinct. RPCL doesn't impose a limit on the length of an identifier. The length is limited by any restrictions that the C compiler imposes on identifiers.

RPCL reserves a set of words for use within the language as keywords. The keyword names may not be reused as identifiers. The keyword identifiers are listed in Figure 7.10.

7.4.4 Remote Program Definitions

Specifying a remote service in a protocol specification is an easy task once you know what all the remote procedures are, including the type of the arguments and result values. The program definition syntax follows:

```
program-def:
        "program" identifier "{"
                version-def
                version-def *
        "}" "=" constant ";"
```

A protocol-specification file can contain one or more program definitions. Appendix 1 covers the procedure for obtaining a program number. The program identifiers are in the same name space as constant and type identifiers. However, *rpcgen* does not check for uniqueness of these identifiers. Reuse of the identifiers is flagged by the C compiler when the generated code is compiled.

The version definition syntax follows:

```
version-def:
        "version" identifier "{"
                procedure-def
                procedure-def *
        "}" "=" constant ";"
```

There can be more than one version for the same program number. Typically, the first version number of a program starts with the number 1 and is incremented each time the program's protocol is changed. A version identifier or version number cannot occur more than once within the scope of a program definition.

The procedure definition syntax follows:

```
procedure-def:
        type-specifier identifier "(" type-specifier ")" "=" constant ";"
```

A procedure definition consists of a specification of the type, called the type-specifier, for the result value, followed by the procedure identifier and then followed by the type-specifier for the procedure argument, which is enclosed in parentheses. There can be more than one procedure for the same version number. Typically, the procedure number 0 is used for the null procedure and procedures are numbered starting with 1. A procedure identifier or procedure number cannot occur more than once within the scope of a version

Time Service Protocol Specification File–time.x

```
/*
 * Time Service Protocol Specification
 *
 * Version 1 Remote Procedures
 *
 *       GET_TIME
 *               Returns the time to the caller.
 *
 * Version 2 Remote Procedures
 *
 *       GET_TIME
 *               Returns the time to the caller.
 *       SET_TIME
 *               This procedure sets the server's time to the value passed in as
 *               the argument and then returns the server's time.
 */
program TIME_PROG {
        version TIME_VERS_1 {
                unsigned int    GET_TIME(void) = 1;
        } = 1;

        version TIME_VERS_2 {
                unsigned int    GET_TIME(void) = 1;
                unsigned int    SET_TIME(unsigned int) = 2;
        } = 2;
} = 0x20000050;
```

FIGURE 7.11

definition. Note that only unsigned constants can be assigned to programs, versions, and procedures.

Figure 7.11 lists a protocol specification file for a time service. You can run the specification through *rpcgen* to generate the files *time_clnt.c, time_svc.c,* and *time_xdr.c*

The protocol specification defines a remote time service that supports two versions. Version one of the service supports the procedure GET_TIME that doesn't have any arguments and returns an *unsigned integer.* Version two of the service also supports the GET_TIME procedure and it supports a SET_TIME procedure that allows you to set the service's time. The SET_TIME procedure takes an *unsigned integer* as an argument, the time to set, and returns an *unsigned integer*, the current time.

The generated file *time_clnt.c* contains the client stubs that actually call the RPC Library routine *clnt_call()* to invoke the remote procedure. Each routine is simply the name of the remote procedure used in the protocol specification, mapped to lowercase characters, with an underscore followed by the version number appended to the routine name. The client stubs take as arguments a pointer to the remote procedure argument and a pointer to the client handle. They return a pointer to the results if the RPC succeeds; if the call doesn't succeed then the pointer is set to NULL. Notice that the memory for the results is statically allocated.

The generated file *time_svc.c* contains the server skeleton which includes the main routine and the dispatch routines. The main routine registers both versions of the service on the UDP and the TCP transports and calls *svc_run()* to wait for RPC requests. There are two dispatch routines, one for version one of the service and one for version two. The generated dispatch routines are similar to those discussed in Chapter 5.

Completion of the time service requires writing a client that uses the client stub routines and writing the actual procedures that would be invoked by the server dispatch routines. The completion of the service is left as an exercise to the reader.

7.4.5 Data Types

In addition to defining interfaces to remote services, RPCL can also generate the XDR routines for the remote service. You can generate the XDR routines by explicitly defining the types for the arguments and results of all the remote procedure calls. This is done by decomposing all the types into the fundamental types supported by the XDR routines in the RPC Library. The supported XDR routines are listed in Chapter 2.

Rpcgen does not do any type checking. If a type is not specified in the protocol specification and an XDR routine does not already exist in the library for the type, then you must write the XDR routine. Otherwise, the XDR routine is listed as undefined when you link all the routines of your service together.

Decomposition of types can best be described by an example.

Suppose you have the following synopsis for a remote procedure that you want to specify in your protocol specification.

```
Entry
return_entry(key)
Keys    key;
```

The procedure definition in the protocol specification would appear as follows:

```
Entry   RETURN_ENTRY(Keys) = 1;
```

If you have not defined the types *Entry* and *Keys* in the protocol specification, then *rpcgen* generates the client stubs and server skeleton that reference the XDR routines *xdr_Entry()* and *xdr_Keys()*. *Rpcgen* will not generate these XDR routines because it does not know how these types are defined. You need to define these types to get *rpcgen* to generate the XDR routines for you. The defined types to include in the protocol specification file are shown below:

```
struct Entry {
        int     refcnt;
        long    indicator;
        u_long  data;
};

struct Keys {
        int     key_type;
        long    data;
};
```

Note that although the types *long* and *u_long* are not XDR data types, the routines *xdr_long()* and *xdr_u_long()* are provided in the RPC Library and you do not need to decompose these types into XDR data types.

Remember that RPCL is a data definition language. You cannot allocate storage within a protocol specification file as you can with C. The following example highlights this fact. Try compiling the following protocol specification file:

```
struct  mytype_decl {
        int     a;
        char    b;
        long    c;
} mytype_def;
int     variable;
```

Of course *rpcgen* reports errors because the example tries to declare storage in a C-like manner for the instance *mytype_def* of type *mytype_decl*. The compile would also fail because the C-like declaration of *variable* does not make sense in the context of RPCL. Note that *rpcgen* stops at the first error; it does not compile the entire input file and report all errors.

The following sections cover the code-generation process for the data types declared in the protocol specification.

7.4.5.1 Constants

A constant is a sequence of one or more decimal digits, optionally preceded by a minus-sign (−). RPCL provides a mechanism for defining integer constants. A constants definition is mapped into a C preprocessor macro in the generated header file. The constant definition syntax is:

"const" identifier "=" integer ";"

Constants may be employed wherever you use an integer constant—for example, in array-size specifications. The following example shows a constant definition for the identifier DOZEN and the generated C preprocessor macro.

```
const DOZEN = 12;     →     #define DOZEN 12
```

7.4.5.2 Void

In a void declaration, the variable is unnamed: The declaration is just void and nothing else. Void declarations can only occur in two places: union definitions, and program definitions as the argument or result of a remote procedure.

7.4.5.3 Enumerations

RPCL enumerations have the same syntax as C enumerations. Here is an example of an RPCL *enum* and the C *enum* into which it is compiled.

```
enum colortype {                 enum colortype {
        RED = 0,                         RED = 0,
        GREEN = 1,                       GREEN = 1,
        BLUE = 2         →               BLUE = 2,
};                               };
                                 typedef enum colortype colortype;
                                 bool_t xdr_colortype();
```

The output is identical to the input, except for the added *typedef* at the end of the definition and the definition of the *xdr_colortype()* routine. The type definition allows you to use *colortype* instead of *enum colortype* when you declare other colortype enumerations. The definition of *enum colortype* must occur before other references to *colortype*. The definition of the XDR routine return type is done for your convenience so that you simply have to include the generated header file, and do not need to type in the external definition in the modules that use the XDR routine.

7.4.5.4 Booleans C has no built-in Boolean type; but RPCL supports the Boolean type called *bool*. RPCL *bool* declarations are compiled into the *bool_t* type in the output header file. The *bool_t* type is defined in *<rpc/types.h>*. The *bool* declaration is only allowed within a structure declaration, a type definition, or as the discriminant declaration in an RPCL union.

The following example shows a RPCL *bool* definition and the generated C code.

```
bool in_use;            →        bool_t in_use;
```

This type is equivalent to:

```
enum {FALSE = 0, TRUE = 1} in_use;
```

7.4.5.5 Fixed-Length Arrays Fixed-length array declarations are just like C array declarations. The following example shows a RPCL fixed-length array declaration and the generated C code.

```
int palette[8];         →        int palette[8];
```

7.4.5.6 Variable-Length Arrays Variable-length array declarations have no explicit syntax in C, so RPCL uses angle-brackets. The maximum size is specified between the angle brackets. The size may be omitted, indicating that the array may be of any size. An array size may not exceed the maximum value that can be represented by an unsigned integer. Example declarations follow:

```
int     heights<12>;        /* at most 12 items */
int     widths<>;           /* any number of items */
```

Because variable-length arrays have no explicit syntax in C, these declarations are actually compiled into structures with a length specifier and a pointer to the array. For example, the heights and widths declarations above get compiled into the following structure:

```
struct {
        u_int   heights_len;          /* # of items in array */
        int     *heights_val;         /* pointer to array */
} heights;

struct {
        u_int   widths_len;           /* # of items in array */
        int     *widths_val;          /* pointer to array */
} widths;
```

Note that the number of items in the array is stored in the *_len*, component and the pointer to the array is stored in the *_val* component. The first part of each of these component's names is the same as the name of the declared array variable.

The maximum size specified in the declaration is used as the *maxsize* argument to the *xdr_array()* routine. If the maximum size is not specified in the RPCL variable length array declaration then the maximum value that can be represented by an unsigned integer is used as the *maxsize* argument.

7.4.5.7 Structures Like its C counterpart, an RPCL structure definition is declared with the *struct* keyword followed by the structure identifier. As an example, here is an RPCL structure to a two-dimensional coordinate and the C structure into which it is compiled in the generated header file.

```
struct coord {                     struct coord {
        int x;                             int x;
        int y;            →                int y;
};                                 };
                                   typedef struct coord coord;
                                   bool_t xdr_coord();
```

The output is identical to the input, except for the added *typedef* at the end of the declaration, which allows you to use *coord* instead of *struct coord* when you declare other coordinate structures. The definition of *struct coord* must occur before other references to *coord*. The components of the structure are XDR-encoded and XDR-decoded in the order of their declaration in the structure.

7.4.5.8 Unions RPCL unions are discriminated unions and are different from C unions. They are more analogous to Pascal variant records than they are to C unions. Discriminated unions are defined in Chapter 2. The discriminant can be either an *int, unsigned int,* or an enumerated type. The "arms" of the union are preceded by the value of the discriminant that implies their encoding. Discriminated unions are declared as follows:

```
union switch (discriminant-declaration) {
        case discriminant-value-A:
                arm-declaration-A;
        case discriminant-value-B:
                arm-declaration-B;

        ...
        default:
                default-declaration;
} identifier;
```

Here is an example of a type that might be returned as the result of a read-data operation. If there is no error, return a block of data. Otherwise, don't return anything.

```
union read_result switch(int errno) {
        case 0:
                opaque data[1024]
        default:
                void;
};
```

The above example gets compiled into the following:

```
struct read_result {
        int errno;
        union {
                char data[1024];
        } read_result_u;
};
typedef struct read_result read_result;
bool_t xdr_read_result();
```

Notice that the union component of the *read_result* structure has the same name as the structure type name, except for the trailing *_u*.

7.4.5.9 Pointers Pointer declarations are made in RPCL exactly as they are in C. Of course sending the address in a pointer to another computer on the network does not make sense since there is no guarantee that what the pointer referenced on one computer is at the same memory location on another computer. This RPCL data type is actually called *optional-data*, instead of *pointer*. You can use RPCL optional-data pointers for sending recursive data types such as lists and trees (discussed in Chapter 2). An example of an RPCL declaration using pointers and the generated C structure follows:

```
struct list {                       struct list {
        int data;                           int data;
        list *nextp;        →               struct list *nextp;
};                                  };
                                    typedef struct list list;
                                    bool_t xdr_list();
```

7.4.5.10 Strings C has no built-in string type, but instead uses the null-terminated *char* pointer convention. In RPCL, strings are declared using the *string* keyword, and compiled into *char* pointers in the output header file. The maximum size contained in the angle brackets specifies the maximum number of characters allowed in the strings (not counting the NULL character). The maximum size may be left off, indicating a string of arbitrary length. Strings cannot be defined with the fixed length array notation.

The following example shows RPCL *string* definitions and the generated C code.

```
string name<32>;        →       char *name;
string longname<>;      →       char *longname;
```

If the maximum size is not specified in the declaration then the maximum size of the string is the maximum value that can be represented by an *unsigned integer*.

7.4.5.11 Opaque Data Opaque data is used to describe untyped data (sequences of arbitrary bytes). The data may be declared either as a fixed or variable length array. The following example shows RPCL *opaque* definitions and the generated C code.

```
opaque diskblock[512];  →       char diskblock[512];
opaque filedata<1024>;  →       struct {
                                        u_int filedata_len;
                                        char *filedata_val;
                                } filedata;
```

7.4.5.12 Typedef RPCL typedefs have the same syntax as C typedefs. Here is an example that defines a *fname_type* used for declaring file name strings that have a maximum length of 255 characters.

```
typedef string fname_type<255>;   →   typedef char *fname_type;
```

7.5 Exercises

1. Complete the implementation of the time service using the protocol specification listed in Figure 7.11.
2. Write protocol specifications for the examples given in Chapter 5 and 6.

Developing RPC-based Distributed Applications

8

The previous chapters have explained how to use the RPC Library and the *rpcgen* compiler. This chapter covers techniques you can use to design, implement, and test a distributed application. It also covers some of the issues associated with this process. An assumption of this chapter is that you are familiar with the design, implementation, and testing of software in general.

Not covered here are distributed application design methodologies that are beyond the scope of this book. The first section of the chapter presents a list of procedures you can follow in designing a distributed application. They are not all-encompassing and are only presented to show you a possible approach.

8.1 Designing a Distributed Application

Typically when you sit down to write a distributed application, you need to answer several questions:

- What functionality is provided by the distributed application?
- What level of security is needed?
- What level of heterogeneity is needed?
- What level of performance is needed?
- Which procedures are remote?
- What are the input and output parameters for the remote procedures?
- What are the machine-independent data types that describe the parameters?

- How will I recover from errors?
- How will I test and debug the distributed application?

The following discussion addresses the above questions. The next section contains an explanation of issues that you should be familiar with before designing a distributed application.

Initially you need to know your goal; in other words, what is the purpose of your distributed application? It is easy to dive into what you believe is the correct solution for your application without fully understanding the problem. Goal definition is an important first step in any engineering task. Once your goal is well defined, you can then specify the functionality of the application.

Security may or may not be an issue in the design of your application. If it is, you can evaluate the authentication types provided by the RPC Library to determine if one of them is satisfactory. If not, you can implement your own authentication flavor or a security layer within your application. In designing your application, some security issues that you may want to consider are:

- Is it all right if the arguments and results of the RPC are visible to other users on the network?
- Does the client need to authenticate the server?
- Does the server need to authenticate or identify the client?
- The security of your application is only as secure as your weakest link. The security should degrade gracefully.

Normally, the arguments and results of your remote procedure calls are readable by anyone monitoring communications between your client and server. To prevent this, you must encrypt the arguments and results before sending them over the network. When designing your application, you need to consider the issue of client and server authentication. Does the client need to verify that it is communicating to the correct server? If so, you need a mechanism to authenticate the server. Does the server need to authenticate the client—that is, does it need to verify that it is communicating with the computer that claims to have made the RPC request? The DES authentication flavor can be used to authenticate the client and the server. An important and obvious security concept is that your security design is only as strong as the weakest link. You should review your security to determine what the weakest link is. Another important concept is that your security should degrade gracefully. The security design should not be configured as an all or nothing setup—i.e., once a piece of the security has been compromised, then the security of the entire system has been compromised. You should try to layer your security if possible. That way, anyone who breaks into one layer has not broken into the entire system. Ideally, you want to detect security leaks at each layer and report them to some authority.

The issue of heterogeneity is important in the design of a distributed application and, typically, the more portable your application, the better. Several kinds of heterogeneity need to be considered: machine-architecture independence, operating-system independence, network-transport independence, release independence, and software-vendor independence. You are probably already aware of the importance of writing software applications that are computer and operating system independent. The C programming language is a good tool to use for doing this. When you write distributed applications, other aspects that affect portability are not related to the programming language or coding style used. Just because a program compiles in a different environment does not mean it will work. A good example is the *talk* program that enables a user on one computer to communicate with a user at another computer. When the two computers were of the same architecture, *talk* worked fine. It failed when the computers had different architectures. The problem was that the software engineers didn't consider the differences in data representations between computers of different architectures. It is important to ensure that the protocol specification does not have dependencies on anything outside the scope of your application. If it does, you could increase the difficulty associated with porting your application to another computer or have interoperability problems with another vendor's version of the same distributed application.

Ideally, you want your application to be independent of the network transport used, and you typically achieve this independence by keeping any transport dependencies isolated in the same layer where the RPC interface is located. Do not let transport dependencies creep out into your application (examples: packet size, time-outs, addresses). Release independence implies that your client should be able to run independently of what version of the service is available. For example, if there are three versions of your distributed application, then a client should be able to work with any version of the server, although the client may limit features available to users, depending on which version of the server it is using. Software-vendor independence is an important consideration. Typically, a software vendor publishes a protocol specification for a distributed application to encourage other software vendors to port the application to their hardware platform.

The protocol specification should be vendor independent—that is, no dependencies should be established that are indigenous to the originating software vendor. Vendor dependencies may increase the difficulty in porting the application. An example of a vendor dependency is the assumption that employee identification numbers always have the format of three characters followed by two digits.

The issue of performance can be complex. Typically, every step of the design process involves some decisions based on performance considerations. These issues are covered in Section 8.2.5.

After you have completed the design of the application, you will probably use structure charts to diagram the procedures you plan to implement. Your particular design methodology may use another type of diagraming technique to represent procedures. Once you have defined the procedures and their arguments, you can then begin partitioning the application. Partioning the application is the process of deciding which procedures are local and which are remote. Once you know which are remote, you can define the protocol specification. This specification should address the underlying information transfer or action request and should not be unduly influenced by implementation decisions.

The only interaction between the client and the server is through the input and output parameters for the remote procedures. The definition of this interaction is in the protocol specification for the distributed application. The protocol specification defines the remote procedures, including the data types of the arguments and the return values. It should contain all the information required for someone to implement a server for your application, including comments and sufficient interface documentation. In general, if a protocol exists for the function you want to perform, it is better to use it than to invent your own proprietary solution. Using standards is crucial to the widespread acceptance of your distributed application. If a protocol does not exist for the function you want to perform, you must develop a new solution, based on existing protocols if possible. Do not introduce machine-architecture, operating-system, or network-transport dependencies into the protocol specification. XDR isolates you from most computer dependencies related to data types. An example of an operating-system dependency is the assumption that all login names are no longer than nine characters. You will have a problem when you port your application to an operating system that allows login names to be as long as 32 characters. An example of a network-transport dependency is the use of a data structure that requires the port number of the transport. Ports are not indigenous to all network transports.

Once you have designed the distributed application, you can begin to implement it. *rpcgen* is used to process the protocol specification file. Remember that *rpcgen* generates the XDR routines, the client stubs, and the server skeleton for you. Next you implement the actual remote procedures and tie in the client side portion of the application to the client stubs. Of course, you may have to modify the client stubs or the server skeleton if you need to add functionality. If you add functionality, make sure you modify your *Makefile* so that when you invoke *rpcgen* you do not accidently overwrite your modified client stubs or server skeleton. If the modifications to the generated files are minor, you can always write a script to post-process the files after *rpcgen* generates the files. This approach is desirable because you do not have to maintain the client stubs and the server skeleton, you just have to maintain the protocol-specification file. Even so, this is not always possible if the modifications to the files are major. After you are through with the implementation, you can move onto the testing phase. Testing procedures are discussed in Section 8.3.

Error recovery is an important issue for distributed applications. Networks go down, computers go down, servers and clients crash. You should design error recovery into your distributed application from the beginning by evaluating all possible failure conditions. Section 8.2.3 covers some of the possible failures that your distributed application should be able to handle.

Planning for debugging and maintenance of your application during the design phase makes things a lot easier in the long run. Section 8.3 discusses the issue of testing and debugging.

Just as a reminder, you should obtain a unique RPC program number from Sun before your application ships to customers. Refer to Appendix 1 for more information.

8.2 Design Issues

The previous section introduced a list of possible steps to use in designing a distributed application. This section covers some issues that you need to be familiar with before you design a distributed application. Not all of these issues may be applicable to the design of your application, but they are useful to know.

8.2.1 Transport Issues

The SunOS 4.0 version of the RPC Library supports remote procedure calls over two types of transports: the connectionless transport called the User Datagram Protocol (UDP) and a reliable connection-oriented transport called the Transmission Control Protocol (TCP). Understanding the significant differences between the two types of transports is crucial.

Think of a reliable connection as a bidirectional pipe that connects the client and the server. When a client starts up, it typically creates a pipe that connects itself to the server. When the client wants to communicate with the server, it simply sends its request down the pipe. The server, in turn, responds to the client by returning the results back to the client through the pipe. The mechanics of the pipe are transparent to users. The pipe guarantees the delivery of data. It ensures that data sent down the pipe is received in the same order it was sent. The pipe also imposes flow control to ensure that one end of the pipe doesn't overload the other end with data at a rate faster than it can handle. There is generally no restriction on the number of bytes in the arguments or the results of your remote procedure. In general, the connection provides a reliable way to send data between the client and the server. A broken connection is the only error condition you need to recover from. This problem is discussed in the error-recovery section. The TCP transport has all the attributes of a reliable connection-oriented transport.

A connectionless transport is the opposite of a reliable connection-oriented transport. Packets of data are independently sent out onto the network, instead of through a pipe. There is no guarantee that the packets are received in the order they were sent. It also does not provide a flow control mechanism. The sender can, therefore, dispatch packets at a rate faster than the receiver can handle. This discrepancy can result in packets being lost or duplicated if the sender tries resending the packet. In an unreliable connectionless transport, the receiver doesn't acknowledge the receipt of packets, so the sender does not know if the packet it sent out was ever received. The UDP transport provides unreliable connectionless delivery.

Users of the UDP transport must put error detection and correction code into their application (see the section on error recovery). The packet size, or the amount of data that can be sent out in one operation, is limited for the UDP transport. On SunOS 4.0, the default maximum size of a UDP packet is 9000 bytes, which includes any packet headers required for transmission. The RPC Library further restricts the maximum size of an RPC request over the UDP transport to 8800 bytes. A rule of thumb is not to exceed 8192 bytes, meaning that you cannot send more than 8192 bytes worth of XDR-encoded arguments to the server or you cannot send more than 8192 bytes worth of XDR-encoded results back to the client. Because not all operating systems have the same maximum size for a UDP packet, it is a good idea for your client to determine the server's maximum UDP packet size. You can do this by sending a RPC to the server querying it for maximum packet size that it can handle. The arguments and results of this RPC call should be minimal, less than 512 bytes, to prevent exceeding the servers maximum packet size. If the server maximum packet size is smaller than the largest packet the client will send out, then you need to break up the request into a size the server can handle. The other alternative is to use the TCP transport.

The following code segment shows how to determine the number of bytes used to XDR-encode data into an XDR stream:

```
...
XDR     xdr_handle;
u_int   pos1, pos2;
```

```
...
pos1 = xdr_getpos(&xdr_handle);
if (pos1 == -1) {
        /* Report error and take appropriate action */
}

/* XDR the data objects here */

pos2 = xdr_getpos(&xdr_handle);
if (pos2 == -1) {
        /* Report error and take appropriate action */
}

printf("Bytes used in XDR stream = %d\n", (int)(pos2 - pos1));
...
```

The code segment calls *xdr_getpos()* to get the position of the XDR stream before and after XDR-encoding the data objects. The ending position is then subtracted from the starting position and the result is printed.

Given the differences between the reliable connection-oriented transport and the connectionless transport, you might wonder why anyone would select UDP instead of TCP. The biggest advantage of UDP over TCP is performance. Connections take time to set up and they require state to be maintained on the computer. The state consumes system resources and may result in a connection attempt failing because no more system resources are available. UDP, on the other hand, does not have startup overhead and only consumes system resources when data is sent or received. If your remote procedures require more than 8192 bytes for either the arguments or the results, you may want to use TCP. You could use UDP if you wanted to break up the argument or the results passed into 8192 byte chunks and then turn the one remote procedure call into a number equal to the number of chunks that you have. If your distributed service is constantly sending data between the client and the server, a TCP connection may be more efficient. If the frequency of communication between the the client and server is low, the UDP transport may be best. You can mix the transports used in your services; for example, you might use UDP most of the time to handle communications between the client and the server, and when you need to make a request to transfer a lot of data, you can set up a TCP connection to handle the transfer.

A common question regarding the RPC Library is, "Why isn't

the transport used invisible to users?" The answer is that the RPC Library is flexible because you can select the transport used, and you have greater control over performance and error recovery. You are free to write a layer on top of the RPC Library to isolate transport dependencies. The High-Level RPC Library interface already isolates these dependencies to a certain degree. In general, a library of flexible routines is superior to one containing inflexible routines.

8.2.2 Idempotency and Execute-At-Most-Once Semantics

Idempotency and execute-at-most-once semantics are important concepts that you need to know. Idempotency basically means "repeatability"; an idempotent remote procedure can be repeated. That means, if you call a procedure multiple times with the same arguments, you should always get the same results. An example of an idempotent routine is a simple addition procedure. For example, 2 + 2 always returns 4. Execute-at-most-once semantics refer to a remote procedure that is guaranteed to be executed at most once per call by a client. An example of a routine that requires execute-at-most-once semantics is a remote procedure that moves a file. You can only move the file once. The second time you call the routine with the same arguments, you get an error because the source file no longer exists, provided that another process did not recreate the file between the two invocations. This remote procedure would be non-idempotent. Idempotent routines don't have to be guaranteed execute-at-most-once semantics.

Figure 8.1 shows a sequence of calls made to the *move file* remote procedure. The first call, request A, asks the server to move file A to file B. The server receives the request and processes it. After the server has finished processing request A, it sends a reply back to the client indicating that the request was processed successfully. This reply, for some reason, does not make it back to the client. The client then times out waiting for request A and resends the request. The server processes request A again and then sends back a *source file doesn't exist* error to the client. This time the client receives the request and believes that the move operation had failed when in fact the move had succeeded. The next section

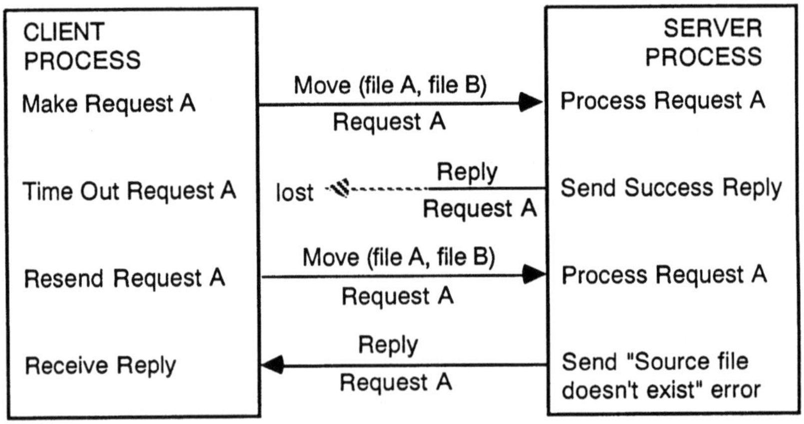

FIGURE 8.1. *Non-idempotent remote procedure example.*

shows how to work around the non-idempotent problem of the *move file* remote procedure.

Idempotency and execute-at-most-once semantics are important in the consideration of the transport to be used and the error-recovery design. If you are using the UDP transport, RPC requests may never arrive at the server, multiple copies may arrive, or requests may arrive out of order. If your remote procedures are idempotent, you don't have to worry about the case of multiple copies arriving or requests arriving out of sequence. There exists an issue of performance, though, which is covered in Section 8.2.5. If you are using the TCP transport, then you are guaranteed that the request arrived, that only one copy of the request arrived, and that multiple requests arrive in the order they were sent. Execute-at-most-once semantics are guaranteed because the remote procedure is only called at most once per request by the client. The only exception is when the TCP connection breaks. This case is discussed in the next section.

8.2.3 Error Recovery

An important issue in designing a distributed application is error recovery. This section deals with errors associated with the use of the RPC Library that were not covered in Chapter 5. These errors deal with the issues discussed in the previous sections regarding transports and with the abnormal termination of either the client or server process. This section only discusses general solutions to the error-recovery problem. Specific solutions are usually application-dependent.

Remember that if you are using the UDP transport, RPC requests may never arrive at the server, multiple copies may arrive, or requests may arrive out of order. If your remote procedures are idempotent, you don't have to worry about the case of multiple copies arriving or requests arriving out of sequence. If your distributed application has non-idempotent remote procedures, then you have a problem. There are ways to work around this problem, but they do not guarantee that you can convert a non-idempotent procedure into an idempotent procedure. One way to work around this problem is to have the server cache replies to a remote procedure request. A reply cache is easy to make. You simply put a unique identifier into every request that the client makes, set up a buffer on the server to cache replies, modify the remote procedure to first check if a reply already exists in the reply cache for the request, and finally have the remote procedure save a reply in the reply cache.

Figure 8.2 shows a client using the *move file* remote procedure that now has a reply cache. This figure is similar to Figure 8.1 except that requests are now numbered, and a reply cache has been added to the server process. The client makes request 1, the server receives request 1 and then checks the reply cache to see if there is a cached reply for request 1. There is no match, so the server processes request 1, in this case successfully. The server copies the request identifier and the success reply to the reply cache and then sends the success reply to the client. This reply is lost, and the client times out on request 1 and resends request 1. The server receives request 1 and checks the reply cache to see if there is a cached reply for request 1. This time there is, so the server sends the cached reply for request 1 back to the client. This algorithm assumes that your server process is single threaded. If your server process is multithreaded you have to modify the above algorithm to take multithreading into account. Also note that the range of the request ID should be much larger than the number of entries in the cache.

By caching the replies, the *move file* remote procedure now

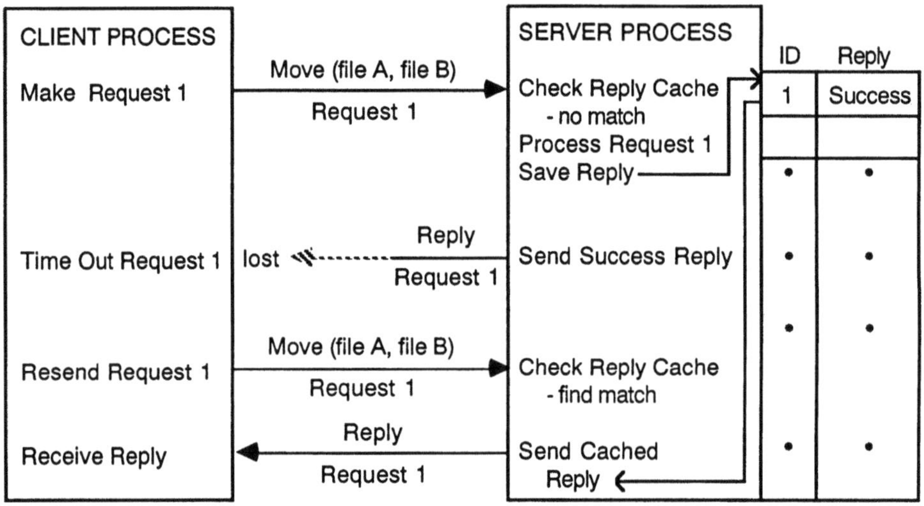

FIGURE 8.2. *Reply cache example.*

appears to be idempotent. Of course, this is not true—the simple protocol can still fail. For example, if the server's reply cache overflows, it will lose cached replies and may repeat a request that should have been satisfied from the cache. Another problem is that the server may crash and then be restarted in which case all the cached replies would be lost. The following discussion will provide some insight to you on the issues associated with using a reply cache. The discussion assumes that the server and client agree on the current time. You can have the client ask the server for the time and compute the time difference between the client's clock and the server's clock, resynchronizing with the server every so often to ensure that the time differential is accurate.

Some issues are associated with the reply-cache approach when it is used in conjunction with a service that employs the UDP transport: What size should the cache be? Should the cache size be static or should it be dynamic? How do you cache large replies? To determine the size of the cache, you need to know the maximum time, in seconds, the client waits for a reply from the server. Let us call this number T. The server can ignore requests that come in that are more than T seconds old because the client has already given up on waiting for a reply from these requests. If you know that the server is processing X requests per second on average then you could allocate a cache that holds (X * T) number of replies. To build a dynamic cache would require keeping a running tab on the number of requests processed per second. Based on the load of the server, you could develop some heuristics to control exactly when the cache would grow and when it would shrink. The value T could be hard-coded in the client and server, but this approach is inflexible. A better way would have the client tell the server what the value of T was when the client first communicated with the server. All clients in a distributed application generally have the same time-out value. If this is not the case, then the server can determine the maximum time-out value, Tmax, given all the time-out values of the clients. The server can then ignore requests that come in that are more than Tmax seconds old. The value of Tmax can change as new clients start communicating with the server and other clients end sessions.

Handling large replies in a reply cache is difficult. Assume that the size of your reply is 8192 bytes; your time-out, T, is 60 seconds; and your server can process 4 requests per second. Your reply cache contains (8192 * 60 * 4) = 1,966,080 bytes—a large cache for just one remote procedure. You could always reduce the number of entries cached, but this could lead to erroneous behavior in your distributed application. If you cannot determine a way to reduce the size of the cache, you may want to use the TCP transport for this remote procedure.

The issue of recovering a reply cache after a server crash is difficult. You could copy the reply cache to a disk drive every few seconds to ensure that a copy of the cache would survive a crash. When the server process comes back up, it could initialize the in-memory reply cache from the copy on the disk drive. The problem with this approach is that there is always a window where the in-memory copy of the cache is newer than the one on the disk drive. As long as this window exists, there is a chance that the network service protocol will fail. Another approach lets the client detect the server crash and take appropriate action to ensure that the protocol functions correctly. You can detect a server crash by having the server return a datum with an RPC reply that is guaranteed to change if the server loses the reply cache. One possible datum is the time that the server was started. The client can then compare the returned datum with the previously returned datum. If they are different, then the client can assume that the server has crashed and that the reply cache was lost. Once the client detects a server crash, it can try to determine if any outstanding RPC requests were executed more than once on the server. This can be difficult to determine depending upon your application.

It is important to remember that a reply cache will not make your non-idempotent procedure idempotent. The cache is simply one possible work around for you when you must implement non-idempotent remote procedures in your distributed application.

Remember that the TCP transport is a reliable connection-oriented transport. It ensures that the packets sent are received in order and that duplicate packets are discarded, and it basically provides a reliable means of sending data between the client and the server. The only error condition that you need to explicitly handle is when the connection is unexpectedly closed, which occurs when either the client or the server process abnormally terminates. If your application tries to send data through the connection, it receives an error. Even worse is that your application process receives the signal *SIGPIPE* if your application persists in writing data in the broken pipe. This signal can result in the termination of your application if you are not prepared to catch it. These semantics depend on the implementation of the sockets mechanism that you are using and are not imposed on you by the RPC Library. The remainder of this discussion refers to a UNIX socket implementation. Refer to your operating-system manual for more information about sockets, signals, and signal handlers.

Re-establishing broken connections between a client and a server when you are using TCP can be tricky. First you must detect the broken connection, and then you can reconnect the client and server. Both your server and your client should always catch the signal *SIGPIPE* to avoid abnormal termination if they try sending data through a broken pipe. You can set a global flag in the signal-catching routine to indicate that the signal has been received. The server can then check this flag if it detected an error while decoding arguments or while sending a reply. The client can detect a broken connection by inspecting the *clnt_stat* value returned after the attempted RPC. The value is set to either *RPC_CANTSEND* or *RPC_CANTRECV*. You can also check to see if the global flag that indicates the receipt of a *SIGPIPE* signal was set. Recovery after a connection breaks on the server is simple. Merely report the error, if desired, and continue on, making sure that you do not try to send data through the broken pipe. You can buffer the data you were going to send the client. If the client reconnects with the server, you can send the data back to the client. Otherwise, the server eventually times the buffer out.

The issue of state recovery is application-dependent. Recovery after a connection breaks on the client can be complicated. You could try to find another server providing the service, you could wait for the server you were using to restart, or you could give up and terminate. If you attempt recovery, you must destroy the client handle that you were using and get a new handle. The reason for destroying the handle is that it contains the port number on which the service was registered (see Chapter 5). You can poll the server computer by calling the *client handle creation* routine every T second intervals. You know the server is back up when the *client handle creation* routine succeeds.

Abnormal termination of the server introduces a recovery problem for your distributed application. The solution to this problem may or may not be difficult depending on your application's design. If your server does not maintain any state about its clients or itself, it can simply be restarted. If the clients didn't make any calls to the server while it was down, they will not even know that the server crashed. If the clients did make calls, they may see some RPC time-outs. If your server maintains state about the clients or about itself, the server must be able to recover this state when it is restarted. The ease of recovery depends on your application and on what is contained in the state.

Server crashes bring up another problem for your distributed application. If you have only one server handling many clients, a server crash can neutralize them all. They may not be able to continue running and just wait for the server to come back up. To improve the fault tolerance of your distributed application, you can have more than one server running on the network. That way when a client detects that its server is no longer responding to RPC requests, it can hunt for another server that provides the same service and use it. This is also referred to as replicating the service. You can refer to [BIRM 89] for more information on replication in distributed systems.

The case of a client's abnormal termination is generally not a problem, other than the client's lack of robustness. The client can

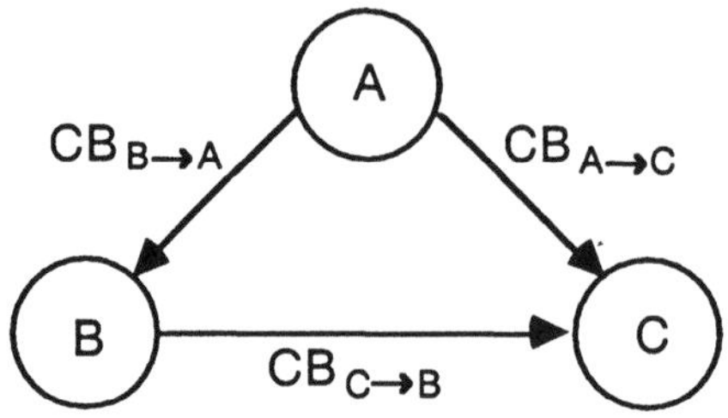

FIGURE 8.3. *Callback RPC deadlock example.*

be restarted, and if the state is saved about the previous client session, the client can load this information and continue from where it left off. This state can be saved on a disk directly accessible by the client or it can be saved on the server. If the state is saved on the server, the client can query the server for any previous state when the client comes up. A problem with this approach is that it assumes the client is restarted. In some situations, the client is not restarted. The server then needs some way to time out the state it is maintaining for the client, so the server can remove the client's state. Otherwise, the server could run out of resources in maintaining the state of crashed clients. For the server to time the client state out, it must know that the client is no longer alive. One way for the server to detect a client's demise is to have the client renew the state on the server. In a physiological analogy, the server feels the client's heartbeat. The server can assume that the client is dead if it hasn't felt a heartbeat in X seconds, where X can be a large or small value, depending on the needs of the distributed application.

8.2.4 Callback Deadlocks

Callback deadlocks can occur when you are using the Callback RPC mechanism. Figure 8.3 shows a scenario that leads to a deadlock. The figure shows three different resources located on computer A, computer B, and computer C. Assume that an RPC service makes the resources available to the network, that it uses callback RPC to access resources on other computers, and that the client calls *svc_run()* when waiting for a callback from the server.

Remember that in callback RPC, the server becomes the client and makes a request to the client which has become a server. In the figure, the network service on computer A becomes a client and makes a call to the network service on computer B that is requesting access to the resource. The network service on computer A cannot process any more requests until its call to computer B is satisfied. In the meantime, the network service on computer B has made a call to the network service on computer C, requesting access to the resource. The service on B cannot process any incoming requests until the request for the resource on computer C is satisfied. In the meantime, the network service on computer C has made a request to the network service on computer A. The service on C will not process any incoming calls until the request to A has been satisfied. A situation now exists where A is waiting for resource B, which is waiting for resource C, which is waiting for resource A. In effect, a callback deadlock exists where the network services on all three computers are waiting for outstanding resource requests that are interdependent on each other. The result is that no resource request is satisfied.

The above example may seem contrived and obvious, but it is important to be careful when you use callback RPC in your application because you may establish interdependencies on resources that could result in a deadlock. A lot of research has been done on deadlocks. The following presents a brief overview of three common techniques for handling deadlocks. They are: avoidance [HAVE 68], detection [OBER 82], and time-out [SPEC 89]. Avoiding deadlocks can be achieved by requesting resources in a canonical order that eliminates cycles. Deadlocks can be detected by analyzing the order of requests and identifying cycles. The time-out approach imposes a maximum amount of time to wait for a callback. If this amount of time is exceeded, then you can assume that a deadlock condition exists.

8.2.5 Performance

As with any software design, performance is an issue in the design of a distributed application. The performance factors this section covers are location of application state, transport used, design of the protocol specification, reduction in the number of

RPC calls made, time-out value selection, client-handle caching, reply caching of idempotent remote procedures, and RPC broadcasts.

Numerous client requests can quickly affect a server's performance when the server has to do a lot of processing for each request. It follows that, by keeping the requests short and the amount of work required by the server for each request low, overall distributed application performance improves. One way of accomplishing this improvement is by letting the client keep track of the progression of requests sent to the server—i.e., letting the client track the state associated with its server interaction. This approach makes sense because in most cases, the client portion of the application is really in charge of the flow of information between the client and the server. The overall workload of the server is reduced, and the server can handle more requests. NFS provides a good example of this concept. The NFS server returns a data object called a *file handle* to the client when a file is accessed for the first time. The client holds on to the *file handle* and returns it as a token in any subsequent request that accesses the same file. The server is thus relieved of the responsibility of maintaining client-specific information about the open file.

As Section 8.2.1 noted, the transport used affects the performance of your distributed application. Sending a UDP packet is currently faster than setting up a TCP connection, sending data, and then tearing down the connection. On the other hand, when you send large bursts of data, it may be faster to use TCP than UDP when you take into account error-detection execution paths that UDP may require and the flow control offered by TCP. Also, the performance of TCP and UDP can vary depending on the implementation of these transports. One way to determine which transport is right for your application is to write a simple program that simulates the RPC calls that your distributed application makes. You can have two versions, one for each transport. Run the program on the computers you intend to use, and measure the performance of the RPC calls. If the performance between the two transports is similar, you can compare the amount of code you would have to write to implement the two different transports. Remember that since transport implementations are constantly being improved, and new transports are being introduced, isolating dependencies on the transport is important so that in the future you can easily switch to another transport.

When you design your client, you may have it create a client handle, make the remote procedure call, and destroy the client handle for every RPC the client makes. The RPC Library routines that create client handles make a RPC to the *portmap* service located on the computer you specified. This means that for every RPC your application makes, two RPCs are actually made to the computer running your server, one implicitly by the client handle creation routine and one by your application. You can improve the performance of your application by caching client handles in the RPC layer of your application. There is one problem that you have to worry about in caching client handles. The client handle contains the port number of your server. In effect, it contains state associated with your server. If your server crashes and comes back up, it most likely has a different port number. To get around this problem, you can simply destroy the client handle, get a new client handle, and retry the operation if you detect an error when you are making a RPC using a cached client handle. This simple enhancement improves the performance of your distributed application.

The design of the protocol specification can affect performance because of the amount of data you want to send over the network and the amount of time it takes to XDR-encode and XDR-decode the data. To maximize performance, you need to minimize the amount of data you send over the network and the frequency at which you send it. The time required to XDR-encode and XDR-decode data is generally not significant. Even so, you can still reduce this time. For example, suppose you have defined the following data type in your protocol specification:

```
struct  user_info {
        char    login[32];
        int     id;
        int     group_ids[32];
};
```

Every time that you send this data type over the network, you XDR-encode and XDR-decode 32 characters for the login, 1 integer for the ID, and 32 integers for the group IDs. The entire 32 characters are encoded for the login regardless of how many characters are actually in the login field. The same is true for the group IDs. This encoding results in 260 bytes being written to the XDR stream. Changing both fields to variable-length declarations reduces the number of potential encodings. This way, only the actual number of elements used would be encoded. The new structure is:

```
struct   user_info {
         char     login<32>;
         int      id;
         int      group_ids<32>;
};
```

The output after using *rpcgen* to compile the declaration is:

```
struct user_info {
        struct {
                u_int login_len;
                char *login_val;
        } login;
        int id;
        struct {
                u_int group_ids_len;
                int *group_ids_val;
        } group_ids;
};
typedef struct user_info user_info;
bool_t xdr_user_info();
```

With this approach you simply set the length value for the login and group IDs members to the actual number contained in the arrays. Now only the amount of data actually being used is XDR-encoded and XDR-decoded. For example if your login name is *jrlogin* and the group IDs are 4, 6, and 8, then the number of bytes XDR-encoded into the stream would be (4 + 7 * 4) + (4) + (4 + 3 * 4) = 52 bytes—a considerable savings over 260 bytes. The parentheses indicate the total encoding size for each member of the structure. Note that 4 bytes was added to the size calculation for the login and group ID members to take into account the 4 byte length specifiers for the variable length arrays that must be encoded into the stream.

You can make another performance enhancement to character-array declarations that store strings. Remember that a character is XDR-encoded into the XDR block size, which is 4 bytes. Instead of declaring strings as character arrays, you can declare them to be string arrays. The result is that the string is copied unencoded into the XDR stream and end-filled so that its length is divisible by the XDR block size. This approach works well if all computers running your distributed application use the ASCII character set. If not, you have to do some type of conversion on incoming and outgoing strings on the computers that do not use ASCII. The preceding example, modified to use the *string* XDR type, is shown below.

```
struct user_info {
        string  login<32>;
        int     id;
        int     group_ids<32>;
};
```

When the login name in the example above is *jrlogin* and the group IDs are 4, 6, and 8, the number of bytes XDR-encoded into the stream is (4 + 7 + 1) + (4) + (4 + 3 * 4) = 32 bytes. Compare this number with the 52 bytes in the previous example. Again, the parentheses indicate the total encoding size for each member of the structure.

Another way to reduce the amount of time your application spends in the XDR routines is by using the XDR In-line macros (covered in Chapter 2). These macros can significantly reduce the amount of time that it takes to encode and decode data. The downside of using these macros is that they are not as robust as the XDR primitive routines they replace because they use single accesses to get the data from the underlying buffer, and fail to operate properly if the data is not correctly aligned. The In-line macros that perform the actual conversions do not return any indication of an error. Also, using these macros requires that you implement your XDR routines instead of having them generated from your protocol specification by *rpcgen*.

You can improve the performance of your server when it is heavily loaded by adding a reply cache to your idempotent routines. This improvement is only useful if you are using the UDP transport. When a server is heavily loaded, RPC requests are being sent from clients and the server is processing the requests as fast as possible, but a backlog develops, and eventually client requests start timing out and the clients resend the requests, making the problem worse. The reply cache helps because the server only processes a request once. If the client resends the request, the server just sends the cached reply.

Once you have implemented your remote procedure, you may be interested in measuring the performance of your distributed application. Many methods of performance measurement are available. You can instrument your application to measure the performance of tasks. For example, to measure the total time of an RPC request, you could get the system time before the RPC call was made and then get the system time after the RPC call was made. The difference between the two time values would yield the time required to make the RPC call. Be sure that the time obtained is sufficiently granular to measure a RPC, which can take less than 5 microseconds to complete. Getting the execution profile of your application is generally an easier method for obtaining a function call graph and timing information about your application. Execution profilers are available with most language compilers. You simply compile your application with the appropriate flags set and then run it. The execution profile data is saved in a file. You can then use a program, such as *prof* or *gprof* on UNIX systems, to display the profile data. The method for execution profiling varies from system to system; consult your operating system and compiler manuals for more information. During the course of performance analysis, you may want to eliminate any overhead associated with the transport. You can use the raw transport to achieve this goal. The raw transport is described in detail in Section 8.3.2.2.

When improperly used by distributed applications, network broadcasts can adversely affect network performance. For example, the network daemon *rwhod* was set up to have each host on the network freely broadcast its user information on the network. This setup proved to be disastrous in a network of diskless computers. Whenever one of these broadcasts was sent, the *rwhod* daemon on all the diskless computers on the network wanted to be swapped in, over the network, at the same time. Multiply this activity by the number of such broadcasts, and you can easily envision the meltdown occurring on the network.

Broadcasts are best used in conjunction with some policy of moderation. The NIS binding program *ypbind* is a good example of this approach. A single broadcast is sent by *ypbind* when it is started. NIS servers only reply if they serve the domain that *ypbind* is interested in, reducing the number of replies to the broadcast. The *ypbind* process binds to a server that responded. All service requests are then directed to that server. If, in the future, the server cannot fulfill the request from the client, *ypbind* starts the binding process again. Note that the *ypbind* process does not broadcast for a server for every request, but only when it is looking for a server.

A better solution to the multidestination network addressing problem is provided by the *multicast* feature. Multicast falls between normal directed network addressing and broadcast addressing by allowing a subset of computers on the network to be assigned common addresses for groups of functions. Only computers that are interested in a particular multicast address receive it when it is sent on the network. Future releases of the RPC Library may have this feature. You could add this feature by modifying the *clnt_broadcast()* routine if you have the source code for the RPC Library, and if the transport provides a way to register for, send, and receive multicasts.

8.2.6 Time-outs

In an ideal network, time-outs would not be necessary because every message sent would be received at the destination. Unfortunately, this is not the case; time-outs are necessary in distributed applications. There are some issues to consider when you determine time-out values for your application. Servers are likely to take varying amounts of time to service individual requests, depending on factors such as server load, network routing, and network congestion. The client should be prepared for a variation of service times. The client should not make loading or congestion problems worse by continually resending requests that have not received replies yet. Rather, one should use some sort of back off strategy of exponentially increasing time-out values.

8.3 Testing Procedures

This section covers testing procedures that you can use in debugging your distributed application. These procedures are not exhaustive, but provide a good introduction and should be used in addition to standard software-testing procedures, such as the implementation of debugging levels and the logging of errors. Thinking about debugging and maintenance issues is useful for all applications but is especially useful in a distributed-application environment in which the distribution of procedures complicates the process of debugging. Planning for these issues while you design your application pays off during the life cycle of your application. Of course, these testing procedures change as new and improved diagnostic tools become available. Also, a good source-code debugger is invaluable for debugging your application.

Two basic ways are available to test your application. The first is to test the application without actually sending requests over the network—referred to as testing without the network component. This way typically involves putting the server and the client into the same process. You can then use a debugger on one computer to test the entire application. This is the recommended way to initially test your application. The second way is with the network component—i.e., having one or more clients communicating with one or more servers. This method can be difficult and is used to debug problems that are not reproducible in single-process testing cases. This section first discusses the utility *rpcinfo* and then covers the two methods of testing.

8.3.1 Rpcinfo

The utility *rpcinfo* is useful for displaying information about network services and testing to see if a particular service has crashed. *Rpcinfo* can be used to list the services registered with the portmapper, to send a remote procedure call to the NULL procedure of a service, or to unregister services with the local portmapper. After obtaining a list of services, you may want to determine if the service has crashed because even though a service shows up on the list, it may have crashed without unregistering itself with the portmapper. To determine if a service has crashed, you can send a remote procedure call to the NULL procedure of a service. If you get a reply then you at least know that the service can accept and dispatch remote procedure calls and that the service has not crashed. If the service has crashed, then you can use *rpcinfo* to unregister the service with the portmapper. To do this, you must have root privileges and be logged into the machine that the service was registered on.

8.3.2 Testing without the Network Component

There are two ways to test without using the actual transport. One is to design the interface to the RPC layer on both the client

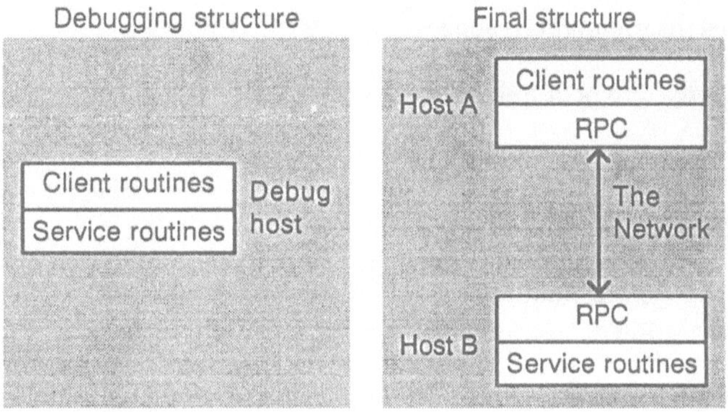

FIGURE 8.4. *Combining client and server routines.*

and server to link them together into a common executable, effectively removing the network. Routine interfaces generated by *rpcgen* are set up to allow you to do this. Figure 8.4 shows a diagram of the union. Another way to test your application without the actual transport is to use the raw transport. A discussion of both approaches, with examples, follows.

8.3.2.1 Linking Client and Server Linking the client program with the server procedures is the easiest approach to testing without the network component. First, you write your protocol specification and run it through *rpcgen*. Then you need to implement all of the client routines, except for the ones *rpcgen* generated for you. Next, build your server procedures. These procedures should have the same functional interface as the client-side routines generated by *rpcgen*. When the coding is complete, link your routines as described in Chapter 7. To generate a debugging version without the network component, simply comment out the client-handle creation calls on the client side and comment out any references to the *rqstp* argument in the server procedures. Then you can link all the client routines (except the ones generated by *rpcgen*) with the server procedures. You can then proceed to debug the testing version of your application. Figure 8.5 shows the *get grade* example from Chapter 7.

Protocol Specification–get_grade.x

```
/*
 * Grade Service Protocol Specification
 *
 * Version 1 Remote Procedures
 *
 *      GET_GRADE
 *              This procedure accepts a student ID number and returns the
 *              corresponding grade. It returns the value NO_GRADE if a
 *              grade was not found.
 */
const   ID_NUM_SIZE = 5;    /* Doesn't include terminating NUL */
const   NO_GRADE = 0;

/*
 * Student ID number
 */
typedef string  stu_id_num<ID_NUM_SIZE>;

program GRADE_PROG {
        version GRADE_VERS_1 {
                char    GET_GRADE(stu_id_num) = 1;
        } = 1;
} = 0x20000000;
```

Grade Client–get_grade.c

```
/*
 * Grade server client, calls the get_grade() remote procedure and prints
 * the results.
 */
#include <stdio.h>
#include <rpc/rpc.h>
#include "get_grade.h"
```

FIGURE 8.5

```
main(argc, argv)
	int	argc;
	char	*argv[]:
{
	CLIENT*clnt_handlep;
	char	*grade;
	int	ret_code;

	if (argc != 3) {
		fprintf(stderr, "usage: %s server_name id#\n", argv[0]);
		return (1);
	}

#ifndef TESTING
	clnt_handlep = clnt_create(argv[1], GRADE_PROG, GRADE_VERS_1,
					"udp");
	if (clnt_handlep == NULL) {
		clnt_pcreateerror(argv[1]);
		return (1);
	}
#endif
	grade = get_grade_1(&argv[2], clnt_handlep);
	if (grade != NULL) {
		if (*grade != NO_GRADE) {
			printf("Your grade is a %c\n", *grade);
			ret_code = 0;
		} else {
			fprintf(stderr, "Could not find your grade\n");
			ret_code = 1;
	}
	} else {
		fprintf(stderr, "Remote procedure call failed\n");
		ret_code = 1;
	}

#ifndef TESTING
	clnt_destroy(clnt_handlep);
#endif
	return (ret_code);
} /* main */
```

FIGURE 8.5 Continued

Server Procedures–grade_proc.c

```
#include <stdio.h>
#include <rpc/rpc.h>
#include "get_grade.h"

#define GRADE_FILE  "grades"
#define NO          0
#define YES         1

char*
get_grade_1 (id_num)
        stu_id_num      *id_num;
{

        static char     grade;
        FILE            *fp;
        char            tmp_id_num[ID_NUM_SIZE + 1];
        int             done;

        done = NO;
        if ((fp = fopen(GRADE_FILE, "r")) !=NULL) {
                while (done == NO && fscanf(fp, "%s %c", tmp_id_num, &grade)
                        != EOF) {
                        if (strncmp(*id_num, tmp_id_num, ID_NUM_SIZE) ==
                           0) {
                                done = YES;
                        }
                }
                fclose(fp);
        } else {
                fprintf(stderr, "Cannot open file: %s\n", GRADE_FILE);
        }

        if (done == NO) {
                grade = NO_GRADE;
        }
        return (&grade);
} /* get_grade */
```

FIGURE 8.5 Continued

Note the addition of the conditional compilation statements in the *get_grade.c* module, which enables you to make an easy transition between the test version and the distributed version. The following line compiles and links the debugging version:

```
% cc -g -DTESTING -c get_grade.c
% cc -g -DTESTING -c grade_proc.c
% cc -g -o tester get_grade.o grade_proc.o
```

You are now ready to debug the *tester* program using a source level debugger.

8.3.2.2 Raw Transport Another way to put the client and server into the same process is by using the raw transport. This transport is provided for testing your application and measuring its performance. It is a memory-based transport, which means that no information actually goes out over the network. It also lets you determine the amount of time it takes for a round trip RPC call, independent of the transport used and any of the associated operating system overhead. You can only use the raw transport if the XDR encoded size of any of the arguments or results does not exceed the value UDPMSGSIZE, the maximum size of a UDP packet. This restriction exists regardless of the transport for which your application was designed.

Below are the synopses for the two raw routines followed by the steps you need to perform to modify your application to use the raw transport.

*SVCXPRT **
svcraw_create()

This routine creates a RPC service transport handle and returns a pointer to it. The routine returns NULL if it fails. The transport is really a buffer within the address space of the calling process. The corresponding RPC client should reside in the same process.

*CLIENT **
clntraw_create(prognum, versnum)
u_long prognum, versnum;

This routine creates a RPC client handle for the argument *prognum*, and *versnum*. The routine returns a pointer to the client handle if it succeeds and NULL if it fails. The transport used to pass messages to the service is actually a buffer within the address space of the calling process. The corresponding RPC client should reside in the same process.

You need to follow several steps to modify your application to run with the raw transport. Figure 8.6 shows the modified modules from the example in the previous section converted to use the raw transport.

As in the previous example, conditional compilation statements were added to the code to facilitate an easy transition between generating the testing version and the distributed version. The client was modified to call the *main* routine in the server, which was renamed to *svc_main()*, and to call the *clntraw_create()* routine to create the client handle. The *main* routine was renamed to prevent a name-space collision with the main routine in the client. On the server side, the remote procedures were renamed to prevent a name-space collision with the client stubs generated by *rpcgen*. In this case there was only one procedure *get_grade_1()*. The *svcudp_create()* call was replaced with a call to *svcraw_create()* and the initialization of a TCP transport was removed. The call to *svc_register()* was modified to pass in a NULL value for the protocol argument because the protocol was bypassed. Also, the call to *svc_run()* was removed because it was not necessary to wait for requests. The only modification to the server procedure module *grade_proc.c* was to add the preprocessor macro definition that changed the name of the server procedure from *get_grade_1()* to *svc_get_grade_1()*.

Note: The raw transport does not work properly in the SunOS 4.0 RPC Library. It has been fixed in the SunOS 4.1 RPC Library and in the Transport Independent RPC source distribution.

Grade Client–get_grade.c

```
/*
 * Grade server client, calls the get_grade() remote procedure and prints
 * the results.
 */
#include <stdio.h>
#include <rpc/rpc.h>
#include "get_grade.h"

main(argc, argv)
        int             argc;
        char            *argv[];
{
```

FIGURE 8.6

```
        CLIENT          *clnt_handlep;
        char            *grade;
        int             ret_code;

#ifdef  TESTING
        svc_main();
#endif

        if (argc != 3) {
                fprintf(stderr, "usage: %s server_name id#\n", argv[0]);
                return (1);
        }

#ifdef  TESTING
        clnt_handlep = clntraw_create(GRADE_PROG, GRADE_VERS_1);
#else
        clnt_handlep = clnt_create(argv[1], GRADE_PROG, GRADE_VERS_1,
                                "udp");
#endif
        if (clnt_handlep == NULL) {
                clnt_pcreateerror(argv[1]);
                return (1);
        }

        grade = get_grade_1(&argv[2], clnt_handlep);
        if (grade != NULL) {
                if (*grade != NO_GRADE) {
                        printf("Your grade is a %c\n", *grade);
                        ret_code = 0;
                } else {
                        fprintf(stderr, "Could not find your grade\n");
                        ret_code = 1;
                }
        } else {
                fprintf(stderr, "Remote procedure call failed\n");
                ret_code = 1;
        }

        clnt_destroy(clnt_handlep);
        return (ret_code);
} /* main */
```

FIGURE 8.6 Continued

Server Skeleton–get_grade_svc.c

```
#include <stdio.h>
#include <rpc/rpc.h>

/*
 * If generating a testing version, then rename the get_grade_1()
 * procedure.
 */
#ifdef  TESTING
#define get_grade_1     svc_get_grade_1
#endif
#include "get_grade.h"

static void grade_prog_1();

#ifdef  TESTING
svc_main()
#else
main()
#endif
{
        SVCXPRT *transp;
#ifdef  TESTING
        transp = svcraw_create();
#else
        (void)pmap_unset(GRADE_PROG, GRADE_VERS_1);
        transp = svcudp_create(RPC_ANYSOCK);
#endif
        if (transp == NULL) {
                (void)fprintf(stderr, "cannot create udp service.\n");
                exit(1);
        }

#ifdef  TESTING
        if (!svc_register(transp, GRADE_PROG, GRADE_VERS_1, grade_prog_1,
           NULL)) {
#else
        if (!svc_register(transp, GRADE_PROG, GRADE_VERS_1,
           grade_prog_1,IPPROTO_UDP)) {
#endif
                (void)fprintf(stderr, "unable to register (GRADE_PROG,
                GRADE_VERS_1, udp).\n");
                exit(1);
        }
```

FIGURE 8.6 Continued

```
#ifndef TESTING
        transp = svctcp_create(RPC_ANYSOCK, 0, 0);
        if (transp == NULL) {
                (void)fprintf(stderr, "cannot create tcp service.\n");
                exit(1);
        }
        if (!svc_register(transp, GRADE_PROG, GRADE_VERS_1, grade_prog_1,
           IPPROTO_TCP)) {
                (void)fprintf(stderr, "unable to register (GRADE_PROG,
                GRADE_VERS_1, tcp).\n");
                exit(1);
        }

        svc_run();
        (void)fprintf(stderr, "svc_run returned\n");
        exit(1);
#endif
}

static void
grade_prog_1(rqstp, transp)
        struct svc_req  *rqstp;
        SVCXPRT         *transp;
{
        union {
                        stu_id_num get_grade_1_arg;
        } argument;
        char            *result;
        bool_t          (*xdr_argument)(), (*xdr_result)();
        char            *(*local)();

        switch (rqstp->rq_proc) {
        case NULLPROC:
                (void)svc_sendreply(transp, xdr_void, (char*)NULL);
                return;

        case GET_GRADE:
                xdr_argument = xdr_stu_id_num;
                xdr_result = xdr_char;
                local = (char *(*)() get_grade_1;
                break;
```

FIGURE 8.6 Continued

```
	default:
		svcerr_noproc(transp);
		return;
	}
	bzero((char *)&argument, sizeof(argument));
	if (!svc_getargs(transp, xdr_argument, &argument)) {
		svcerr_decode(transp);
		return;
	}
	result = (*local)(&argument, rqstp);
	if (result != NULL && !svc_sendreply(transp, xdr_result, result)) {
		svcerr_systemerr(transp);
	}
	if (!svc_freeargs(transp, xdr_argument, &argument)) {
		(void)fprintf(stderr, "unable to free arguments\n");
		exit(1);
	}
}
```

Server Procedures–grade_proc.c

```
#include <stdio.h>
#include <rpc/rpc.h>
#include "get_grade.h"

#define GRADE_FILE	"grades"
#define NO		0
#define YES		1

char *
get_grade_1(id_num)
	stu_id_num	*id_num;
{

	static char grade;
	FILE	*fp;
	char	tmp_id_num[ID_NUM_SIZE + 1];
	int	done;

	done = NO;
```

FIGURE 8.6 Continued

```
	if ((fp = fopen(GRADE_FILE, "r")) != NULL) {
		while (done == NO && fscanf(fp, "%s %c", tmp_id_num,
			&grade) != EOF) {
			if (strncmp(*id_num, tmp_id_num, ID_NUM_SIZE) ==
			   0) {
				done = YES;
			}
		}
		fclose(fp);
	} else {
		fprintf(stderr, "Cannot open file: %s\n", GRADE_FILE);
	}

	if (done == NO) {
		grade = NO_GRADE;
	}
	return (&grade);
} /* get_grade */
```

FIGURE 8.6 Continued

8.3.3 Testing with the Network Component

You are now ready to test your application with the network component—once you have verified that it works by testing without the network component. You may find that you still have bugs in the server and the client. Generally these bugs are due to sequence and/or state issues related to your distributed application. In other words, the bug is only seen when more than one client and potentially more than one server are involved. Sometimes these bugs can be difficult to isolate. It is important to have sufficient debugging levels and error reporting in both the server and the client to help you in isolating the cause of the bug. This section provides some useful procedures for debugging your application over the network.

An important thing to know when debugging your distributed application is whether or not your server is running, and if not, why. You can verify that the operating system kernel on the computer on which your server is running is up by using the *ping* program that is available on most computers that run with networks. The *ping* program sends a network low level echo request, "ping," to the computer specified as its argument. If the ping is successful, you know that the computer is up and accepting network requests and that the network itself is operational. You can now verify that the *portmap* program is running on the remote computer and that your server program responds to requests to the NULL procedure by using the *rpcinfo* program. Here is an example invocation:

```
rpcinfo -u servername 100003 1
```

This example results in a request to the *portmap* program on the computer named *servername* to determine the port number to use for the RPC service registered as program number 100003 and version number 1. The program number and version number are interpreted as decimal numbers. The *rpcinfo* program then uses this information to send a request to the NULL procedure, using the UDP transport—indicated by the *-u* flag. If the reply comes back, you know that all your application-dispatching code is operational and that your application is ready to work. If there is still a problem, it is most likely in the application itself; it might be useful to debug it by removing the network component as discussed in Section 8.3.2. Asking the *portmap* program if a service is up or not does not always provide reliable information because servers may die without informing the *portmap* program. You really need to ping the NULL procedure of the service to determine whether the service is actually up or not.

Debugging server problems can be tricky. You quickly find out that your client times out on RPC requests when you set breakpoints in your server procedures. This is not a problem when you just want to catch one procedure call to the server. It becames a problem when a sequence of RPC requests to the server is required before the server fails. You need to determine what this sequence of calls is or a way to detect the problem through the analysis of data within the server. If you know the sequence or the byte(s) of data that are modified that result in the server failure, you can then add a condition statement within your server that detects the failure condition. You can set your breakpoint within this condition to examine the state of the server and when the breakpoint is hit, stop all clients and related servers to evaluate the current state of your distributed application. The information provided should help you to locate the problem, or at the least help you to determine a better place to set the breakpoint.

A protocol tester can be a useful tool when you debug your server. In the context of RPCs, a protocol tester is simply a program or set of programs that exercises the remote procedures provided by a service. Protocol testers can be simple or they can be complex. Simple testers verify that the remote procedure properly interpreted requests. A complex tester verifies that a related sequence of requests executed properly.

8.4 Exercises

1. Implement a network service that maintains a schedule for conference room usage. The service should let you reserve the conference room for a specified amount of time. What happens when the test to see if the conference room has already been scheduled for the specified time does not occur in the same remote procedure call that reserves the conference room?
2. Implement a network service that provides your application with the information necessary to build a map showing the computers on the network.
3. What can be done to make the examples in Chapters 5 and 6 more robust?

Future Directions of RPC Programming

9

Distributed computing is the wave of the future. More and more users are connecting their computers over networks. Small networks are being interconnected to form larger networks. Corporate-wide networks are now commonplace, as are campus-wide networks at universities. These networks are typically connected with outside networks to a global computer network.

Distributed computing enables you to construct a flexible computing environment. It allows information to flow between your computer and other computers on the network. Distributed computing gives you access to resources that might not be available on your computer. The exchange of information between computers that are not interconnected takes place through other media, typically magnetic tape, which is usually not as fast as sending the data over a network. Of course, sending certain types of information via magnetic tape, such as the distribution of a new operating system, can be more practical than sending it over the network. For other types of information, though, magnetic tape is impractical—for example, sending electronic mail.

This chapter covers some improvements that can be made to the existing RPC Library. It provides an overview of RPC-related standardization efforts, examines the Transport Independent (TI) version of the RPC Library, and concludes with a discussion of useful tools for distributed-application developers.

9.1 RPC Library

The RPC mechanism is a fundamental part of distributed computing. This mechanism or a similar message-passing scheme will serve as the building blocks of tomorrow's distributed applications, so the mechanism must be flexible. Sun's RPC protocol specification and RPC Library give you this flexibility. The RPC protocol can be modified via a version scheme similar to what you use to build a new version of your distributed application. Because this protocol specification is publicly available, you are free to develop your own version of the RPC Library. You can even get the source code for the current Library as a model for your own; you do not have to start from scratch.

The current RPC Library has served and continues to serve the user community well, especially considering that it was released in 1985. Some additional capabilities that would be desirable in a new implementation of the RPC Library are: manycast support, asynchronous RPC Library routines, support in a lightweight process environment, providing execute-at-most-once semantics, and removing the packet size restriction for the datagram transport (UDP). A manycast RPC is similar to a broadcast RPC except that instead of going to all computers on the local network, the caller simply supplies a list of computers to send the RPC to. Manycasting is more flexible than broadcasting because it puts no restrictions on the location of the servers. With broadcast RPC, the servers must be on the same physical network. Manycasting is also less demanding on networking resources. Asynchronous RPC Library routines perform the request portion of an RPC but do not wait for the reply; instead they return control to the caller of the library routine. The caller then calls another RPC Library routine to determine when the results from the RPC have been returned by the server. Depending on your application needs, this mechanism may be more convenient than Callback RPC. Lightweight process environments are becoming popular and are available on many different operating systems. In a lightweight process environment, the server can generate a new process thread for each incoming RPC request, allowing the server to process more than one request at a time. This is more convenient and computationally cheaper than forking a new process for every incoming request. The client could also take advantage of threads, generating a new process thread for a RPC request and allowing the client to continue processing while waiting for a response from the request.

You can probably think of some other features that you would like to see in an RPC implementation. The problem with everybody implementing their own version of the RPC Library is that porting your distributed application to other computers that have a different RPC Library becomes difficult. Of course, if you ported your version of the RPC Library first, then your application would run; but this is not a good idea as it wastes time having to port your library to other computers. It would be simpler if every software vendor sold a version of the RPC Library that used a standard RPC Library API. If this standard existed and you still wanted to add new functionality, you could always do so, but you would have to keep in mind that adding new functionality may be nonportable. It is best to isolate dependencies on the nonportable functionality to make the job of porting to another platform easier. You simply have to evaluate the delimited nonportable code to determine how to port it. The rest of the code ports without effort. The next section discusses the RPC standardization efforts.

9.2 Standardization

As the use of the different RPC mechanisms becomes more widespread, the need for a standard increases. Not only does the RPC protocol need to be standardized, but so does the API. The standardization of the RPC protocol will allow distributed applications using different RPC mechanisms to interoperate. The beneficiaries of a protocol standard are end-users. The standardization of the API will increase the portability of distributed applications to different platforms that have different RPC libraries. The beneficiaries of an API standard are distributed-application developers.

The bottom line is that standards can save both end-users and distributed application developers time. This savings in time translates to monetary savings. If an RPC protocol standard existed, you could then write clients for other vendors' servers, or you could write servers for other vendors' clients. You would not have to worry about the interoperability of different RPC mechanisms. An API standard would allow you to simply take the source of your application over to a different vendor's computer and recompile it. You could be assured that the RPC library calls were supported on the other vendor's computer and that the semantics of the calls were the same.

Two fundamental types of standards are found in the computing industry: *de facto* and *de jure* [STAL 87]. De facto (Latin for "according to the fact") standards arise out of user support. In the world of distributed file systems (DFS), NFS became the most widely used DFS and therefore became the de facto standard for DFSs. De jure (Latin for "according to law") standards are generated by standards organizations. These organizations may be supported by national governments, corporations, or users. De jure standards can be further subdivided into voluntary and involuntary. Voluntary standards do not compel users to use them. The standards are adapted by industry if it perceives a benefit to employing them. By contrast involuntary, or regulatory, standards are developed by government agencies to satisfy a public objective. Industry is required by law to use these standards.

UNIX has become a popular operating system, and System V Release 4 (SVR4) by AT&T is the de facto standard for UNIX operating systems. SVR4 includes a modified version of Sun's RPC Library. This version of the library is sometimes referred to as Transport Independent RPC or simply TI RPC. TI RPC may become the de facto standard for RPC, at least in the UNIX arena, because of the widespread acceptance of SVR4 and the popularity of Sun's RPC Library.

Of the several standards organizations in the world today, the two that are most likely to steer the RPC standardization efforts are the International Organization for Standardization (ISO) and the Institute of Electrical and Electronics Engineers (IEEE) P1003 Portable Operating Systems Environment Committee (POSIX). ISO is an international agency that develops a wide range of standards. It is a voluntary, nontreaty organization whose members are designated standards bodies of participating nations and nonvoting observer organizations. IEEE is the largest professional organization in the world. In addition to publishing journals and running conferences, IEEE has a standardization group that develops standards in the area of electrical engineering and computing. IEEE formed the P1003 committee to define a portable operating systems environment. Voting status is given to members of the committee that are members of IEEE or the IEEE Computer Society. Work is under way to get the POSIX standards adapted by ISO. The following sections give a brief overview of the RPC standardization efforts of both organizations.

9.2.1 RPC and ISO

In 1984, the ISO developed the Open Systems Interconnection (OSI) model, a computer communications architecture. This

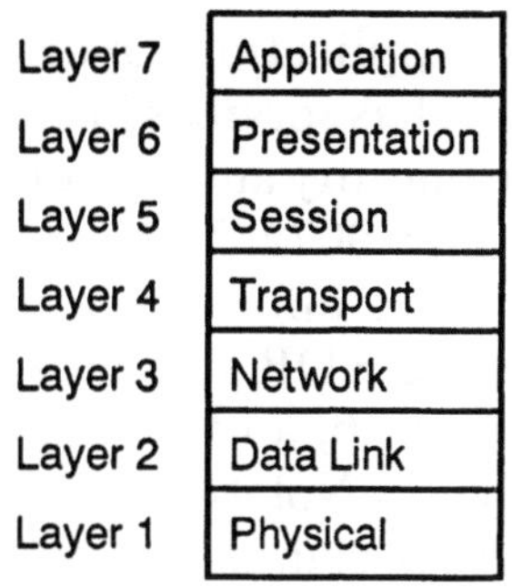

FIGURE 9.1. *OSI reference model.*

model contains seven conceptual layers and is illustrated in Figure 9.1. Layer seven, the Application Layer, is the window between the OSI model and the local system environment where the distributed applications reside. Layer six, the Presentation Layer, provides independence to your application process from data-representation differences between the different computers your application runs on; the XDR mechanism provides a similar service. Layer five, the Session Layer, provides the control structure for communication between applications and establishes, manages, and terminates connections between applications. The RPC mechanism provides a similar service. Figure 9.2 shows where RPC and XDR might fit into the OSI model. Although the current RPC mechanism does not fit the OSI model, it could be rewritten so that it does.

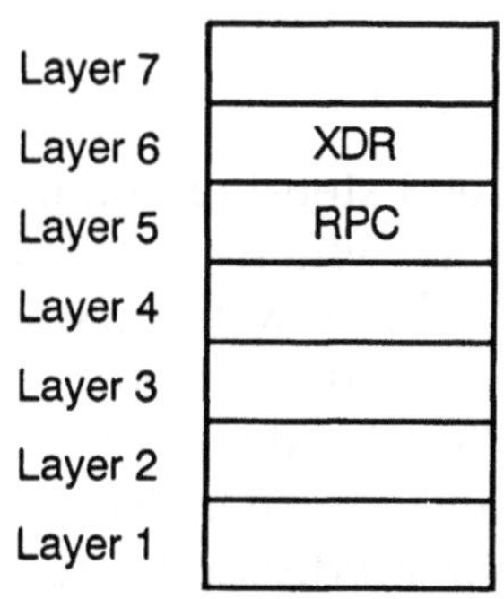

FIGURE 9.2. *RPC and XDR in the OSI model.*

ISO has adopted the Remote Operations Service Element (ROSE), which is an application layer entity similar to an RPC mechanism. The ROSE has services for interactive types of communications that involve enquiry and response actions. ROSE is specified in the ISO/IEC DIS 9072. You can refer to these documents or to [FOLT 89] for more information on ROSE.

As noted above, the XDR standard is comparable to the OSI Presentation Layer, layer 6, and is roughly analogous in purpose to the ISO Abstract Syntax Notation 1 (ASN.1). The ASN.1 notation is described in the ISO standard 8824. The rules for encoding ASN.1 data structures to a bit stream for transmission are described in the ISO standard 8825. The major difference between these two is that XDR uses implicit typing, while ASN.1 uses explicit typing. Implicit typing means that both the sender and receiver know the format of the data. A protocol defines the data type of the information—i.e., the RPC protocol specification. Explicit typing means that the data being transmitted is self-describing—that is some information at the beginning indicates the data type of the information to follow. With ASN.1 you can develop a distributed application that can handle a dynamic protocol. In other words, the parameters or results of a remote procedure do not have to be of a fixed type. With ASN.1, the parameters and results can be self-describing. You could also use XDR to implement a dynamic protocol by defining data type identifiers that went into the XDR stream followed by the data type. The XDR decode routine could then decode the data type identifier and determine how to decode the data type that follows. Flexibility is an important difference between ASN.1 and XDR. With XDR you can implement explicit typing. You cannot implement implicit typing with ASN.1.

9.2.2 RPC and POSIX

In 1988, the P1003 steering committee started several new working groups, one of which would develop an IEEE POSIX networking standard. This new group was called the P1003.8 working group. Under the P1003 standards organization, the working group actually specifies the standard, and the balloting group approves it. The balloting group consists of the voting members. This working group further subdivided into several subcommittees to handle the different aspects of the networking standard. One of the subcommittees was given the task of standardizing remote procedure call mechanisms. The exact charter and goals for this subcommittee remain to be defined, but the hope is that it will deliver a timely draft of the standard. You can obtain more information on the current status of the working group from IEEE.

9.3 Transport-Independent RPC

The original implementation of the Sun RPC Library used only the UDP and TCP transports. The implementation was not based on particular aspects of the underlying transport, but rather on a class of transports. UDP represented the datagram, or connectionless, transport class and TCP represented the connection-oriented transport. However, as the RPC implementation progressed, certain TCP/IP specific features, mainly addressing, found their way into the RPC Library and the application writer had to be aware of some of the low level details of network communication. The Transport Independent (TI) version of the RPC Library was introduced to remove any transport dependencies from the RPC Library and is currently being shipped with AT&T's SVR4.

TI RPC permits selection of the transports at runtime, depending on configurable options. The programming interface is backward-compatible with older versions of the RPC Library, while providing the flexibility of a newer model. Instead of using a socket-based mechanism, the TI RPC Library uses the Transport Layer Interface (TLI) which is based upon the STREAMS input/output mechanism. The new TI RPC architecture allows transports to be added as they become available, without the need to modify existing transport-independent RPC-based applications.

This section provides a brief overview of TI RPC. Refer to [SAMA 89] for more detailed information on the TI RPC architecture and implementation.

9.3.1 Transport Selection Mechanism

The transport selection mechanism provides a way to choose the transport to be used by the application. Each transport belongs to a class, such as datagram or circuit-oriented. You can specify either a specific transport required for the application or a particular class of transport, or you could leave the decision up to the user at runtime. Each computer has a configuration file, */etc/netconfig*, which lists the available transports, and each user can specify a personal preference list of transports with an environment variable, *NETPATH*. If you do not specify a transport, transport selection occurs at runtime when your distributed application creates a transport handle. For this case *NETPATH* is used in conjunction with the */etc/netconfig* file to determine the appropriate transport to use.

The existing *clnt_create()* call is used to access a given transport from a specified class of transports. The *nettype* argument specifies the choice and can be one of the following values:

- VISIBLE — Selects *visible* transports from */etc/netconfig*. Visible transports are available to applications. Some transports may not be specified as visible because the transport is being tested or is only for experimental use. VISIBLE should be used by applications that want to use the transports listed in the *netconfig* file and do not care about the user's preference.
- CIRCUIT_V — Same as *VISIBLE*, except that it restricts the choice to connection-oriented transports.
- DATAGRAM_V — Same as *VISIBLE*, except that it restricts the choice to datagram transports.
- NETPATH — Selects transports from *NETPATH* environment variable, defaults to *VISIBLE* if *NETPATH* is not set. This should be used by those applications that care about the user's preference.
- CIRCUIT_N — Same as *NETPATH*, except that it restricts the choice to connection-oriented transports.
- DATAGRAM_N — Same as *NETPATH*, except that it restricts the choice to datagram transports.
- udp — Uses the UDP transport (provided for backward compatibility).
- tcp — Uses the TCP transport (provided for backward compatibility).

Old Routines	New Routines
clnttcp_create(), clntudp_create()	clnt_tli_create()
svctcp_create(), svcudp_create()	svc_tli_create()
callrpc()	rpc_call()
registerrpc()	rpc_reg()
clnt_broadcast()	rpc_broadcast()

FIGURE 9.3. *Comparison of some of the old and new library routines.*

A new RPC Library routine *svc_create()* uses similar semantics for transport-independent RPC on the server.

9.3.2 Rpcbind

The program *rpcbind* provides a registry of addresses of RPC servers running on a computer. This eliminates the need for each RPC service to have a well known transport address. *rpcbind* provides a convienent way to do RPC binding. Clients can find out the address of the service at run time by contacting the *rpcbind* program running on the remote computer. The client can then find service addresses, and convert to the format required by the transport used for the RPC request. However, its usage is not required if the client has some other means of finding the server address.

9.3.3 Backward Compatibility

The TI RPC Library is backward compatible with earlier versions of the RPC Library. The routines from the SunOS 4.0 RPC Library have been implemented in terms of the newer TLI-based interface. Figure 9.3 lists some of the old and new library routines.

Remember that the 4.0 implementation is based on sockets. Applications that do not make explicit socket system calls on socket descriptors that are used by the RPC Library are source compatible with the TI RPC Library. Applications that make socket system calls require some minor changes.

The new binding service *rpcbind* (version 3) is backward compatible with *portmap* (version 2). Services using the UDP or

TCP transports that are registered with *portmap* also get registered with *rpcbind* and vice-versa.

9.4 Distributed Development Tools

Currently, the software industry does not provide a complete set of tools to distributed-application developers. To develop distributed applications effectively, you need an integrated environment that takes an idea from conception to production. The environment should provide the following functions:

- Functional Specification
- Design Specification and Validation
- Prototyping
- Simulation
- Code Generation
- Testing
- Debugging
- Performance Analysis

The first step in any engineering task is the definition of goals. A tool should exist that allows you to put your goals into the system and use them later to verify that you have satisfied them. The tool could also verify that you are staying focused as your project progresses. Not every software project starts out with well-defined goals, but you should be able to specify your initial goals and update them as the project develops. This process would be similar to a directed search strategy for your goals.

The design specification and validation tool would allow you to specify your design. The tool should work with a variety of methodologies and allow you to select the best one for the problem you were trying to solve. The design-validation tool would validate your design. Because the design and prototyping phases of a project are interrelated, as you are specifying the design, you will have questions about the best possible approach for solving a given problem. Use of the prototyping tool would answer your questions.

With a prototyping tool, you could quickly test different approaches that would satisfy your goals. The prototypes would not have to be full-scale; ideally they could consist of the minimum functions required to simulate them. You wouldn't have to write any code, you could just provide the specifications you wanted. The prototyping tool would link with the simulator and the performance-analysis tools. The simulator would let you analyze the behavior of the prototype. The performance analysis tool would give you the anticipated performance of this approach. Both pieces of information are necessary to make an informed decision about the best approach to use.

A simulation tool would simulate a design or prototype, and would give you a chance to analyze the behavior of your design before you had written any code. Ideally the simulator should support local and remote interaction. A local simulation would only run on one computer. A remote simulation would run on more than one computer and would send requests over the network. The simulator could help you detect and remove any bugs in your design.

A code-generation tool would take your design specification and generate the actual code. The tool would be flexible and give you the ability to post-process the generated code or write your own functions to be included with the generated code. The code generator needs to generate high quality code—otherwise nobody would use it.

A testing tool would process your design specification and determine the best way to test your application. It would then generate an automated tester you could use to verify the correctness of your application. Because a distributed application might require many test cases to verify the correctness of the implementation, a prohibitive amount of time would be required to fully test the application. The tester could prioritize the tests and let you specify how much time you wanted to spend testing the application.

A distributed application debugger should be able to handle more than one debugging session concurrently and should allow debugging at the source code level. The processes being debugged could either be local or remote. You should be able to set breakpoints in one process based on an event in another process. A debugger with these functions would be invaluable to you.

A performance analysis tool should be able to generate performance numbers for your application. This tool would be invaluable in verifying that your application satisfied the performance requirements set in your goal specification. This tool should also integrate with the simulator and prototyping tool.

The environment described above will allow distributed applications to be developed in a short period of time. Some of the tools discussed above are already available today. For example, design specification and validation tools are available, as are basic debuggers and simulators. Not everybody may agree on what goes into the "ideal" distributed application development environment, but most will agree that this environment is needed.

Sun RPC Information

Appendix
1

A1.1 RPC Source Code Availability

The source code for the SunOS 4.0 RPC and XDR Library, referred to as RPCSRC 4.0, is a license-free version of Sun's RPC and XDR Library. RPCSRC is available free to anyone with access to the Internet via an anonymous file-transfer program (ftp) login from one of the RPCSRC archive sites. Because the archive sites change over time, consult your local system administrator for more information on locating an archive site and on using the Internet. You can also obtain RPCSRC 4.0 directly from Sun for a nominal processing fee. The part numbers are:

RPC-4.0-X-X-5 RPCSRC on 1/4-inch tape
RPC-4.0-X-X-6 RPCSRC on 1/2-inch tape

In the future, new releases of the RPC and XDR Library will be available from RPCSRC archive sites.

A1.2 RPC Program Numbers

Program numbers are assigned in groups of 0x20000000 according to the following chart:

Program Number	Description
0x00000000 - 0x1FFFFFFF	Defined by Sun Microsystems
0x20000000 - 0x3FFFFFFF	Defined by User
0x40000000 - 0x5FFFFFFF	Transient
0x60000000 - 0x7FFFFFFF	Reserved
0x80000000 - 0x9FFFFFFF	Reserved
0xA0000000 - 0xBFFFFFFF	Reserved
0xC0000000 - 0xDFFFFFFF	Reserved
0xE0000000 - 0xFFFFFFFF	Reserved

Sun Microsystems administers the first group of numbers, which should be identical for all users of Sun's RPC Library, to ensure that the global program numbers are unique. If you develop an application that might be of general interest, or that might become a product, then you should obtain a program number from the first range. The second group of numbers is reserved for applications specific to you, in that these applications are only running on your network. This range is intended primarily for developing new programs. If you develop internal distributed applications, then somebody within your organization should maintain these numbers to ensure that two different applications do not try to use the same program number. The third group is reserved for applications that generate program numbers dynamically, such as applications that use Callback RPC. The final groups are reserved for future use, and should not be used. Blocks of numbers are also available for assignment to companies for use internally or for assignment to your customers.

To obtain a unique RPC program number and to optionally register a protocol specification, send a request by electronic mail to *rpc@sun* or write to: RPC Administrator, Sun Microsystems, 2550 Garcia Ave., Mountain View, CA 94043

Below is a list of the RPC program numbers that have been assigned and are public. On Unix systems, these program numbers are usually found in the file */etc/rpc*.

portmapper	100000 portmap sunrpc
rstatd	100001 rstat rup perfmeter
rusersd	100002 rusers
nfs	100003 nfsprog
ypserv	100004 ypprog
mountd	100005 mount showmount
ypbind	100007
walld	100008 rwall shutdown
yppasswdd	100009 yppasswd
etherstatd	100010 etherstat
rquotad	100011 rquotaprog quota rquota
sprayd	100012 spray
3270_mapper	100013
rje_mapper	100014
selection_svc	100015 selnsvc
database_svc	100016
rexd	100017 rex
alis	100018

sched	100019	
llockmgr	100020	
nlockmgr	100021	
x25.inr	100022	
statmon	100023	
status	100024	
bootparam	100026	
ypupdated	100028	ypupdate
keyserv	100029	keyserver
tfsd	100037	
nsed	100038	
nsemntd	100039	
Netlicense	100062	rpc.netlicd

The following chart lists the currently used authentication numbers:

Authentication Number	Description
0	None
1	UNIX-style
2	Short hand UNIX-style
3	DES

Sun Microsystems administers the entire range of authentication numbers. If you develop a new authentication flavor and wish to reserve the authentication number, then you should obtain a unique authentication number. Blocks of numbers are also available for assignment to companies. The procedure for obtaining an authentication number is the same as for obtaining a program number.

External Data Representation Standard: Protocol Specification

Appendix 2

A2.1 Status of This Standard

Note: This appendix specifies a protocol that Sun Microsystems, Inc., and others are using. It has been designated RFC1014 by the ARPA Network Information Center.

A2.2 Introduction

XDR is a standard for the description and encoding of data. It is useful for transferring data between different computer architectures, and has been used to communicate data between such diverse machines as the Sun Workstation, VAX, IBM-PC, and Cray. XDR fits into the ISO presentation layer, and is roughly analogous in purpose to X.409, ISO Abstract Syntax Notation. The major difference between these two is that XDR uses implicit typing, while X.409 uses explicit typing.

XDR uses a language to describe data formats. The language can be used only to describe data; it is not a programming language. This language allows one to describe intricate data formats in a concise manner. The alternative of using graphical representations (itself an informal language) quickly becomes incomprehensible when faced with complexity. The XDR language itself is similar to the C language [1], just as Courier [4] is similar to Mesa. Protocols such as Sun RPC (Remote Procedure Call) and the NFS (Network File System) use XDR to describe the format of their data.

The XDR standard makes the following assumption: that bytes (or octets) are portable, where a byte is defined to be 8 bits of data. A given hardware device should encode the bytes onto the various media in such a way that other hardware devices may decode the bytes without loss of meaning. For example, the Ethernet standard suggests that bytes be encoded in "little-endian" style [2], or least significant bit first.

Basic Block Size

The representation of all items requires a multiple of four bytes (or 32 bits) of data. The bytes are numbered 0 through n − 1. The bytes are read or written to some byte stream such that byte m always precedes byte m + 1. If the n bytes needed to contain the data are not a multiple of four, then the n bytes are followed by enough (0 to 3) residual zero bytes, r, to make the total byte count a multiple of 4.

We include the familiar graphic box notation for illustration and comparison. In most illustrations, each box (delimited by a plus sign at the 4 corners and vertical bars and dashes) depicts a byte. Ellipses (...) between boxes show zero or more additional bytes where required.

A Block

```
+--------+--------+...+--------+--------+...+--------+
| byte 0 | byte 1 |...|byte n-1|    0   |...|    0   |
+--------+--------+...+--------+--------+...+--------+
|<-----------n bytes---------->|<------r bytes------>|
|<-----------n+r (where (n+r) mod 4 = 0)------------>|
```

A2.3 XDR Data Types

Each of the sections that follow describes a data type defined in the XDR standard, shows how it is declared in the language, and includes a graphic illustration of its encoding.

For each data type in the language we show a general paradigm declaration. Note that angle brackets (⟨ and ⟩) denote variable length sequences of data and square brackets ([and]) denote fixed-length sequences of data. "n", "m" and "r" denote integers. For the full language specification and more formal definitions of terms such as "identifier" and "declaration", refer to The XDR Language Specification presented later.

For some data types, more specific examples are included. A more extensive example of a data description is in *An Example of an XDR Data Description* that follows.

Integer

An XDR signed integer is a 32-bit datum that encodes an integer in the range [-2147483648,2147483647]. The integer is represented in two's complement notation. The most and least significant bytes are 0 and 3, respectively. Integers are declared as follows:

Integer

```
(MSB)                      (LSB)
+-------+-------+-------+-------+
| byte 0 | byte 1 | byte 2 | byte 3 |
+-------+-------+-------+-------+
<-----------32 bits----------->
```

Unsigned Integer

An XDR unsigned integer is a 32-bit datum that encodes a nonnegative integer in the range [0,4294967295]. It is represented by an unsigned binary number with most and least significant bytes of 0 and 3, respectively. An unsigned integer is declared as follows:

Unsigned Integer

```
(MSB)                      (LSB)
+-------+-------+-------+-------+
| byte 0 | byte 1 | byte 2 | byte 3 |
+-------+-------+-------+-------+
<-----------32 bits----------->
```

Enumeration

Enumerations have the same representation as signed integers. Enumerations are handy for describing subsets of the integers. Enumerated data is declared as follows:

```
enum { name-identifier = constant, ... } identifier;
```

For example, the three colors red, yellow, and blue could be described by an enumerated type:

```
enum { RED = 2, YELLOW = 3, BLUE = 5 } colors;
```

It is an error to encode as an enum any other integer than those that have been given assignments in the enum declaration.

Boolean

Booleans are important enough and occur frequently enough to warrant their own explicit type in the standard. Booleans are declared as follows:

```
bool identifier;
```

This is equivalent to:

```
enum { FALSE = 0, TRUE = 1 } identifier;
```

Hyper Integer and Unsigned Hyper Integer

The standard also defines 64-bit (8-byte) numbers called hyper integer and unsigned hyper integer. Their representations are the obvious extensions of integer and unsigned integer defined above. They are represented in two's complement notation. The most and least significant bytes are 0 and 7, respectively. Their declarations:

Hyper Integer
Unsigned Hyper Integer

```
(MSB)                                                   (LSB)
+-------+-------+-------+-------+-------+-------+-------+-------+
| byte 0 | byte 1 | byte 2 | byte 3 | byte 4 | byte 5 | byte 6 | byte 7 |
+-------+-------+-------+-------+-------+-------+-------+-------+
<---------------------------64 bits---------------------------->
```

Floating-point

The standard defines the floating-point data type "float" (32 bits or 4 bytes). The encoding used is the IEEE standard for normalized single-precision floating-point numbers [3]. Three fields describe the single-precision floating-point number. The first field, which takes ((uses?)) one bit, refers to the sign of the number; values 0 and 1 represent positive and negative, respectively. The second field describes the exponent of the number to the base 2, with the exponent biased by 127. Eight bits are devoted to the second field. The third field refers to the fractional part of the number's mantissa with base 2; 23 bits are devoted to this field.

Therefore, the floating-point number is described by:

(−1)**S * 2**(E-Bias) * 1.F

It is declared as follows:

Single-Precision Floating-Point

```
+------+------+------+------+
| byte 0 | byte 1 | byte 2 | byte 3 |
S|   E   |          F          |
+------+------+------+------+
1|<- 8 ->|<----- 23 bits ----->|
<---------- 32 bits ---------->
```

Just as the most and least significant bytes of a number are 0 and 3, the most and least significant bits of a single-precision floating-point number are 0 and 31. The beginning bit (and most significant bit) offsets of S, E, and F are 0, 1, and 9, respectively. Note that these numbers refer to the mathematical positions of the bits, and NOT to their actual physical locations (which vary from medium to medium).

The IEEE specifications should be consulted concerning the encoding for signed zero, signed infinity (overflow), and denormalized numbers (underflow) [3]. According to IEEE specifications, the "NaN" (not a number) is system dependent and should not be used externally.

Double-precision Floating-point

The standard defines the encoding for the double-precision floating-point data type "double" (64 bits or 8 bytes). The encoding used is the IEEE standard for normalized double-precision floating-point numbers [3]. The standard encodes the following three fields, which describe the double-precision floating-point number. The first field, which takes one bit, refers to the sign of the number; values 0 and 1 represent positive and negative, respectively. The second field describes the exponent of the number to the base 2, with the exponent biased by 1023. Eleven bits are devoted to the second field. The third field refers to the fractional part of the number's mantissa with base 2; 52 bits are devoted to this field. Therefore, the floating-point number is described by:

```
(-1)**S * 2**(E-Bias) * 1.F
```

It is declared as follows:

Double-Precision Floating-Point

```
+------+------+------+------+------+------+------+------+
| byte 0 | byte 1 | byte 2 | byte 3 | byte 4 | byte 5 | byte 6 | byte 7 |
S|   E   |                    F                                       |
+------+------+------+------+------+------+------+------+
1|<- 11 ->|<------------------- 52 bits ------------------->|
<----------------------- 64 bits ----------------------->
```

Just as the most and least significant bytes of a number are 0 and 3, the most and least significant bits of a double-precision floating-point number are 0 and 63. The beginning bit (and most significant bit) offsets of S, E , and F are 0, 1, and 12, respectively. Note that these numbers refer to the mathematical positions of the bits, and NOT to their actual physical locations (which vary from medium to medium).

The IEEE specifications should be consulted concerning the encoding for signed zero, signed infinity (overflow), and denormalized numbers (underflow) [3]. According to IEEE specifications, the "NaN" (not a number) is system dependent and should not be used externally.

Fixed-length Opaque Data

At times, fixed-length uninterpreted data needs to be passed among machines. This data is called "opaque" and is declared as follows:

```
opaque identifier[n];
```

where the constant n is the (static) number of bytes necessary to contain the opaque data. If n is not a multiple of four, then the n bytes are followed by enough (0 to 3) residual zero bytes, r, to make the total byte count of the opaque object a multiple of four.

Fixed-Length Opaque

```
0        1     ...
+--------+--------+...+--------+--------+...+--------+
| byte 0 | byte 1 |...|byte n-1|    0   |...|    0   |
+--------+--------+...+--------+--------+...+--------+
|<-----------n bytes---------->|<------r bytes------>|
|<-----------n+r (where (n+r) mod 4 = 0)------------>|
```

Variable-length Opaque Data

The standard also provides for variable-length (counted) opaque data, defined as a sequence of n (numbered 0 through n – 1) arbitrary bytes to be the number n encoded as an unsigned integer (as described below), and followed by the n bytes of the sequence.

Byte m of the sequence always precedes byte m + 1 of the sequence, and byte 0 of the sequence always follows the sequence's length (count). Enough (0 to 3) residual zero bytes, r, to make the total byte count a multiple of four. Variable-length opaque data is declared in the following way:

```
opaque identifier<m>;
```

or

```
opaque identifier<>;
```

The constant m denotes an upper bound of the number of bytes that the sequence may contain. If m is not specified, as in the second declaration, it is assumed to be (2**32) – 1, the maximum length. The constant m would normally be found in a protocol specification. For example, a filing protocol may state that the maximum data transfer size is 8192 bytes, as follows:

```
opaque filedata<8192>;
```

This can be illustrated as follows:

Variable-Length Opaque

```
0     1     2     3     4     5   ...
+-----+-----+-----+-----+-----+-----+...+-----+-----+...+-----+
|        length n       |byte0|byte1|...| n-1 |  0  |...|  0  |
+-----+-----+-----+-----+-----+-----+...+-----+-----+...+-----+
|<-------4 bytes------->|<------n bytes------>|<---r bytes--->|
|<----------4+n+r (where (n+r) mod 4 = 0)-------------------->|
```

It is an error to encode a length greater than the maximum described in the specification.

String

The standard defines a string of n (numbered 0 through n − 1) ASCII bytes to be the number n encoded as an unsigned integer (as described above), and followed by the n bytes of the string. Byte m of the string always precedes byte m + 1 of the string, and byte 0 of the string always follows the string's length. If n is not a multiple of four, then the n bytes are followed by enough (0 to 3) residual zero bytes, r, to make the total byte count a multiple of four. Counted byte strings are declared as follows:

```
string object<m>;
```

or

```
string object<>;
```

The constant m denotes an upper bound of the number of bytes that a string may contain. If m is not specified, as in the second declaration, it is assumed to be (2**32) − 1, the maximum length. The constant m would normally be found in a protocol specification. For example, a filing protocol may state that a file name can be no longer than 255 bytes, as follows:

```
string filename<255>;
```

Which can be illustrated as:

A String

```
0     1     2     3     4     5   ...
+-----+-----+-----+-----+-----+-----+...+-----+-----+...+-----+
|        length n       |byte0|byte1|...| n-1 |  0  |...|  0  |
+-----+-----+-----+-----+-----+-----+...+-----+-----+...+-----+
|<-------4 bytes------->|<------n bytes------>|<---r bytes--->|
|<----------4+n+r (where (n+r) mod 4 = 0)----------------->|
```

It is an error to encode a length greater than the maximum described in the specification.

Fixed-length Array

Declarations for fixed-length arrays of homogeneous elements are in the following form:

type-name identifier[n];

Fixed-length arrays of elements numbered 0 through n − 1 are encoded by individually encoding the elements of the array in their natural order, 0 through n − 1. Each element's size is a multiple of four bytes. Though all elements are of the same type, the elements may have different sizes. For example, in a fixed-length array of strings, all elements are of type "string", yet each element will vary in its length.

Fixed-Length Array

```
+---+---+---+---+---+---+---+---+...+---+---+---+---+
|   element 0   |   element 1   |...|  element n-1  |
+---+---+---+---+---+---+---+---+...+---+---+---+---+
|<-------------------- n elements ------------------>|
```

Variable-length Array

Counted arrays provide the ability to encode variable-length arrays of homogeneous elements. The array is encoded as the element count n (an unsigned integer) followed by the encoding of each of the array's elements, starting with element 0 and progressing through element n − 1. The declaration for variable-length arrays follows this form:

type-name identifier⟨m⟩;

or

type-name identifier⟨⟩;

The constant m specifies the maximum acceptable element count of an array; if m is not specified, as in the second declaration, it is assumed to be (2**32) − 1.

Counted Array

```
0  1  2  3
+--+--+--+--+--+--+--+--+--+--+--+--+...+--+--+--+--+
|     n     | element 0 | element 1 |...|element n-1|
+--+--+--+--+--+--+--+--+--+--+--+--+...+--+--+--+--+
|<--4 bytes-->|<-------------- n elements ------------->|
```

It is an error to encode a value of n that is greater than the maximum described in the specification.

Structure

Structures are declared as follows:

```
struct {
        component-declaration-A;
        component-declaration-B;
        ...
} identifier;
```

The components of the structure are encoded in the order of their declaration in the structure. Each component's size is a multiple of four bytes, though the components may be different sizes.

Structure

```
+-----------+-----------+...
| component A | component B | ...
+-----------+-----------+...
```

Discriminated Union

A discriminated union is a type composed of a discriminant followed by a type selected from a set of prearranged types according to the value of the discriminant. The type of discriminant is either "int", "unsigned int", or an enumerated type, such as "bool". The component types are called "arms" of the union, and are preceded by the value of the discriminant which implies their encoding. Discriminated unions are declared as follows:

```
union switch (discriminant-declaration) {
        case discriminant-value-A:
        arm-declaration-A;
        case discriminant-value-B:
        arm-declaration-B;
        ...
        default: default-declaration;
} identifier;
```

Each "case" keyword is followed by a legal value of the discriminant. The default arm is optional. If the discriminant is not specified, then a valid encoding of the union cannot take on unspecified discriminant values. The size of the implied arm is always a multiple of four bytes.

The discriminated union is encoded as its discriminant followed by the encoding of the implied arm.

Discriminated Union

```
0   1   2   3
+---+---+---+---+---+---+---+---+
|  discriminant  |  implied arm  |
+---+---+---+---+---+---+---+---+
|<----4 bytes---->|
```

Void

An XDR void is a 0-byte quantity. Voids are useful for describing operations that take no data as input or no data as output. They are also useful in unions, where some arms may contain data and others do not. The declaration is simply as follows:

```
void;
```

Voids are illustrated as follows:

```
++
||
++
--><-- 0 bytes
```

Constant

The data declaration for a constant follows this form:

```
const name-identifier = n;
```

"const" is used to define a symbolic name for a constant; it does not declare any data. The symbolic constant may be used anywhere a regular constant may be used. For example, the following defines a symbolic constant DOZEN, equal to 12.

```
const DOZEN = 12;
```

Typedef

"typedef" does not declare any data either, but serves to define new identifiers for declaring data. The syntax is:

```
typedef declaration;
```

The new type name is actually the variable name in the declaration part of the typedef. For example, the following defines a new type called "eggbox" using an existing type called "egg":

```
typedef egg eggbox[DOZEN];
```

Variables declared using the new type name have the same type as the new type name would have in the typedef, if it were considered a variable. For example, the following two declarations are equivalent in declaring the variable "fresheggs":

```
eggbox  fresheggs;
egg     fresheggs[DOZEN];
```

When a typedef involves a struct, enum, or union definition, there is another (preferred) syntax that may be used to define the same type. In general, a typedef of the following form:

```
typedef <<struct, union, or enum definition>> identifier;
```

may be converted to the alternative form by removing the "typedef" part and placing the identifier after the "struct", "union", or "enum" keyword, instead of at the end. For example, here are the two ways to define the type "bool":

```
typedef enum {          /* using typedef */
        FALSE = 0,
        TRUE = 1
        } bool;

enum bool {             /* preferred alternative */
        FALSE = 0,
        TRUE = 1
        };
```

The reason for preferring this syntax is that one does not have to wait until the end of a declaration to figure out the name of the new type.

Optional-data

Optional-data is one kind of union that occurs so frequently that we give it a special syntax of its own for declaring it. It is declared as follows:

```
type-name *identifier;
```

This is equivalent to the following union:

```
union switch (bool opted) {
        case TRUE:
        type-name element;
        case FALSE:
        void;
} identifier;
```

It is also equivalent to the following variable-length array declaration, since the boolean "opted" can be interpreted as the length of the array:

```
type-name identifier⟨1⟩;
```

Optional-data is not so interesting in itself, but it is very useful for describing recursive data-structures such as linked-lists and trees. For example, the following defines a type "stringlist" that encodes lists of arbitrary length strings:

```
struct *stringlist {
        string item⟨⟩;
        stringlist next;
};
```

It could have been equivalently declared as the following union:

```
union   stringlist switch (bool opted) {
        case TRUE:
                struct {
                        string item⟨⟩;
                        stringlist next;
                } element;
        case FALSE:
                void;
};
```

or as a variable-length array:

```
struct stringlist⟨1⟩ {
        string item⟨⟩;
        stringlist next;
};
```

Both of these declarations obscure the intention of the stringlist type, so the optional-data declaration is preferred over both of them. The optional-data type also has a close correlation to how recursive data structures are represented in high-level languages such as Pascal or C by use of pointers. In fact, the syntax is the same as that of the C language for pointers.

Areas for Future Enhancement

The XDR standard lacks representations for bit fields and bitmaps, since the standard is based on bytes. Also missing are packed (or binary-coded) decimals.

The intent of the XDR standard was not to describe every kind of data that people have ever sent or will ever want to send from machine to machine. Rather, it only describes the most commonly used data-types of high-level languages such as Pascal or C so that applications written in these languages will be able to communicate easily over some medium.

One could imagine extensions to XDR that would let it describe almost any existing protocol, such as TCP. The minimum necessary for this are support for different block sizes and byte-orders. The XDR discussed here could then be considered the 4-byte big-endian member of a larger XDR family.

A2.4 Discussion

Why a Language for Describing Data?

There are many advantages in using a data-description language such as XDR versus using diagrams. Languages are more formal than diagrams and lead to less ambiguous descriptions of data. Languages are also easier to understand and allow one to think of other issues instead of the low-level details of bit-encoding. Also, there is a close analogy between the types of XDR and a high-level language such as C or Pascal. This makes the implementation of XDR encoding and decoding modules an easier task. Finally, the language specification itself is an ASCII string that can be passed from machine to machine to perform on-the-fly data interpretation.

Why Only One Byte-Order for an XDR Unit?

Supporting two byte-orderings requires a higher level protocol for determining in which byte-order the data is encoded. Since XDR is not a protocol, this cannot be done. However, an advantage of supporting two byte-orderings is that data in XDR format can be written to a magnetic tape, and any machine will be able to interpret it, since no higher level protocol is necessary for determining the byte-order.

Why Does XDR Use Big-Endian Byte-Order?

Yes, it is unfair, but having only one byte-order means you have to be unfair to somebody. Many architectures, such as the Motorola 68000 and IBM 370, support the big-endian byte-order.

Why Is the XDR Unit Four Bytes Wide?

There is a tradeoff in choosing the XDR unit size. Choosing a small size such as two makes the encoded data small, but causes alignment problems for machines that aren't aligned on these boundaries. A large size such as eight means the data will be aligned on virtually every machine, but causes the encoded data to grow too big. We chose four as a compromise. Four is big enough to support most architectures efficiently, except for rare machines such as the eight-byte aligned Cray. Four is also small enough to keep the encoded data restricted to a reasonable size.

Why Must Variable-Length Data Be Padded with Zeros?

It is desirable that the same data encode into the same thing on all machines, so that encoded data can be meaningfully compared or checksummed. Forcing the padded bytes to be zero ensures this.

Why Is There No Explicit Data-Typing?

Data-typing has a relatively high cost for what small advantages it may have. One cost is the expansion of data due to the inserted type fields. Another is the added cost of interpreting these type fields and acting accordingly. Since most protocols already know what type they expect, data-typing supplies only redundant information. However, one can still get the benefits of data-typing using XDR. One way is to encode two things: first a string which is the XDR data description of the encoded data, and then the encoded data itself. Another way is to assign a value to all the types in XDR, and then define a universal type which takes this value as its discriminant and for each value describes the corresponding data type.

A2.5 The XDR Language Specification

Notational Conventions

This specification uses an extended Backus-Naur Form notation for describing the XDR language. Here is a brief description of the notation:

- The characters |, (,), [,], , and * are special.
- Terminal symbols are strings of any characters surrounded by double quotes.
- Non-terminal symbols are strings of non-special characters.
- Alternative items are separated by a vertical bar ("|").
- Optional items are enclosed in brackets.
- Items are grouped together by enclosing them in parentheses.
- A * following an item means 0 or more occurrences of that item.

For example, consider the following pattern:

```
"a " "very" (", " " very")* [" cold" "and"] " rainy " ("day" | "night")
```

An infinite number of strings match this pattern. A few of them are:

```
"a very rainy day"
"a very, very rainy day"
"a very cold and rainy day"
"a very, very, very cold and rainy night"
```

Lexical Notes

- Comments begin with '/*' and terminate with '*/'.
- White space serves to separate items and is otherwise ignored.
- An identifier is a letter followed by an optional sequence of letters, digits or underbar ('_'). The case of identifiers is not ignored.

- A constant is a sequence of one or more decimal digits, optionally preceded by a minus-sign ('–').

Syntax Information

```
declaration:
        type-specifier identifier
        | type-specifier identifier "[" value "]"
        | type-specifier identifier "<" [ value ] ">"
        | "opaque" identifier "[" value "]"
        | "opaque" identifier "<" [ value ] ">"
        | "string" identifier "<" [ value] ">"
        | type-specifier "*" identifier
        | "void"

value:
        constant
        | identifier

type-specifier:
          [ "unsigned" ] "int"
        | [ "unsigned" ] "hyper"
        | "float"
        | "double"
        | "bool"
        | enum-type-spec
        | struct-type-spec
        | union-type-spec
        | identifier

enum-type-spec:
        "enum" enum-body

enum-body
        "{"
        ( identifier "=" value )
        ( "," identifier "=" value )*
        "}"

struct-type-spec:
        "struct" struct-body

struct-body:
        "{"
        ( declaration ";" )
        ( declaration ";" )*
        "}"
```

```
union-type-spec:
        "union" union-body

union-body:
        "switch" "(" declaration ")" "{"
        ( "case" value ":" declaration ";" )
        ( "case" value ":" declaration ";" )*
        [ "default" ":" declaration ";" ]
        "}"

constant-def:
        "const" identifier "=" constant ";"

type-def:
        "typedef" declaration ";"
        | "enum" identifier enum-body ";"
        | "struct" identifier struct-body ";"
        | "union" identifier union-body ";"

definition:
        type-def
        | constant-def

specification:
        definition *
```

Syntax Notes

1. The following are keywords and cannot be used as identifiers: "bool", "case", "const", "default", "double", "enum", "float", "hyper", opaque", "string", "struct", "switch", "typedef","union", "unsigned" and "void".
2. Only unsigned constants may be used as size specifications for arrays. If an identifier is used, it must have been declared previously as an unsigned constant in a "const" definition.
3. Constant and type identifiers within the scope of a specification are in the same name space and must be declared uniquely within this scope.
4. Similarly, variable names must be unique within the scope of struct and union declarations. Nested struct and union declarations create new scopes.

5. The discriminant of a union must be of a type that evaluates to an integer. That is, "int", "unsigned int", "bool", an enumerated type or any typedefed type that evaluates to one of these is legal. Also, the case values must be one of the legal values of the discriminant. Finally, a case value may not be specified more than once within the scope of a union declaration.

A2.6 An Example of an XDR Data Description

Here is a short XDR data description of a thing called a "file", which might be used to transfer files from one machine to another.

```
const MAXUSERNAME = 32;     /* max length of a user name */
const MAXFILELEN = 65535;   /* max length of a file */
const MAXNAMELEN = 255;     /* max length of a file name */


/*
 * Types of files:
 */

enum filekind {
        TEXT  = 0,          /* ascii data */
        DATA  = 1,          /* raw data */
        EXEC  = 2           /* executable */
};

/*
 * File information, per kind of file:
 */

union filetype switch (filekind kind) {
        case    TEXT:
                void;                            /* no extra information */
        case    DATA:
                string creator<MAXNAMELEN>;      /* data creator */
        case    EXEC:
                string interpretor<MAXNAMELEN>;  /* program interpretor */
};

/*
 * A complete file:
 */
```

```
struct file {
        string filename<MAXNAMELEN>;  /* name of file */
        filetype type;                /* info about file */
        string owner<MAXUSERNAME>;    /* owner of file */
        opaque data<MAXFILELEN>;      /* file data */
};
```

Suppose now that there is a user named "john" who wants to store his lisp program "sillyprog" that contains just the data "(quit)". His file would be encoded as follows:

Offset	Hex Bytes	ASCII	Description
0	00 00 00 09	....	Length of filename = 9
4	73 69 6c 6c	sill	Filename characters
8	79 70 72 6f	ypro	... and more characters ...
12	67 00 00 00	g...	... and 3 zero-bytes of fill
16	00 00 00 02	....	Filekind is EXEC = 2
20	00 00 00 04	....	Length of interpretor = 4
24	6c 69 73 70	lisp	Interpretor characters
28	00 00 00 04	....	Length of owner = 4
32	6a 6f 68 6e	john	Owner characters
36	00 00 00 06	....	Length of file data = 6
40	28 71 75 69	(qui	File data bytes ...
44	74 29 00 00	t)..	... and 2 zero-bytes of fill

References

[1] Brian W. Kernighan & Dennis M. Ritchie, "The C Programming Language", Bell Laboratories, Murray Hill, New Jersey, 1978.

[2] Danny Cohen, "On Holy Wars and a Plea for Peace", IEEE Computer, October 1981.

[3] "IEEE Standard for Binary Floating-Point Arithmetic", ANSI/IEEE Standard 754-1985, Institute of Electrical and Electronics Engineers, August 1985.

[4] "Courier: The Remote Procedure Call Protocol", XEROX Corporation, XSIS 038112, December 1981.

Remote Procedure Call: Protocol Specification

Appendix 3

A3.1 Status of this Memo

Note: This appendix specifies a protocol that Sun Microsystems, Inc., and others are using. It has been designated RFC1057 by the ARPA Network Information Center.

A3.2 Introduction

This appendix specifies a message protocol used in implementing Sun's Remote Procedure Call (RPC) package. (The message protocol is specified with the External Data Representation (XDR) language. See the *External Data Representation Standard: Protocol Specification* Appendix 3 for the details. Here, we assume that the reader is familiar with XDR and do not attempt to justify it or its uses.) The paper by Birrell and Nelson [1] is recommended as an excellent background to and justification of RPC.

Terminology

This chapter discusses servers, services, programs, procedures, clients, and versions. A server is a piece of software where network services are implemented. A network service is a collection of one or more remote programs. A remote program implements one or more remote procedures; the procedures, their parameters, and results are documented in the specific program's protocol specification (see the *Port Mapper Program Protocol* below, for an example). Network clients are pieces of software that initiate remote procedure calls to services. A server may support more than one version of a remote program in order to be forward compatible with changing protocols.

For example, a network file service may be composed of two programs. One program may deal with high-level applications such as file system access control and locking. The other may deal with low-level file IO and have procedures like "read" and "write". A client machine of the network file service would call the procedures associated with the two programs of the service on behalf of some user on the client machine.

The RPC Model

The remote procedure call model is similar to the local procedure call model. In the local case, the caller places arguments to a procedure in some well-specified location (such as a result register). It then transfers control to the procedure, and eventually gains back control. At that point, the results of the procedure are extracted from the well-specified location, and the caller continues execution.

The remote procedure call is similar, in that one thread of control logically winds through two processes – one is the caller's process, the other is a server's process. That is, the caller process sends a call message to the server process and waits (blocks) for a reply message. The call message contains the procedure's parameters, among other things. The reply message contains the procedure's results, among other things. Once the reply message is received, the results of the procedure are extracted, and the caller's execution is resumed.

On the server side, a process is dormant awaiting the arrival of a call message. When one arrives, the server process extracts the procedure's parameters, computes the results, sends a reply message, and then awaits the next call message.

Note that in this model, only one of the two processes is active at any given time. However, this model is only given as an example. The RPC protocol makes no restrictions on the concurrency model implemented, and others are possible. For example, an implementation may choose to have RPC calls be asynchronous, so that the client may do useful work while waiting for the reply from the server. Another possibility is to have the server create a task to process an incoming request, so that the server can be free to receive other requests.

Transports and Semantics

The RPC protocol is independent of transport protocols. That is, RPC does not care how a message is passed from one process to another. The protocol deals only with specification and interpretation of messages.

It is important to point out that RPC does not try to implement any kind of reliability and that the application must be aware of the type of transport protocol underneath RPC. If it knows it is running on top of a reliable transport such as TCP/IP[6], then most of the work is already done for it. On the other hand, if it is running on top of an unreliable transport such as UDP/IP[7], it must implement its own retransmission and time-out policy as the RPC layer does not provide this service.

Because of transport independence, the RPC protocol does not attach specific semantics to the remote procedures or their execution. Semantics can be inferred from (but should be explicitly specified by) the underlying transport protocol. For example, consider RPC running on top of an unreliable transport such as UDP/IP. If an application retransmits RPC messages after short time-outs, the only thing it can infer if it receives no reply is that the procedure was executed zero or more times. If it does receive a reply, then it can infer that the procedure was executed at least once.

A server may wish to remember previously granted requests from a client and not regrant them in order to insure some degree of execute-at-most-once semantics. A server can do this by taking advantage of the transaction ID that is packaged with every RPC request. The main use of this transaction is by the client RPC layer in matching replies to requests. However, a client application may choose to reuse its previous transaction ID when retransmitting a request. The server application, knowing this fact, may choose to remember this ID after granting a request and not regrant requests with the same ID, thus achieving some degree of execute-at-most-once semantics. The server is not allowed to examine this ID in any other way except as a test for equality.

On the other hand, if using a reliable transport such as TCP/IP, the application can infer from a reply message that the procedure was executed exactly once, but if it receives no reply message, it cannot assume the remote procedure was not executed. Note that even if a connection-oriented protocol like TCP is used, an application still needs time-outs and reconnection to handle server crashes.

There are other possibilities for transports besides datagram- or connection-oriented protocols. For example, a request-reply protocol such as VMTP[2] is perhaps the most natural transport for RPC. At Sun, RPC is currently implemented on top of both TCP/IP and UDP/IP transports.

Binding and Rendezvous Independence

The act of binding a client to a service is NOT part of the remote procedure call specification. This important and necessary function is left up to some higher-level software. (The software may use RPC itself—see the *Port Mapper Program Protocol* below).

Implementors should think of the RPC protocol as the jump-subroutine instruction ("JSR") of a network; the loader (binder) makes JSR useful, and the loader itself uses JSR to accomplish its task. Likewise, the network makes RPC useful, using RPC to accomplish this task.

Authentication

The RPC protocol provides the fields necessary for a client to identify itself to a service and vice-versa. Security and access control mechanisms can be built on top of the message authentication. Several different authentication protocols can be supported. A field in the RPC header indicates which protocol is being used. More information on specific authentication protocols can be found in the *Authentication Protocols* below.

A3.3 RPC Protocol Requirements

The RPC protocol must provide for the following:

- Unique specification of a procedure to be called.
- Provisions for matching response messages to request messages.
- Provisions for authenticating the caller to service and vice-versa.

In addition to these requirements, features that detect the following are worth supporting because of protocol roll-over errors, implementation bugs, user error, and network administration:

- RPC protocol mismatches.
- Remote program protocol version mismatches.
- Protocol errors (such as misspecification of a procedure's parameters).
- Reasons why remote authentication failed.
- Any other reasons why the desired procedure was not called.

Programs and Procedures

The RPC call message has three unsigned fields: remote program number, remote program version number, and remote procedure number. The three fields uniquely identify the procedure to be called. Program numbers are administered by some central authority (like Sun). Once an implementor has a program number, he can implement his remote program; the first implementation would most likely have the version number of 1. Because most new protocols evolve into better, stable, and mature protocols, a version field of the call message identifies which version of the protocol the caller is using. Version numbers make speaking old and new protocols through the same server process possible.

The procedure number identifies the procedure to be called. These numbers are documented in the specific program's protocol specification. For example, a file service's protocol specification may state that its procedure number 5 is "read" and procedure number 12 is "write".

Just as remote program protocols may change over several versions, the actual RPC message protocol could also change. Therefore, the call message also has in it the RPC version number, which is always equal to two for the version of RPC described here.

The reply message to a request message has enough information to distinguish the following error conditions:

- The remote implementation of RPC does speak protocol version 2. The lowest and highest supported RPC version numbers are returned.
- The remote program is not available on the remote system.
- The remote program does not support the requested version number. The lowest and highest supported remote program version numbers are returned.
- The requested procedure number does not exist. (This is usually a caller side protocol or programming error.)
- The parameters to the remote procedure appear to be garbage from the server's point of view. (Again, this is usually caused by a disagreement about the protocol between client and service.)

Authentication

Provisions for authentication of caller to service and vice-versa are provided as a part of the RPC protocol. The call message has two authentication fields, the credentials and verifier. The reply message has one authentication field, the response verifier. The RPC protocol specification defines all three fields to be the following opaque type:

```
enum    auth_flavor     {
        AUTH_NULL   = 0,
        AUTH_UNIX   = 1,
        AUTH_SHORT  = 2,
        AUTH_DES    = 3
        /* and more to be defined */
};

struct  opaque_auth {
        auth_flavor flavor;
        opaque body<400>;
};
```

In simple English, any *opaque_auth* structure is an *auth_flavor* enumeration followed by bytes which are opaque to the RPC protocol implementation.

The interpretation and semantics of the data contained within the authentication fields is specified by individual, independent authentication protocol specifications. (See *Authentication Protocols* below, for definitions of the various authentication protocols.)

If authentication parameters were rejected, the response message contains information stating why they were rejected.

Program Number Assignment

Program numbers are given out in groups of 0x20000000 (decimal 536870912) according to the following chart:

Program Number	Description
0x00000000 - 0x1FFFFFFF	Defined by Sun Microsystems
0x20000000 - 0x3FFFFFFF	Defined by User
0x40000000 - 0x5FFFFFFF	Transient
0x60000000 - 0x7FFFFFFF	Reserved
0x80000000 - 0x9FFFFFFF	Reserved
0xA0000000 - 0xBFFFFFFF	Reserved
0xC0000000 - 0xDFFFFFFF	Reserved
0xE0000000 - 0xFFFFFFFF	Reserved

The first group is a range of numbers administered by Sun Microsystems and should be identical for all sites. The second range is for applications peculiar to a particular site. This range is intended primarily for debugging new programs. When a site develops an application that might be of general interest, that application should be given an assigned number in the first range. The third group is for applications that generate program numbers dynamically. The final groups are reserved for future use, and should not be used.

Other Uses of the RPC Protocol

The intended use of this protocol is for calling remote procedures. That is, each call message is matched with a response message. However, the protocol itself is a message-passing protocol with which other (non-RPC) protocols can be implemented. Sun currently uses, or perhaps abuses, the RPC message protocol for the following two (non-RPC) protocols: batching (or pipelining) and broadcast RPC. These two protocols are discussed but not defined below.

Batching. Batching allows a client to send an arbitrarily large sequence of call messages to a server; batching typically uses reliable byte stream protocols (like TCP/IP) for its transport. In the case of batching, the client never waits for a reply from the server, and the server does not send replies to batch requests. A sequence of batch calls is usually terminated by a legitimate RPC in order to flush the pipeline (with positive acknowledgement).

Broadcast RPC. In broadcast RPC-based protocols, the client sends a broadcast packet to the network and waits for numerous replies. Broadcast RPC uses unreliable, packet-based protocols (like UDP/IP) as its transports. Servers that support broadcast protocols only respond when the request is successfully processed, and are silent in the face of errors. Broadcast RPC uses the Port Mapper RPC service to achieve its semantics. See the *Port Mapper Program Protocol* below, for more information.

A3.4 The RPC Message Protocol

This section defines the RPC message protocol in the XDR data description language. The message is defined in a top-down style.

```
enum   msg_type    {
       CALL        = 0,
       REPLY       = 1
};

/*
 * A reply to a call message can take on two forms:
 * The message was either accepted or rejected.
 */
enum reply_stat {
   MSG_ACCEPTED = 0,
   MSG_DENIED   = 1
};

/*
 * Given that a call message was accepted, the following is the
 * status of an attempt to call a remote procedure.
 */
enum accept_stat {
       SUCCESS         = 0, /* RPC executed successfully */
       PROG_UNAVAIL    = 1, /* remote hasn't exported program */
       PROG_MISMATCH   = 2, /* remote can't support version # */
       PROC_UNAVAIL    = 3, /* program can't support procedure */
       GARBAGE_ARGS    = 4 /* procedure can't decode params */
};
```

```
/*
 * Reasons why a call message was rejected:
 */
enum reject_stat {
        RPC_MISMATCH  = 0, /* RPC version number != 2 */
        AUTH_ERROR    = 1  /* remote can't authenticate caller */
};
/*
 * Why authentication failed:
 */
enum auth_stat {
        AUTH_BADCRED          = 1, /* bad credentials */
        AUTH_REJECTEDCRED     = 2, /* client must begin new session */
        AUTH_BADVERF          = 3, /* bad verifier */
        AUTH_REJECTEDVERF     = 4, /* verifier expired or replayed */
        AUTH_TOOWEAK          = 5  /* rejected for security reasons */
};

/*
 * The RPC message:
 * All messages start with a transaction identifier, xid,
 * followed by a two-armed discriminated union. The union's
 * discriminant is a msg_type which switches to one of the two
 * types of the message. The xid of a REPLY message always
 * matches that of the initiating CALL message. NB: The xid
 * field is only used for clients matching reply messages with
 * call messages or for servers detecting retransmissions; the
 * service side cannot treat this xid as any type of sequence
 * number.
 */ .
struct rpc_msg {
        unsigned int xid;
        union switch (msg_type mtype) {
                case CALL:
                     call_body cbody;
                     case REPLY:
                          reply_body rbody;
        } body;
};

/*
 * Body of an RPC request call:
 * In version 2 of the RPC protocol specification, rpcvers must
 * be equal to 2. The fields prog, vers, and proc specify the
 * remote program, its version number, and the procedure within
 * the remote program to be called. After these fields are two
 * authentication parameters: cred (authentication credentials)
```

```
 * and verf (authentication verifier). The two authentication
 * parameters are followed by the parameters to the remote
 * procedure, which are specified by the specific program
 * protocol.
 */
struct call_body {
        unsigned int rpcvers;      /* must be equal to two (2) */
        unsigned int prog;
        unsigned int vers;
        unsigned int proc;
        opaque_auth cred;
        opaque_auth verf;
        /* procedure specific parameters start here */
};

/*
 * Body of a reply to an RPC request:
 * The call message was either accepted or rejected.
 */
union reply_body switch (reply_stat stat) {
        case MSG_ACCEPTED:
                accepted_reply areply;
        case MSG_DENIED:
                rejected_reply rreply;
} reply;

/*
 * Reply to an RPC request that was accepted by the server:
 * there could be an error even though the request was accepted.
 * The first field is an authentication verifier that the server
 * generates in order to validate itself to the caller. It is
 * followed by a union whose discriminant is an enum
 * accept_stat. The SUCCESS arm of the union is protocol
 * specific. The PROG_UNAVAIL, PROC_UNAVAIL, and GARBAGE_ARGP
 * arms of the union are void. The PROG_MISMATCH arm specifies
 * the lowest and highest version numbers of the remote program
 * supported by the server.
 */
struct accepted_reply {
        opaque_auth verf;
        union switch (accept_stat stat) {
                case    SUCCESS:
                        opaque results[0];
                        /* procedure-specific results start here */
                case    PROG_MISMATCH:
                        struct {
```

```
                        unsigned int low;
                        unsigned int high;
                } mismatch_info;
        default:
                /*
                 * Void. Cases include PROG_UNAVAIL,
                PROC_UNAVAIL,
                 * and GARBAGE_ARGS.
                 */
                void;
    } reply_data;
};

/*
 * Reply to an RPC request that was rejected by the server:
 * The request can be rejected for two reasons: either the
 * server is not running a compatible version of the RPC
 * protocol (RPPC_MISMATCH), or the server refuses to
 * authenticate the caller (AUTH_ERROR). In case of an RPC
 * version mismatch, the server returns the lowest and highest
 * supported RPC version numbers. In case of refused
 * authentication, failure status is returned.
 */
union rejected_reply switch (reject_stat stat) {
    case RPC_MISMATCH:
        struct {
            unsigned int low;
            unsigned int high;
        } mismatch_info;
    case AUTH_ERROR:
        auth_stat stat;
};
```

A3.5 Authentication Protocols

As previously stated, authentication parameters are opaque, but open-ended to the rest of the RPC protocol. This section defines some "flavors" of authentication implemented at (and supported by) Sun. Other sites are free to invent new authentication types, with the same rules of flavor number assignment as there is for program number assignment.

Null Authentication

Often calls must be made where the caller does not know who he is or the server does not care who the caller is. In this case, the flavor value (the discriminant of the *opaque_auth 's* union) of the RPC message's credentials, verifier, and response verifier is *AUTH_NULL*. The bytes of the opaque_auth's body are undefined. It is recommended that the opaque length be zero.

UNIX Authentication

The caller of a remote procedure may wish to identify himself as he is identified on a UNIX system. The value of the credential's discriminant of an RPC call message is *AUTH_UNIX*. The bytes of the credential's opaque body encode the following structure:

```
struct auth_unix {
        unsigned int stamp;
        string machinename<255>;
        unsigned int uid;
        unsigned int gid;
        unsigned int gids<10>;
};
```

The *stamp* is an arbitrary ID which the caller machine may generate. The *machinename* is the name of the caller's machine (like "krypton"). The *uid* is the caller's effective user ID. The *gid* is the caller's effective group ID. The *gids* is a counted array of groups which contain the caller as a member. The verifier accompanying the credentials should be of *AUTH_NULL* (defined above).

The value of the discriminant of the response verifier received in the reply message from the server may be *AUTH_NULL* or *AUTH_SHORT*. In the case of *AUTH_SHORT*, the bytes of the response verifier's string encode an opaque structure. This new opaque structure may now be passed to the server instead of the original *AUTH_UNIX* flavor credentials. The server keeps a cache which maps shorthand opaque structures (passed back by way of an *AUTH_SHORT* style response verifier) to the original credentials of the caller. The caller can save network bandwidth and server cpu cycles by using the new credentials.

The server may flush the shorthand opaque structure at any time. If this happens, the remote procedure call message will be rejected due to an authentication error. The reason for the failure will be *AUTH_REJECTEDCRED*. At this point, the caller may wish to try the original *AUTH_UNIX* style of credentials.

DES Authentication

UNIX authentication suffers from two major problems:

- The naming is too UNIX-system oriented.
- There is no verifier, so credentials can easily be faked.

DES authentication attempts to fix these two problems.

Naming. The first problem is handled by addressing the caller by a simple string of characters instead of by an operating system specific integer. This string of characters is known as the "netname" or network name of the caller. The server is not allowed to interpret the contents of the caller's name in any other way except to identify the caller. Thus, netnames should be unique for every caller in the internet.

It is up to each operating system's implementation of DES authentication to generate netnames for its users that insure this uniqueness when they call upon remote servers. Operating systems already know how to distinguish users local to their systems. It is usually a simple matter to extend this mechanism to the network. For example, a UNIX user at Sun with a user ID of 515 might be assigned the following netname: "unix.515@sun.com". This netname contains three items that serve to insure it is unique. Going backwards, there is only one naming domain called "sun.com" in the internet. Within this domain, there is only one UNIX user with user ID 515. However, there may be another user on another operating system, for example VMS, within the same naming domain that, by coincidence, happens to have the same user ID. To insure that these two users can be distinguished we add the operating system name. So one user is "unix.515@-sun.com" and the other is "vms.515@sun.com".

The first field is actually a naming method rather than an operating system name. It just happens that today there is almost a one-to-one correspondence between naming methods and operating systems. If the world could agree on a naming standard, the first field could be the name of that standard, instead of an operating system name.

DES Authentication Verifiers. Unlike UNIX authentication, DES authentication does have a verifier so the server can validate the client's credential (and vice-versa). The contents of this verifier are primarily an encrypted timestamp. The server can decrypt this timestamp, and if it is close to what the real time is, then the client must have encrypted it correctly. The only way the client could encrypt it correctly is to know the "conversation key" of the RPC session. And if the client knows the conversation key, then it must be the real client.

The conversation key is a DES [5] key which the client generates and notifies the server of in its first RPC call. The conversation key is encrypted using a public key scheme in this first transaction. The particular public key scheme used in DES authentication is Diffie-Hellman [3] with 192-bit keys. The details of this encryption method are described later.

The client and the server need the same notion of the current time in order for all of this to work. If network time synchronization cannot be guaranteed, then the client can synchronize with the server before beginning the conversation, perhaps by consulting the Internet Time Server (TIME[4]).

The way a server determines if a client timestamp is valid is somewhat complicated. For any other transaction but the first, the server simply checks for two things:

- the timestamp should be greater than the one previously seen from the same client.
- the timestamp should not have expired.

A timestamp is expired if the server's time is later than the sum of the client's timestamp plus what is known as the client's "window". The "window" is a number the client passes (encrypted) to the server in its first transaction. You can think of it as a lifetime for the credential.

This explains everything but the first transaction. In the first transaction, the server checks only that the timestamp has not expired. However, if this was all that was done, then it would be quite easy for the client to send random data in place of the timestamp with a fairly good chance of succeeding. As an added check, the client sends an encrypted item in the first transaction known as the "window verifier" which must be equal to the window minus 1, or the server will reject the credential.

The client too must check the verifier returned from the server to be sure it is legitimate. The server sends back to the client the encrypted timestamp it received from the client, minus one second. If the client gets anything different than this, it will reject it.

Nicknames and Clock Synchronization. After the first transaction, the server's DES authentication subsystem returns in its verifier to the client an integer "nickname" which the client may use in its further transactions instead of passing its netname, encrypted DES key and window every time. The nickname is most likely an index into a table on the server which stores for each client its netname, decrypted DES key and window.

Although they originally were synchronized, the client's and server's clocks can get out of sync again. When this happens the client RPC subsystem most likely will get back *RPC_AUTHERROR*, at which point it should resynchronize.

A client may still get the *RPC_AUTHERROR* error even though it is synchronized with the server. The reason is that the server's nickname table is a limited size, and it may flush entries whenever it wants. A client should resend its original credential in this case and the server will give it a new nickname. If a server crashes, the entire nickname table gets flushed, and all clients will have to resend their original credentials.

DES Authentication Protocol (in XDR language)

```
/*
 * There are two kinds of credentials: one in which the client uses
 * its full network name, and one in which it uses its "nickname"
 * (just an unsigned integer) given to it by the server. The
 * client must use its fullname in its first transaction with the
 * server, in which the server will return to the client its
 * nickname. The client may use its nickname in all further
 * transactions with the server. There is no requirement to use the
 * nickname, but it is wise to use it for performance reasons.
 */
```

```
enum authdes_namekind {
        ADN_FULLNAME = 0,
        ADN_NICKNAME = 1
};

/*
 * A 64-bit block of encrypted DES data
 */
typedef opaque des_block[8];

/*
 * Maximum length of a network user's name
 */
const MAXNETNAMELEN = 255;

/*
 * A fullname contains the network name of the client, an encrypted
 * conversation key and the window. The window is actually a
 * lifetime for the credential. If the time indicated in the
 * verifier timestamp plus the window has past, then the server
 * should expire the request and not grant it. To insure that
 * requests are not replayed, the server should insist that
 * timestamps are greater than the previous one seen, unless it is
 * the first transaction. In the first transaction, the server
 * checks instead that the window verifier is one less than the
 * window.
 */
struct authdes_fullname {
        string name<MAXNETNAMELEN>;  /* name of client */
        des_block key;               /* PK encrypted conversation key */
        unsigned int window;         /* encrypted window */
};

/*
 * A credential is either a fullname or a nickname
 */
union authdes_cred switch (authdes_namekind adc_namekind) {
        case ADN_FULLNAME:
                authdes_fullname adc_fullname;
        case ADN_NICKNAME:
                unsigned int adc_nickname;
};

/*
 * A timestamp encodes the time since midnight, January 1, 1970.
 */
```

```
struct timestamp {
        unsigned int seconds;   /* seconds */
        unsigned int useconds;  /* and microseconds */
};

/*
 * Verifier: client variety
 * The window verifier is only used in the first transaction. In
 * conjunction with a fullname credential, these items are packed
 * into the following structure before being encrypted:
 *
 * struct {
 *  adv_timestamp;          —one DES block
 *  adc_fullname.window;    —one half DES block
 *  adv_winverf;            —one half DES block
 * }
 * This structure is encrypted using CBC mode encryption with an
 * input vector of zero. All other encryptions of timestamps use
 * ECB mode encryption.
 */
struct authdes_verf_clnt {
        timestamp adv_timestamp; /* encrypted timestamp */
        unsigned int adv_winverf; /* encrypted window verifier */
};

/*
 * Verifier: server variety
 * The server returns (encrypted) the same timestamp the client
 * gave it minus one second. It also tells the client its nickname
 * to be used in future transactions (unencrypted).
 */
struct authdes_verf_svr {
        timestamp adv_timeverf;     /* encrypted verifier */
        unsigned int adv_nickname;  /* new nickname for client */
};
```

Diffie-Hellman Encryption. In this scheme, there are two constants, *BASE* and *MODULUS*. The particular values Sun has chosen for these for the DES authentication protocol are:

```
const BASE = 3;
const MODULUS = "d4a0ba0250b6fd2ec626e7efd637df76c716e22d0944b88b"; /*
hex */
```

The way this scheme works is best explained by an example. Suppose there are two people "A" and "B" who want to send encrypted messages to each other. So, A and B both generate "secret" keys at random which they do not reveal to anyone. Let these keys be represented as SK(A) and SK(B). They also publish in a public directory their "public" keys. These keys are computed as follows:

```
PK(A) = ( BASE ** SK(A) ) mod MODULUS
PK(B) = ( BASE ** SK(B) ) mod MODULUS
```

The "**" notation is used here to represent exponentiation. Now, both A and B can arrive at the "common" key between them, represented here as CK(A, B), without revealing their secret keys.

A computes:

```
CK(A, B) = ( PK(B) ** SK(A)) mod MODULUS
```

while B computes:

```
CK(A, B) = ( PK(A) ** SK(B)) mod MODULUS
```

These two can be shown to be equivalent:

```
(PK(B) ** SK(A)) mod MODULUS = (PK(A) ** SK(B)) mod MODULUS
```

We drop the "mod MODULUS" parts and assume modulo arithmetic to simplify things:

```
PK(B) ** SK(A) = PK(A) ** SK(B)
```

Then, replace PK(B) by what B computed earlier and likewise for PK(A).

```
((BASE ** SK(B)) ** SK(A) = (BASE ** SK(A)) ** SK(B)
```

which leads to:

```
BASE ** (SK(A) * SK(B)) = BASE ** (SK(A) * SK(B))
```

This common key CK(A, B) is not used to encrypt the timestamps used in the protocol. Rather, it is used only to encrypt a conversation key which is then used to encrypt the timestamps. The reason for doing this is to use the common key as little as possible, for fear that it could be broken. Breaking the conversation key is a far less serious offense, since conversations are relatively short-lived.

The conversation key is encrypted using 56-bit DES keys, yet the common key is 192 bits. To reduce the number of bits, 56 bits are selected from the common key as follows. The middle-most 8-bytes are selected from the common key, and then parity is added to the lower order bit of each byte, producing a 56-bit key with 8 bits of parity.

A3.6 Record Marking Standard

When RPC messages are passed on top of a byte stream protocol (like TCP/IP), it is necessary, or at least desirable, to delimit one message from another in order to detect and possibly recover from user protocol errors. This is called record marking (RM). Sun uses this RM/TCP/IP transport for passing RPC messages on TCP streams. One RPC message fits into one RM record.

A record is composed of one or more record fragments. A record fragment is a four-byte header followed by 0 to (2**31) − 1 bytes of fragment data. The bytes encode an unsigned binary number; as with XDR integers, the byte order is from highest to lowest. The number encodes two values—a boolean which indicates whether the fragment is the last fragment of the record (bit value 1 implies the fragment is the last fragment), and a 31-bit unsigned binary value which is the length in bytes of the fragment's data. The boolean value is the highest-order bit of the header; the length is the 31 low-order bits. (Note that this record specification is NOT in XDR standard form!)

A3.7 The RPC Language

Just as there was a need to describe the XDR data-types in a formal language, there is also need to describe the procedures that operate on these XDR data-types in a formal language as well. We use the RPC Language for this purpose. It is an extension to the XDR language. The following example is used to describe the essence of the language.

An Example Service Described in the RPC Language

Here is an example of the specification of a simple ping program.

```
/*
 * Simple ping program
 */
program PING_PROG {
        /* Latest and greatest version */
        version PING_VERS_PINGBACK {
        void
        PINGPROC_NULL(void) = 0;
```

```
        /*
         * Ping the caller, return the round-trip time
         * (in microseconds). Returns -1 if the operation
         * timed out.
         */
        int
        PINGPROC_PINGBACK(void) = 1;
} = 2;

/*
 * Original version
 */
version PING_VERS_ORIG {
        void
        PINGPROC_NULL(void) = 0;
        } = 1;
} = 1;

const PING_VERS = 2;          /* latest version */
```

The first version described is *PING_VERS_PINGBACK* with two procedures, *PINGPROC_NULL* and *PINGPROC_PINGBACK*. *PINGPROC_NULL* takes no arguments and returns no results, but is useful for computing round-trip times from the client to the server and back again. By convention, procedure 0 of any RPC protocol should have the same semantics, and never require any kind of authentication. The second procedure is used for the client to have the server do a reverse ping operation back to the client, and it returns the amount of time (in microseconds) that the operation used. The next version, *PING_VERS_ORIG*, is the original version of the protocol and it does not contain *PINGPROC_PINGBACK* procedure. It is useful for compatibility with old client programs, and as this program matures it may be dropped from the protocol entirely.

The RPC Language Specification

The RPC language is identical to the XDR language, except for the added definition of a *program-def* described below.

```
program-def:
        "program" identifier "{"
                version-def
                version-def *
        "}" "=" constant ";"
```

```
version-def:
        "version" identifier "{"
                procedure-def
                procedure-def *
        "}" "=" constant ";"

procedure-def:
        type-specifier identifier "(" type-specifier ")" "=" constant ";"
```

Syntax Notes

- The following keywords are added and cannot be used as identifiers: "program" and "version";
- A version name cannot occur more than once within the scope of a program definition. Nor can a version number occur more than once within the scope of a program definition.
- A procedure name cannot occur more than once within the scope of a version definition. Nor can a procedure number occur more than once within the scope of version definition.
- Program identifiers are in the same name space as constant and type identifiers.
- Only unsigned constants can be assigned to programs, versions and procedures.

A3.8 Port Mapper Program Protocol

The port mapper program maps RPC program and version numbers to transport-specific port numbers. This program makes dynamic binding of remote programs possible.

This is desirable because the range of reserved port numbers is very small and the number of potential remote programs is very large. By running only the port mapper on a reserved port, the port numbers of other remote programs can be ascertained by querying the port mapper.

The port mapper also aids in broadcast RPC. A given RPC program will usually have different port number bindings on different machines, so there is no way to broadcast directly to all of these programs. The port mapper, however, does have a fixed port number. So, to broadcast to a given program, the client actually sends its message to the port mapper located at the broadcast address. Each port mapper that picks up the broadcast then calls the local service specified by the client. When the port mapper gets the reply from the local service, it sends the reply on back to the client.

Port Mapper Protocol Specification (in RPC Language)

```
const PMAP_PORT = 111;          /* portmapper port number */

/*
 * A mapping of (program, version, protocol) to port number
 */
struct mapping {
        unsigned int prog;
        unsigned int vers;
        unsigned int prot;
        unsigned int port;
};

/*
 * Supported values for the "prot" field
 */
const IPPROTO_TCP = 6;          /* protocol number for TCP/IP */
const IPPROTO_UDP = 17;         /* protocol number for UDP/IP */

/*
 * A list of mappings
 */
struct *pmaplist {
        mapping map;
        pmaplist next;
};

/*
 * Arguments to callit
 */
struct call_args {
        unsigned int prog;
        unsigned int vers;
        unsigned int proc;
        opaque args<>;
};
```

```
/*
 * Results of callit
 */
struct call_result {
        unsigned int port;
        opaque res<>;
};

/*
 * Port mapper procedures
 */
program PMAP_PROG {
        version PMAP_VERS {
                void
                PMAPPROC_NULL(void)             = 0;

                bool
                PMAPPROC_SET(mapping)           = 1;

                bool
                PMAPPROC_UNSET(mapping)         = 2;

                unsigned int
                PMAPPROC_GETPORT(mapping)       = 3;

                pmaplist
                PMAPPROC_DUMP(void)             = 4;

                call_result
                PMAPPROC_CALLIT(call_args)      = 5;
        } = 2;
} = 100000;
```

Port Mapper Operation

The portmapper program currently supports two protocols (UDP/IP and TCP/IP). The portmapper is contacted by talking to it on assigned port number 111 (SUNRPC [8]) on either of these protocols. The following is a description of each of the portmapper procedures:

PMAPPROC_NULL:

This procedure does no work. By convention, procedure zero of any protocol takes no parameters and returns no results.

PMAPPROC_SET:

When a program first becomes available on a machine, it registers itself with the port mapper program on the same machine. The program passes its program number "prog", version number "vers", transport protocol number "prot", and the port "port" on which it awaits service request. The procedure returns a boolean response whose value is *TRUE* if the procedure successfully established the mapping and *FALSE* otherwise. The procedure refuses to establish a mapping if one already exists for the tuple "(prog, vers, prot)".

PMAPPROC_UNSET:

When a program becomes unavailable, it should unregister itself with the port mapper program on the same machine. The parameters and results have meanings identical to those of *PMAPPROC _SET*. The protocol and port number fields of the argument are ignored.

PMAPPROC_GETPORT:

Given a program number "prog", version number "vers", and transport protocol number "prot", this procedure returns the port number on which the program is awaiting call requests. A port value of zero means the program has not been registered. The "port" field of the argument is ignored.

PMAPPROC_DUMP:

This procedure enumerates all entries in the port mapper's database. The procedure takes no parameters and returns a list of program, version, protocol, and port values.

PMAPPROC_CALLIT:

This procedure allows a caller to call another remote procedure on the same machine without knowing the remote procedure's port number. It is intended for supporting broadcasts to arbitrary remote programs via the well-known port mapper's port. The parameters "prog", "vers", "proc", and the bytes of "args" are the program number, version number, procedure number, and parameters of the remote procedure. Note:

1. This procedure only sends a response if the procedure was successfully executed and is silent (no response) otherwise.
2. The port mapper communicates with the remote program using UDP/IP only.

The procedure returns the remote program's port number, and the bytes of results are the results of the remote procedure.

References

[1] Birrell, Andrew D. & Nelson, Bruce Jay; "Implementing Remote Procedure Calls"; XEROX CSL-83-7, October 1983.

[2] Cheriton, D.; "VMTP: Versatile Message Transaction Protocol", Preliminary Version 0.3; Stanford University, January 1987.

[3] Diffie & Hellman; "Net Directions in Cryptography"; IEEE Transactions on Information Theory IT-22, November 1976.

[4] Harrenstien, K.; "Time Server", RFC 738; Information Sciences Institute, October 1977.

[5] National Bureau of Standards; "Data Encryption Standard"; Federal Information Processing Standards Publication 46, January 1977.

[6] Postel, J.; "Transmission Control Protocol—DARPA Internet Program Protocol Specification", RFC 793; Information Sciences Institute, September 1981.

[7] Postel, J.; "User Datagram Protocol", RFC 768; Information Sciences Institute, August 1980.

[8] Reynolds, J. & Postel, J.; "Assigned Numbers", RFC 923; Information Sciences Institute, October 1984.

Differences Between the RPC Library on SunOS 4.0 and SunOS 4.1

Appendix 4

This appendix covers the differences between the SunOS 4.0 and the SunOS 4.1 versions of the RPC Library, the *portmap* service, and the *rpcgen* program. Only a brief summary of the changes are presented. More detailed information can be obtained from the SunOS 4.1 documentation.

A4.1 RPC Library

The following new features were added to the RPC Library:

- The routine *xdrrec_readbytes()* was added to the Library. This routine can only be used on streams created by *xdrrec_create()*. The routine attempts to read a specified number of bytes from the XDR stream into a specified buffer.
- The routine *clntudp_bufcreate()* is now documented and available to the user. This routine is in the SunOS 4.0 version of the Library but is for internal use by the Library. This routine is the same as *clntudp_create()* except that you can now specify the size of the send and receive buffers.
- The routine *clnt_create_vers()* was added to the Library. This routine is a generic client creation routine which also checks for the version available. Remember that the *clnt_create()* routine returns a valid client handle even if the specified version number supplied to the routine is not registered with the *portmap* service. However, *clnt_create_vers()* does this for you and returns a valid handle only if a version within the range supplied is supported by the server.

- New request values have been added to the *clnt_control()* routine. The new request values, their associated argument types, and what the requests do follows:

CLGET_FD	int	get socket descriptor associated with the client handle
CLSET_FD_CLOSE	void	close socket when *clnt_destroy()* is called
CLSET_FD_NCLOSE	void	leave socket open when *clnt_destroy()* is called

- You need to include ⟨*rpc/raw.h*⟩ when using the raw transport creation routines.

The following fixes were added to the SunOS 4.1 version of the Library:

- The routine *clnt_call()* now does an exponential back off when retrying RPC requests.
- The *clnt_broadcast()* routine now uses an exponential back off on the retry time-out. In SunOS 4.0 version, it used a linear series for retry time-outs.
- The *svc_run()* routine now ignores all error codes returned from *select()* except for EBADF. The *svc_run()* in the SunOS 4.0 version of the Library ignores only the EINTR error code. This change was made because EBADF is the only error that should result in svc_*run()* returning. This change also makes *svc_run()* more tolerant of applications that handle signals and inadvertently modify the global variable *errno* inside their signal handling routine. The problem exists in *svc_run()* because the return from *select()* and the test of the *errno* variable is not an atomic operation and, in fact, control may be passed to a signal handling routine during this sequence of operations. The SunOS 4.1 version of the *svc_run()* routine was covered in Chapter 6.
- The raw transport creation routines have been fixed.

A4.2 Portmap Service

The following fixes were made to the *portmap* service:

- Disallows PMAP_SET and PMAP_UNSET operations from remote hosts.

- Disallows PMAP_SET and PMAP_UNSET of reserved ports from non-reserved ports.
- The PMAP_RMTCALL procedure no longer forks. This provides a significant performance improvement for the processing of broadcast requests.

A4.3 Rpcgen

The following features were added to *rpcgen*:

- Can generate servers which can be invoked by the *inetd* program.
- Allows for -DDEFINE statements on the command line to define macros.
- Allows for server error messages to be logged using the syslog mechanism.
- Can generate an indexed-by-procedure table.

Source for Examples

Appendix 5

The examples used in this book can be obtained in a computer readable form. To order the examples, specify the type of media desired and the format to be used on the disk. The media, media formats supported, and prices are listed below.

3.5″	Floppy Disk UNIX *tar* Format	\$8.00(US)
5.25″	Floppy Disk UNIX *tar* Format	\$8.00(US)
1/4″	Streaming Tape Unix *tar* Format	\$12.00(US)
3.5″	Floppy Disk MS-DOS Format	\$8.00(US)
5.25″	Floppy Disk MS-DOS Format	\$8.00(US)

Send your order along with payment to:

RPC Programming Examples
P.O. Box 12474
El Paso, TX 79912

Bibliography

Bergan, E.S., Tolchin, S.G.: Using Remote Procedure Calls (RPC) for a Distributed Clinical Information System. Proceedings of the UniForum Conference, 1986

Birman, K.P., Joseph, T.A.: Exploiting Replication in Distributed Systems. In: Mullender, S.(ed.): Distributed Systems. Reading (Mass.): Addison-Wesley 1989, pp. 191 - 214

Birrell, A.D., Nelson, B.J.: Implementing Remote Procedure Calls. ACM Transactions on Computer Systems 2:1, 39 - 59 (1984)

Comer, D.: Internetworking With TCP/IP -- Principles, Protocols and Architectures. Englewood Cliffs (New Jersey): Prentice Hall 1988

Coulouris, G.F., Dollimore, J.: Distributed Systems -- Concepts and Design. Reading (Mass.): Addison-Wesley 1988

Diffie, W., Hellman, M.E.: New Directions in Cryptography. IEEE Transactions on Information Theory *IT-22*, 644 - 654 (1976)

Folts, H.: Open Systems Standards -- OSI Remote and Reliable Operations. IEEE Network 3:3, (1989)

Havender, J.W.: Avoiding Deadlock in Multitasking Systems. IBM Systems Journal 7:2, 74 - 84 (1968)

Leffler, S.J., et al.: The Design and Implementation of the 4.3BSD UNIX Operating System. Reading (Mass.): Addison-Wesley 1989

Lyon, B.: Sun Remote Procedure Call Specification. Sun Microsystems, Inc., Mountain View (Calif.), 1984.

Lyon, B.: Sun External Data Representation Specification. Sun Microsystems, Inc., Mountain View (Calif.), 1984.

National Bureau of Standards: Data Encryption Standard. Federal Information Processing Standards Publication 46, January 15, 1977

Needham, R.M., Schroeder, M.D.: Using Encryption for Authentication in Large Networks of Computers. Communications of the ACM *21*:12, (1978)

Obermarck, R.: Distributed Deadlock Detection Algorithm. ACM Transactions on Database Systems 7:2, 187 - 208 (1982)

Samar, V., McManis, C.: Sun Remote Procedure Call Implementation Made Transport Independent. Sun Microsystems, Mountain View (Calif.), December 1989.

Spector, A.Z.: Distributed Transaction Processing Facilities. In: Mullender, S.(ed.): Distributed Systems. Reading (Mass.): Addison-Wesley 1989, pp. 191 - 214

Stallings, W.: Handbook of Computer-Communications Standards (Volume 1). New York (New York): Macmillan 1987

Sun Microsystems: Network Programming. Mountain View (Calif.): Sun Microsystems 1988

Sun Microsystems: SunOS Reference Manual. Mountain View (Calif.): Sun Microsystems 1988

Sun Microsystems: Security Features Guide. Mountain View (Calif.): Sun Microsystems 1988

Taylor, B., Goldberg, D.: Secure Networking in the Sun Environment. Proceedings of the USENIX Summer Conference, 1986

Weihl, W.E.: Remote Procedure Call. In: Mullender, S.(ed.): Distributed Systems. Reading (Mass.): Addison-Wesley 1989, pp. 65 - 86

White, J.E.: A High-level Framework For Network-based Resource Sharing. Proceedings of the National Computer Conference, June 1976

Xerox Corporation: Courier: The Remote Procedure Call Protocol -- Xerox System Integration Standard XSIS-038112. Stamford (Conn.): Xerox Corporation 1981

Index

MIX
Papier aus verantwortungsvollen Quellen
Paper from responsible sources
FSC® C105338

If you have any concerns about our products,
you can contact us on
ProductSafety@springernature.com

In case Publisher is established outside the EU,
the EU authorized representative is:
Springer Nature Customer Service Center GmbH
Europaplatz 3, 69115 Heidelberg, Germany

Printed by Libri Plureos GmbH
in Hamburg, Germany